interrogating travel

interro

LOUISIANA STATE UNIVERSITY PRESS   BATON ROUGE

GUIDANCE
FROM A
RELUCTANT
TOURIST

gating
travel

PAUL LINDHOLDT

Published by Louisiana State University Press
lsupress.org

LSU Press Paperback Original

Designer: Barbara Neely Bourgoyne
Typeface: FreightText Pro

Several chapters, extensively revised here, appeared first in the following book and periodicals:

"The Spray and the Slamming Sea," in *On Nature: Great Writers on the Great Outdoors* (2002), reprinted by permission of the Creative Nonfiction Foundation; "Shooters and the Tools They Use," *Sewanee Review* 122, no. 4 (fall 2014); "Paddling Lake Missoula," *Spokesman-Review* (2015); "The Trumpets of Solitude," *Terrain.org* (2015); "Shrub-Steppe, Pothole, Ponderosa Pine," *Numéro Cinq* (2017); "Hawk Watching," *Kenyon Review* 40, no. 3 (2018); "The Security of Dirt," *Smart Set* (2018); and "Making Landfall," *Terrain.org* (2019).

Cover illustration courtesy iStock.com/francescoch.

Cataloging-in-Publication Data are available from the Library of Congress.

ISBN 978-0-8071-7949-9 (paperback)
ISBN 978-0-8071-8019-8 (epub)
ISBN 978-0-8071-8020-4 (pdf)

What benefit has travel of itself ever been able to give anyone? No restraint upon pleasure, no bridling of desire, no checking of bad temper, no crushing of the wild assaults of passion, no opportunity to rid the soul of evil. Travelling cannot give us judgment or shake off our errors; it merely holds our attention for a moment by a certain novelty, as children pause to wonder at something unfamiliar.

—SENECA THE YOUNGER, CA. 63 CE, TRANS. RICHARD GUNMERE

If you didn't know the TV footage was a video from January the 6th, you would actually think it was a normal tourist visit.

—REP. ANDREW CLYDE (R-GEORGIA), 2021

contents

among the beloved

among the predatory

among the indigenous

interrogating travel

Introduction

Traveling with my family in Belize, I first heard the assertion "Sustainable travel is an oxymoron." Tourist-wrangler Judy du Plooy said it. She owned an all-inclusive resort. Her clients flew to a US airline hub and then jetted to Belize City. There they clambered aboard a bumpy puddle-jumper, winged it to the city of San Ignacio, piled into a ten-person shuttle van, and wound their way past the town of tiny Santa Elena to arrive at Judy's resort.

In 1987, she moved to Belize with her husband, Ken, and their five daughters from South Carolina and bought a riverside farm. Ken died in 2001 from heart disease; Judy bravely raised their daughters on her own. The girls learned "to ride in the back of the bus" to get to school, an image Judy shared with me to illustrate her family's lives in their Central American home.

For thirty years she ran their resort of forty-eight employees named du Plooy's Jungle Lodge. Sun supplies the power for its forty-five acres of arboretum and another 160 acres of cabins and jungle. Guanacaste trees shade the grounds—towering, flowering deciduous giants that resemble live oaks. The resort's cabins blend into the foliage. During our 2012 visit, fruit bats roosted in an observation dome above the Macal River. Agoutis, known as bush rabbits by the locals, proved so adaptable to human presence that they resembled statues on the grounds.

During breakfast on the day that I remember best, Judy's staff served hibiscus juice, the first time my family had tasted it. Outside the window of the dining hall, a flock of aracari toucans swiveled upside down and plucked fruit from a palm tree. Judy sat down with us and chatted. "Sustainable travel is an oxymoron," she looked me in the eye and said a second time. I had already confided to her how our carbon-intensive voyage from Seattle had unsettled me.

Throughout the world I had been sleepwalking, till Judy's assertion woke me up. To hear a resort owner say it was encouraging. Her opinion confirmed the squeamish feeling at my core.

Five years later, in 2017, twin pictures woke me further to the complex travel trade. On the cover of a *New Yorker* magazine, a gigantic man and woman are seen trampling a landscape. The woman is engrossed by her smartphone, the man distracted by a map. The kicker comes in the couple's cartoonish outsized shoes. Like the Grateful Dead Truckin' logo, those clodhoppers dwarf the countryside. They crush villages, roads, and landscapes. They send villagers fleeing.

The second picture to waken me in 2017 arrived from Iceland. That nation's prime minister and others were conducting a funeral for the Okjökull Glacier. That ice field had died five years before, but the community hoped it somehow would regrow. To commemorate its permanent loss, civic leaders in Iceland installed a plaque. The plaque expressed the nation's promise to combat the global climate change that had reduced their massive glacier to a stain.

Those twin pictures—tramping tourists and a funeral for a glacier— came together like crossed hairs on a riflescope. My family was packing up just then for a trip to French Polynesia. We would follow the French people to remote islands and enjoy their food and culture. More than pleasure was motivating our trip, though. A steady violence of rising seawater, bleaching coral, extreme weather, and atmospheric acidification was afflicting those low-lying islands.

To explain our Tahitian travel to family and friends, we said we were checking an item off our bucket list. We were also fulfilling a tender agenda to visit places on the planet that are at most risk of extinction. Leaders in Tahiti were taking desperation measures to stymie sea rise. Those measures included the approval of floating harbor islands, as detailed below in chapter 17, "Island Time." On Switzerland's famous ski slopes that same year, fleece blankets the breadth of fourteen football fields were being draped to slow the pace of the glaciers' melting.

Our travels often take the shape of bittersweet farewells today. Near our home in Washington State, Glacier National Park has seen its namesake ice fields retreat by 85 percent—as spelled out in chapter 8, "My Climate Change," and in other chapters here that catalogue ecological crises. *Solastalgia* is a new coinage, or neologism, meant to underscore stressors generated by firsthand experience of ecological degradation. That new word is closely related to *nostalgia*, the melancholy suffered by individuals when severed from a beloved home.

At-risk endpoints on our home globe often smack of humans withering from disease—whether it be bleaching coral, burning forests, shrinking glaciers, or rising seas. Ecologies are not the only sad casualty of travel to catch at my attention. Indigenous people everywhere are feeling desperate when tourist and energy-development pressures overrun their societies and lifeways.

The *New Yorker* cover of the tramping man and woman asked its readers to ponder the ethics of international travel, which is an activity for the most privileged alone. Only 4 percent of the global population undertakes such trips, travel promoter Rick Steves has estimated. We 4-percenters underwrite pollutants from cruise ships, trash from overpackaged meals on jets, the transport of exotic foodstuffs to far-flung resorts, and millions of gallons of deicing chemicals that foul waterways. Studies of climate change are bringing the airline industry under greater scrutiny than ever before. Most of that attention has arisen from within Western nations.

One climate activist is George Monbiot in England. His article titled "Flying Is Dying" explores the connection between airline travel and climate change. Building larger airports and adding runways become self-fulfilling causeways to ever-more-excessive flights. Worse, Monbiot says, the widely ratified 1944 Chicago Convention on Civil Aviation decrees that "no government may levy tax on aviation fuel." Diesel and gasoline— polluting fuels for cars and cargo trucks—are heavily taxed around the planet, but air carriers are getting a free pass.

Bill McKibben, at Middlebury College in Vermont, founded 350.org with his students in 2007. The group's name derives from a NASA scientist's finding that 350 parts per million (ppm) of atmospheric carbon is the sustainable threshold. At the present time, global carbon ppm is 420. Not content merely to lobby or raise funds, 350.org has led protests around the nation and fostered affiliate groups in 188 countries. Its organizing influence is international in scope.

The most high-profile activist is the Swedish woman Greta Thunberg. She refused to fly to the 2019 United Nations General Assembly in New York where she had been asked to speak. She chose to go by solar boat. As someone on the autism spectrum, she fell into a funk as a teenager over climate issues. For weeks she would not eat. Her family feared she was going to die. She rallied herself by organizing a school strike and enlisting others her age. Her example, and a growing awareness of the high stakes of climate change, are fueling movements known variously as Flight Free UK, Flight Free USA, and an international No-Fly Travel Club.

Closer to home, the Pacific Northwest suffered a thousand-year weather event in June 2021. In Oregon and Washington, some two hundred people died in a heat dome. Meteorologists define a heat dome as ocean air that functions like a cap or a lid. Portland's record of 107°F had stood for fifty years before being broken three times in one month. Its temperature rose to 108°F on Friday, June 26, to 112°F on Sunday, and to 116°F on Monday. The little town of Lytton in British Columbia experienced 121°F that same week. Dozens of wildfires also smoldered around our Far Northwest. A Catholic friend exclaimed, "Sweet suffering Jesus! Is this what the gates of Hell look like?" How far travel is implicated in the conditions that caused that record heat dome no one certainly may say. This book intends to broaden dialogues on the topic.

To critique travel is a privilege, an entitlement I am not taking lightly. Nor are my partner and I blind to the irony of our desires. At-risk planetary meccas grow more squalid with every batch of tourists like us that arrives. The best way to reduce one's carbon footprint is to drive and fly less. That is what I aim to do—whether constrained by another pandemic, barred by host countries, or by choosing to chill more often near our home.

My spouse, as a pro bono lawyer, represented protesters charged on Standing Rock Sioux Tribe lands in 2017. The Dakota Access Pipeline there was put on hold in 2021 but was soon reactivated after a judge ruled that an environmental review had to be conducted. The pipeline jeopardizes aquifers and rivers across three states, it desecrates tribal burial grounds, and it heightens reliance on hydrocarbon extraction and consumption across the continent.

* * *

As I began to write this book, I promised myself it would not travel-shame. It would not offend friends, generate enemies, or advance a holier-than-thou attitude. It would not scold or dictate, guilt-trip or impugn. Nor would it goad those industrious individuals whose livelihoods rely on the travel trade—businesspeople who offer consumers pleasing services as hosts, travel agents, writers, or promoters. My family and I are implicated in the hot mess that is commercial tourism. We are cohorts in all the forces I analyze and describe. Nevertheless, as Gustave Flaubert wrote long ago, "You don't make art out of good intentions."

This book of literary nonfiction balances international voyages with outings close to home. "Vertical travel," as scholars in England are calling it, happens when travelers slow their pace and subject their surroundings to the close inspection that comes from burrowing deep within a place. Chapter 9, "Survivor Tree," and chapter 4, "Shrub-Steppe, Pothole, Ponderosa Pine," are purposeful instances of vertical journeying in Spokane County, Washington. In all these eighteen chapters, my aim is primarily to delight and instruct, not to grind a political ax.

Commentators throughout the ages who have taken a dim view of travel are the minority. Like the opening epigraphs here—the quotations by Roman statesman Seneca and Rep. Andrew Clyde—my research is selective. My rationale for cherry-picking research sources is simple. Elite travelers have always been the tastemakers. Only the most privileged have gotten their opinions into print. They alone have had the wherewithal and the leisure to tour and travel internationally. That minuscule sample size has come to stand in for the whole of humankind.

A certain blurring of the terms *travel* and *tourism* is unavoidable. Some of my cues come from Paul Fussell's book *Class: A Guide through the American Status System*. Tourists pursue a set agenda, often, whether sightseeing in groups or going it alone. Travelers are more likely to be spontaneous and to welcome whatsoever might unfold. Tourists value souvenirs—T-shirts, mugs, curios, mementos—so that "life becomes a travelogue of picture-postcard charms," as Joni Mitchell sang it on her album of travel angst *Hejira*. If tourists as a rule hold loyal to their native tongues, dedicated travelers will sample the regional language and diminish the distance between themselves and locals. Tourists in a stereotypical picture also dress garishly, caring little whether they stand out. Travelers, by contrast, are more likely to avoid corporate logos and floral prints in their wardrobes. Fussell's class marker, "legible clothing," has central relevance here.

If the traveler proves willing to try the local cuisine and take culinary risks, the tourist—both in practice and in popular culture—seeks comfort food, familiar food, thus generating markets for those gilded arches in whichever sector of the planet he plunks down. The tourist also proves more vulnerable to being gulled. Destinations capitalizing on tourism as a spending sector lower quality, increase costs, and neutralize experiences for all comers. Tourism can be an aspect of travel, then, though it need not be. In the 2021 documentary film *Roadrunner*, Anthony Bourdain poses before a handprinted sign that advises viewers, "Be a traveler not a tourist."

People travel for a multitude of reasons—to attend weddings or funerals, to visit family or friends, to receive medical care, chase jobs, pay homage to saints and holy lands, and to escape from oppressive governments. This year, family love will compel me to fly to Florida for a wedding. As one who is able-bodied, heterosexual, and white, I feel confident as I undertake such junkets, whether they be international or domestic. Race, sex, and gender can make travel exclusionary. Safe sojourns are privileges afforded to different people in differing degrees. Scholar Sara Ahmed has noted keenly, "The idealisation of movement, or transformation of movement into a fetish, depends upon the exclusion of others who are already positioned as not free in the same way." Travel, that is, often pivots on invisible prohibitions.

Public lands as an antidote to global travel are more accessible to certain publics than to others. Aware of the freedoms I enjoy, I was stunned by the 2020 ordeal of Christian Cooper, the Black writer and bird-watcher who was wrongly reported to authorities in Central Park. That incident exemplifies both the challenge and the privilege of recreating in public spaces (as the online video and poem "9 Rules for the Black Birdwatcher" foretold). The person who reported Cooper, a white woman walking her dog, was first charged with a misdemeanor for filing a false police report, but her charges were dropped as a swap for taking an educational course. The Central Park ordeal has become a watershed instance of disparities inherent in public-lands play.

Writer Amy Irvine explores the hazards faced by solitary women who live, recreate, or travel in public spaces, much less try to raise their children alone. Male writers such as Edward Abbey, she says, rarely acknowledge their privileges. They idealize public sojourns as natural rights. Rebecca Solnit put it succinctly in her excellent history of walking as the primordial form of mobility: "Travel, whether local or global, has remained a largely masculine prerogative."

People following a path of faith call for special recognition. Hundreds of writings, from Hui-li to Geoffrey Chaucer to Annie Dillard, pivot on religious journeys. The Hajj is the yearly pilgrimage to Mecca, the holiest city for Muslims. If pilgrims and religious disciples do not think of their journeys as tourism, the nimble industry handles them as tourists all the same. Consider, likewise, the Indian mystic Mohan Das, aka Lotan Baba or "Rolling Saint." No holidaymaker, he has tumbled sidelong on hips, elbows, and knees—chafed, scraped, and bandaged—traversing his nation through more than thirty thousand kilometers in humble efforts to advocate for peace.

The tourist, distinct from voyagers like these, is chiefly a leisure traveler. Still, the seams between the tourist and the traveler are blurry, the fabric porous, the divisions rarely watertight.

By what measure may we gauge the scale of global travel? If by earnings, that would be impossible due to a dearth of self-reporting by host countries. If by the numbers of travelers served, must one measure transits only from country to country, or also within a given country after a traveler has arrived? If by the numbers of people whom the industry employs, then the connective tissue between the disparate sectors grows wafer-thin, and the vexing matter of an absence of accountability intercepts the truth again. Especially if one factors in those independent promoters known as influencers, many travel statistics are unattainable.

What about hunting and fishing, rodeos, spectator sports, bachelor and bachelorette parties, or visits to patronize the arts? Most such outings are intranational by contrast with the international, short haul rather than long haul. But they also must be tallied to compile elusive truths. Again, the numbers for gauging travel's size on a global scale are unavailable, the requisite definitions missing, and the capacity to gather exacting data nowhere to be found.

Occasions to take tours are multiplying every year. One may indulge historical tourism by visiting sites where momentous events have taken place. Adventure tourism includes skiing, surfing, hunting, scuba, fishing, mountain climbing, bird-watching, photo safaris, and much more. Flying from the Bahamas, I saw men on planes hold precious fly-fishing rod tubes close. One may enjoy days at beachside for medical tourism and come out money ahead. In Mexico, Costa Rica, Thailand, Malaysia, and Israel, self-care costs less than in the United States. Two women judges of my acquaintance, always in the public eye, travel to Mexico for cosmetic care.

There are so many alibis or opportunities to travel—some predatory, some philanthropic, some elitist. The Road Scholar program began as Elderhostel in 1975. The Backroads, for active adventure tours on bicycles, began in 1979. Ecotourism has a lengthy history that goes back to the early 1980s. Tourists can hunt wolves today in Alberta—a furry trophy all but guaranteed. Voluntourism allows humanitarian types to see the sights and help to rebuild villages or offer aid to ecological or political refugees. My friends have gone on retreats to practice yoga in Greece, Costa Rica, Mexico, and Iceland. If Virgin Galactic CEO Michael Colglazier sees the future clearly, the wealthiest people might soon go boldly where no humans have gone before. Virgin Galactic, founded by Sir Richard Branson in 2004, is billed as "a space tourism venture."

Dark tourism—however dubious or ghoulish—has inspired dozens of articles and books. It is defined as an affinity for places or events allied with mass tragedy and death. Some dark tourists visit sites of genocidal atrocities by the Nazis, the Khmer Rouge, and the Serbs. Other favorite spots include the post-Katrina Ninth Ward in New Orleans and the path of Medellin Cartel drug lord Pablo Escobar through Colombia. Some dark tourists travel to see executions, pay homage to sites like Auschwitz, gaze at monuments or graves, reenact battles, or survey well-known slums to appreciate how the other half gets by. Dark tourism goes by a variety of names—black-spot tourism, disaster tourism, grief tourism, holocaust tourism, doom tourism, and war tourism. The Greek personification of death, Thanatos, has even inspired the cognate expression *thanatourism*. Dark tourism is so new, coined only in 1996, that no one yet can seem to agree on how to name it. It is only history with a twist, I was told about a visit to Dallas to pay homage to the site where JFK died. It can be enlightening in the right frame of mind.

One may also reverence deceased artists by paying homage to their graves or homes. It is as if an atmospheric osmosis can confer insights unavailable by reading novels or biographies alone. Pulitzer Prize–winner Marilynne Robinson refuses to visit the domiciles of writers who have passed from this world. "They feel like mausoleums," she says. "I prefer to think of my favorite writers off somewhere writing."

* * *

One device to gauge travel is the growth of international arrivals over the last seventy years. My source is the United Nations World Tourism Organization. In 1950, it says, some twenty-five million inbound international tourists took overnight journeys of less than a year to countries outside the locales where they live. By 2018, 1.4 billion tourists were making such trips every year—an increase of 5,500 percent. In that same period, we 2,556 billion humans grew to 7,600 billion. From 1950 to 2018, then, planet Earth increased its human population by 197 percent. If we juxtapose those twin rates of increase, we see that international tourism grew 2,687 percent more than the planetary population in that period of seventy years.

A multitude of factors contribute to that exponential upsurge. First, air travel grew safer and more affordable. In 1970, some five million air passengers were flying per death. In 2017, ninety million were flying on commercial airlines for every passenger that died. From 1950 to 2020, commercial air travel became less expensive and more accessible to a wider cross-section of people, in part through subsidies given airlines to boost international exchanges of cash. Wealth and disposable income also grew within first-world nations. To say "safer and more affordable" about air travel is to ignore the heavy costs shifted to later generations and ecologies.

The relative ease of travel by jet plane carries hidden hazards for the planet. A wing of the United Nations (UN) forecast that airplane emissions of the most concerning sort—the greenhouse gas, carbon dioxide—would exceed 900 million metric tons in 2018. And those tons, the UN projected, are on pace to triple by 2050. Such stunning numbers might explain the hodophobia, or aversion to the path, some flyers instinctively suffer. "The Security of Dirt," chapter 3, examines that aversion. The global pandemic has only increased unease. Not only is Earth more at risk from those jet airliners today, but so are the huddled masses of us passengers when we consider congested airports and jets as breeding grounds for bacteria and viruses.

Travel writer Rick Steves recommends we travelers stray from standard destinations to experience homegrown cultures and less-frequented locales. That credo inspired him to write *Travel as a Political Act*. Its third edition appeared two years before the pandemic swept the globe—before objections to masks and vaccinations devolved into political acts of their own. Steves, a tour promoter, champions visits to developing nations instead of first-world tourist traps to enlarge our comfort zones and conserve shekels. Instead of voyaging always in lavish abandon, he says, allow some adversity to acquaint you with the locals. My first trip to Paris was taken on a pauper's budget, an outing I narrate here as "Broncos in the Salon," chapter 7.

Chimamanda Ngozi Adichie warned about "the danger of a single story." Her warning applies to popular conceptions of travel. A single travel story has drawbacks, whether intended as an earned privilege, as a self-improvement, or as a sort of noblesse oblige extended toward developing nations. The narrating self often outfoxes the experiential self during unreflective sojourns abroad. No matter what we do or where we travel, we often become the beneficiaries of our self-generated sagas. It is normal, it is customary, to promote adventures that will outlast us.

Sleeping in a frosty orchard at dawn, I have relished songs by migrant workers rallying themselves to pick fruit. Miles from ready rescue in Costa Rica, I have straddled a coral snake, the most poisonous reptile in the Western Hemisphere. Stricken by a norovirus in a Caribbean resort, I have taken turns with other members of my family above a toilet. In the frigid waters of Lake Tahoe, I have watched an overweight swim-racer flail, drop beneath the chop, and expire before a crowd of watchers on the shore. Riding the Paris Metro, I have been pickpocketed, and on a second visit to that self-same City of Light I have fallen for my spouse all over again.

Which experiences ring most true? Like all whose narrating selves stow away with them to foreign lands, I need to be on guard against perilous partialities and a limited worldview.

*   *   *

To develop remedies or cures for tourist travel, I turned to *National Geographic* for my guidance. Rupert Murdoch's 21st Century Fox bought *NatGeo*'s media properties in 2015 and brought the magazine entirely online in 2020. Its NatGeo Expeditions® organizes "250+ Trips Around the World." Online advice *NatGeo* shared in 2021 sounded savvy: "Travel slowly, spend locally, stay in homes, and go off the beaten path." If I choose to follow that advice, though, how slow is just right and how fast is too fast? How will I know if my outlays help the locals? Do the profits from my homestay or short-let rental remain in the host country, or mostly flow away to absentee investors? Such considerations have always badgered me. Given the overtourism pressures that are being acknowledged worldwide, what are the best ways to rethink travel?

COVID-19 and its staying power have accelerated the urgency of such questions. No one anymore may travel with entire abandon. Though mask mandates for air travel have been lifted for the time being, Calanques National Park in France recently began to discourage visitors and Instagram influencers due to overcrowding dangers. My family visited that park in 2016. We rented a small boat and skippered it from Cassis to explore those icy Mediterranean limestone inlets. We briefly swam there and watched our sons gasping in the chill. Since the pandemic, too, new business models have amended past practices to address demands for environmentally responsible vacations. Major air carriers have committed to improving targets for carbon neutrality. They include American Airline, Delta Airline, and United Airline. Carriers are working to calm consumer qualms about sustainability and germs.

The pandemic changed the terms of travel and gave this book an unexpected timeliness, as chapter 12, "Tidings from the Virus," shows.

COVID-19 and its restrictions supplied a set of unintended consequences, a baseline from which to assess the effects of human mobility. Internal combustion throttled down, air pollution precipitated out, and water quality briefly improved.

NatGeo's guidance, though it appears simple, can prove prohibitive to put into practice. Instead of always traveling slowly, with the added costs such a lucky pace entails, another solution is to reinvestigate local environs. Visas, vaccines, and passports will never be needed on local outings. By absorbing the intricacies of our provincial vicinities, by traveling vertically, one may assuage or cure the tourist urge. The joys of vertical travel embed my "Hawk Watching" (chapter 11) below. If exploring local environs seems like a too-easy solution to the lure of tourism, some will find it dull. The Stoic philosopher Seneca, two millennia ago, noticed that certain individuals travel to escape themselves and their cares. He wrote, "travel won't make a better or saner man of you."

Like my aesthetic and political avatar Henry David Thoreau, his mentor Ralph Waldo Emerson merits a mention. Both men were dubious of tourism's virtues. Emerson dubbed it "a fool's paradise." He disliked conformity and emulating others. Emerson's essay "Self-Reliance" criticizes global tourist travel: "It is for want [absence] of self-culture that the superstition of Travelling, whose idols are Italy, England, Egypt, retains its fascination for all educated Americans." To self-enculturate is to discover one's natural gifts, cultivate them, and transfigure them into a new persona, a work of art, or a fusion of life and art in a seamless whole. The philosopher Emerson, by categorizing travel as a superstition, was dismissing it as doctrine.

Building on his mentor Emerson, Thoreau originated an aphorism that reduces travel to enumeration. "It is not worth the while," he wrote at the end of *Walden,* "to go round the world to count the cats in Zanzibar." An island off the east coast of Africa, Zanzibar traces its local cats to pets kept on ships to curb rats. Many of Zanzibar's felines went feral. It is a chump's errand, a fool's paradise, to travel just to count them. Thoreau's analogy puts me in mind of those global maps some homeowners stud with pushpins and display to enumerate the places they have seen.

* * *

Three themes structure these narrative chapters. First, I assess travel's impacts on beloved individuals, on people who are closest to me. "The Spray and the Slamming Sea" and "Paddling Lake Missoula" focus on ordeals my sons underwent on hazardous sojourns. Second, I look at predation as an aspect of travel. Roadkill and bird strikes show commercial tourism and travel can be predatory acts, as cars, planes, and trains become weapons. The third set of chapters profiles Indigenous people, for whom the tourism and energy industries often prove hazardous. Such gradual violence can be inconspicuous to everyday eyes. "Loved Badly on Your Bank" honors Indigenous Americans in the Far Northwest, while "Nomads of the Sea" visits among the shrinking population of the Urak Lawoi people in Thailand. Throughout this book, I try to crack the shiny façade of first-world privilege to examine the excesses that shelter beneath that shell.

The journeys in these pages will whisk you to places far and near. From a tiny island off Malaysia to the Sorbonne Université in Paris. From Hawai'i to Caribbean ports of call, from Tahiti to Belize. Between those foreign destinations, you will plunge deep in the Far Northwest. Pluck psilocybin mushrooms and taste wild duck. View salmon, mergansers, moose, and hawks up close. If you accept this invitation, you will cast for trout and paddle kayaks in whitewater.

That trusty culture critic Thoreau wrote in "Civil Disobedience," his blisteringly relevant 1849 essay, "Let your life be a counter-friction to stop the machine." The machine for Thoreau was a warmongering US government that disdained and even jailed pacificists like him. The machine of most concern for me is a commercial tourism that endangers climates, ecologies, and Indigenous people around the planet. The guidance I extend here includes superior forms of education, a base of solid information, and a resolution to appreciate the pleasures of the local.

among
the beloved

1

The Spray and the Slamming Sea

For five days a choppy bay has hidden the body of my son. Braden is twenty. The newspapers say he is presumed drowned. My reverence for water deepens by the hour. The blood sounds in my ears like the waves that pound on the shore—salt for salt, thud for thud.

Braden was kayaking with his best friend, Jim, on the Salish Sea at Larrabee Beach, a spot unusual for its sandstone cliffs, whose wave-etched scarps remind my eye of veins and ribs. Early March, the weather still unstable, an ill time for anyone to go paddling. The men were not planning to stray far from where they launched outside Bellingham on the coast of Washington State. Making up for the life vest neither wore, they assured their moms they would stay close to shore. That was the last anyone saw of them. The next day their boats washed up across the bay.

Six feet and four inches tall, buzzcut and bullet-headed, he plays basketball with skill and flair. *Played!* Before he vanished, he was going to college. A paper lay on his desk, ready to hand in, some research about our relationship with the chimpanzees. An artist of the pen, he taught himself to sketch. At the age of three, he sketched me—the wire-rim glasses askew, the bed-head hair, the whiskered neck unshamed by blade. Savagely we cared for one another, father and son. Now every glimpse of seawater rocks me, menaces me, unlike any other vision ever did.

When I was a child, my father saved me from death by drowning. Fishing on a river beside him, I slipped and plunged into the drink. Minnows swam past me and regarded the clumsy creature flung into their nimble midst. Those several seconds spent estranged in water somehow did not terrorize me, though. The swim was liberating, almost sensual, though I was scarcely four. Before the water could carry me away, sweep me out to sea, my daddy's ready arm unbent. He collared me and hauled me back to wholesome light and air.

Two decades later I asked my father for details about that narrow escape. He was as surprised as I had ever seen him. He told me it never happened, I did not slip, the ordeal took place only in my head. How could that be? My memory of the swim was much too vivid to discredit. I might have died in a previous life—if I choose to open the door to reincarnation. Or was it all a dream, a precaution, a harbinger of some sudden plunge to come?

Some one hundred searchers, all volunteers, tramp the beaches, knock on doors, and ply the waters of the Salish Sea in the days after Jim and Braden disappear. Helicopter pilots scan the San Juan archipelago, giving their time freely, taking more than twenty flights. *Disappeared. Presumed drowned. Missing.* Lacking any certainty or evidence, his mother, Vicki, and I can plan no funeral, no memorial. We wait in mystery and limbo, no closure coming into view.

Braden's favorite watch cap is found upon a beach. Vicki clings to her friends, drops rapid tears, and wrings the damp cap dry. Her sorrow has no bottom. I have traveled across the Cascade Range to join her, the first time we have met in two years. Her face is swollen, ravaged by tranquilizers and grief. She stoops. In years to come she will become a medium, one who communicates with her only child via a variety of electronic media. Baseboard heat makes for more discomfort than I already feel, so I go outside for a hike above Larrabee Beach.

Hikers hike at different rates. Some like to hustle from start to stop, vying for elapsed times, covering ground. Not me, though, I go slow, snuff the air, overhear birdcalls, try to name each species in flight. I poke along, scrutinizing insects, inviting the lay of the land to invest itself in me. I can stare at a tuft of lupines for a long time, charged by the way each leaf cup cradles rain, guessing when the tip-top of the flower head might grow ponderous enough to nod.

A trail terracing a hill above Larrabee is shaded by maples and firs. Through the Earth's thin crust, tough mushrooms shove, splintering fallen trees, even crumbling concrete where their spores embed. In my fragile state, those fungi wield tremendous power. I pluck one of them, a prince, *Agaricus augustus*, its broad cap curving to upturned gills. It smells like trees. How fully mushrooms, those torpid flesh-flowers, flourish on death and decay.

The Kiowa writer N. Scott Momaday encourages "reciprocal appropriation" of the land. By that process, a being can respectfully surrender to the landscape and take it into his or her experience. Maybe that's what Braden did—too enthusiastically. If *scape* means *scope*, and *scope* suggests the acquisition of knowledge, Braden knows the watery landscape at Larrabee Beach too well. Knows it organically not consciously. Knows it like a fallen leaf knows rain.

During his time in the womb, Mount St. Helens blew. We were camping near the town of Oroville, some 250 miles from the exploded mountain. We heard the blast as though it were a mining charge a mile away. A transistor radio report told us what had happened. Good thing Vicki insisted we pack up and flee, south and west, across Stevens Pass to get back to Seattle. The sheltering Cascades rose to the west above the mile-high curtain of advancing ash.

We camped and hiked a lot in those days. In bear country, because she had been afraid, I packed a handgun with us on some outings. One night in the Olympic Peninsula, in tornado season and terrain, a thunderstorm passed close by. The lightning's flash and the thunder's crack were simultaneous events. The tent poles shone like ribs, the nylon sheath like a thin red skin.

The Jewish prayer book the Haggadah tells the story of the Passover. A pharaoh, Ramses II, refused to free the Israelites he had enslaved. In retribution, God sent the angel of death to kill the Egyptians' firstborn sons. God instructed Moses to tell the families of the Israelites to sacrifice a lamb and smear the blood on the door of their houses. The angel would recognize the Israelite houses and "pass over" them that way. The pistol inside our pack, the tool I toted for safety, afforded us no comfort from the passing storm. She yodeled fear in dreams and could not sleep.

She and I grieve the absence of our son at different rates. Hers is swift and physical, groaning, low, a blow as though from a kayak paddle jabbed to her solar plexus. My own pace on the path toward calm is a fumbling and tunneled vision, numb and vulnerable in open space.

* * *

Ten days have passed. Water haunts my rest each night. Allured by it, repulsed as well, I hear its call—Triton, Shiva, a vengeful lord out of Leviticus, all anger and caprice. From my waking dream I watch the ocean's fluid moods. To try to escape it I cower, the water booming, flashing, a tsunami poised to slam above my puny spit of sand. A dream-steed rides me, a nag whose hoofs keep relaxation at a distance, who rejoices the fact that rivers never sleep, waves will not relent, the moon pulls irrepressibly. Rain falls and evaporates, with or without me.

Water has two moods: life and death. On many occasions I have cheated the second one. The closest scrape came while salmon fishing as a teenager off the Strait of Juan de Fuca. It was May. The king salmon were running. Black mouths, silver sides, full of hunger and fight. They schooled beyond the opening of the rowdy Salish Sea. There the warlike Pacific throws its weight around. We nosed toward naked ocean aboard an eighteen-foot inboard.

The boat's owner, Fred, had some knowledge of ocean waves. To earn his aqualungs, he had worked as a skipper for dudes out of Westport before he sold his birthright to the Boeing Company. Fred liked to get too stoned, though, for most comfort zones. With frantic care he guided his boat one-handed, smoking a reefer with the other, often tilting a beer at the same time.

The waves loomed large after we left the harbor at Neah Bay, the same harbor that gained later fame as a put-in point for whalers in the Makah Tribe. We headed out that day in May, plunging along the whale-road, the sky clear, Vancouver Island at our backs, no wind to cause us concern, balancing on swells that rose already human-high. Tatoosh Island passed to starboard, and we entered open sea. Wine-dark, it was *la mere*, the prehistoric mother of us all.

Fred set aside his drink and smoke to thread a cut-plug herring on his line. One hook passed through the hollow gut of the baitfish to reappear near its anal vent; the other bristled where the head of the fish would be. A five-ounce lead weight plummeted the line, sinking the baitfish through the wave chop, which now was towering higher than our staggered craft.

"Put your lines in!" Fred hissed, his words an audible function of the spray and the slamming sea. The skipper knew the fish were there. He had seen a riptide where they feed. The phantoms of king salmon agitated him. Presently his pole bent, and he handed the steering wheel to me. "Keep it facing the waves," he commanded, his feet wide, horsing in the slug Chinook.

Cresting and lunging with random shifts in pitch, the boat mounted the wall of each successive swell, then plunged back to flounder in the channel before the next wave came. Seasick weather, our faces paled. A kind of suffocation can ensue in heavy seas. Walls of water rise on every side, the sky shuts down, and the light grows emerald and probes. The foremost source of motion sickness in the human body is the salty and responsive water in the ear.

The rollers came sloping, eighteen and twenty feet in height. Backlit walls of green foam filtered light from the hidden sky. The waves silhouetted fish like bugs in amber. Our stomachs compressed. Schools of herring swam above us, bent on spawning in the calm of the Salish Sea. As if jeering, shapes of Chinook salmon overtopped the deck, wave-tossed, heedless of the threat posed to our boat of getting caught broadside. Half the time our lines were slanting up above us. Weary and scared, my mates and I feared another boat might broadside us, wind might rise and slash the wave crests, whitecaps hurl heavy water to the deck.

We threatened mutiny. Fred capitulated with a sorry snarl and wheeled the boat around.

* * *

Thoughts of Braden's final moments taunt me. My stomach cracks and growls like far-off thunder, gnawing at itself, fraying the sleeves of sleep. I have been trying to read philosophy to gain relief, just turned off the lamp in bed, and a tide of advice from the *Enchiridion* rises.

Epictetus, the Roman slave who wrote that book of consolation, spoke in loaded language about the transience of life. His words comfort me. "On a voyage," he wrote, "when the ship is at anchor, if you disembark to get water, you may amuse yourself by picking up a stone or a shell on the beach. But your thoughts ought to be on the ship every minute, to be always attentive, for fear the captain should call, and then you must leave all your things behind."

Unlike the Greek and Roman Stoics, I rely on spoken words to float me through. If the ancient mariner told his story to absolve himself of shame, I lean on speech to ventilate my grief. My mouth becomes a valve, a compression release to ease the tension in my head. The mariner in the poem by Coleridge kills an albatross and pays hard penance by wearing its corpse around his neck. Fated to wander the high seas and tell his pain to anyone who will pay him heed.

"The Ancient Mariner" is a sonorous swatch of sorrow about the sea. So is a lot of America's greatest literature—from Poe's Pym, to Melville's Ishmael, to Whitman's cradle endlessly rocking. The reckless sea, creator and destroyer, redeemer and swift doom.

* * *

Two weeks after Braden's cap turns up on the sand, I am buckling on a life jacket. Alex, Derrick, Neil, and I have toted our canoes and kayaks to the bank of Rock Creek. That stream is bony in the best of times. My hands are trembling at the jacket clasps. These young men, former students first and now my friends, have scanned the maps and hiked the cliffs above that Eastern Washington stream. Alex and Derrick are thrilled to be here. For seven hours we will dodge rocks, portage past falls and logs, and clamber slopes to pictographs scrawled on basalt walls.

No one knows for sure where we're going, only where we parked the shuttle car. No one in our party has paddled this stream before. At the shuttle drop-off spot a farmer, a red-faced Marlboro smoker with bare swollen ankles and scared hair, calls us crazy for tackling this stretch of water, this stony plunge through canyons fed by Rock Lake. All the same he agrees to let us to park our vehicles on his land.

I push the bow of my boat out. Flycatchers and magpies gather sticks for nests. This month of March is still proving cruel. Storm clouds threaten rain, though Rock Creek in this drought year is barely navigable—narrow, twisting, boulder-strewn, swift. Fences cross it. Fallen trees can stop unwatchful boaters and swamp them with the current's force. Herds of mule deer file the hillsides, ears twitching, gazing at us over shoulders as they go. Someplace in some sudden canyon, none of us sure exactly where, fifteen-foot Towell Falls will obstruct our way.

My kayak knifes its way downstream. Sitting just above water level, I feel like part of the flow, an integer in nature's equation. I stroke right, gouge left, and lean the molded plastic craft before each turn. We're in class-one whitewater, nontechnical, a piece of cake. Waves spray over the gunwale, wetting faces and arms and legs. Aside from our personal flotation devices, or PFDs, we are wearing no special helmets, dry suits, or other safety gear. Hanging branches scrape and bruise us. Our muscles strain. Exhilaration and anxiety mix freely, compounding the fatigue and chill.

On one sudden right-hand hairpin, in a pool scooped at the base of steepling basalt columns, Alex and Neil capsize. Instantly they bob to the surface, holding paddles in one hand and the canoe in the other. They ride out the turn, before pulling up on a grassy bank to pour the stream back out. Their clothing will be dampish for the day.

Neil, like me, has water issues to confront. He too trembles. Seven years before this trip, he watched his younger brother and his best friend go down in Lake Roosevelt, the reservoir formed from the Columbia River behind Grand Coulee Dam.

Near the burg of Keller, all three boys were hand-paddling big inner tubes for tractor tires to reach an island bared by the overregulated dam flows. Midchannel a wicked wind rose. That wind stripped the inner tubes from their grip, sent the tubes rolling end over end, leaving the guys to trust their muscle power alone. Neil at the time was a weightlifter and football player. He urged the others to work the water hard, he urged them to keep the faith, but no amount of urging could confer upon them the strength and warmth to stroke to shore. They cried out several times and then surrendered, Neil recalled, "almost peaceful," to hypothermia and fatigue.

My tortured imagination tells me this is the way that Braden and Jim went down. Neil wisely did not try to rescue his drowning kin. The drowning swimmer sometimes drowns the stronger one who would save him. Panic sets in. It might have been that Jim, who had broken his legs in a motorcycle crash two years before, was flailing and Braden tried to help.

Or maybe a similar wind set in, and both men were dashed unconscious on the cliffs by waves.

* * *

A month has passed. It's April 12. To get better rest, I conjure fond memories of him.

My son was plucky enough to travel the West in a series of low-budget adventures with me. In an Eastern Oregon desert, I cooked us oysters over a juniper fire. That bummer of a supper never slowed his appetite. Those oysters quivered on his plate. They were snotty and chewy, charred outside and underdone within, but he ate them and told me I was a good cook.

Another time, alongside a tent high in Nevada, at Great Basin National Park where millennia-old bristlecone pines grow, a herd of beef cows came thundering through our camp and almost flattened him. He was scared. He wet his pants. At least that's what an old photo shows. Nonetheless he slept there with me in that tent, and I remember he slept well.

He also rested on a thin canvas cot, spindly with aluminum legs, beside me for a week in Deary, Idaho, while we pulled weeds to care for an eighty-acre organic farm. Each night before we got in bed, we watched the mountains purple up and heard the great horned owls hoot. Then we checked each other's scalp for ticks that helped themselves to suppers of our blood.

There was another time, another long drive, all the way to Disneyland, sleeping at campgrounds and eating fast food. The first night in that plastic province we ordered some fish at a restaurant and within hours took turns heaving at the motel toilet till after midnight. The next day he was cheerful enough to mug for my camera beside a wax-museum figure of Mr. T.

And we had dangerous times together—like driving the North Cascades Highway and hitting a mule deer that nearly crashed through the car windshield. Like colliding with a runaway pickup wheel that disabled our Honda wagon on Interstate 5. Across that international freeway's six busy lanes we traveled together, southbound and northbound alike, after dark on foot, holding hands and running hard and dodging cars, to reach a lighted rest stop on the other side.

Sleep returns after two months. It knits back my tattered sleeves. In Bellingham we hold a memorial service. At that service Braden's friends and family speak. I stand up and speak, unsure at first if I can pull it off. Karen's and my four-year-old son, Reed, takes the hand of his sobbing aunt Jill and looks her in the eye. Reed and Braden had swum together in the Pacific.

Now it is July. Vicki says she hopes he won't be found, skeletal, decayed—rather that he be left alone. If only for her sake, I agree. Let him rest in the Salish Sea, cushioned by water weeds, rocked by storms and tides. Finding him would irrupt the organic cycle.

Instead, the parents will erect a bench above the beach with photos of Braden and his friend Jim. The city will outfit that site with PFDs free for the taking. Photos and a script will offer warnings to the ill-equipped, the innocent, and the invincible. And it will honor our sons.

Throughout the fever of that loss, I felt a tangible gratitude to have my new family beside me. Without them, I might have gone spinning off some precipice into an emotional unknown. Outdoor exercise also aided my recovery. The flood of endorphins bathed me, helped me battle grief, and conducted me into sleep.

2

Paddling Lake Missoula

With the third of my three sons, I have traveled far by car to paddle the Clark Fork River. We are crossing a bridge where the river's burly current compels a spell of vertigo in me. The girders of the old suspension platform shimmer, its taut cables whine, and the wooden deck tosses like a drunken boat. I halt the Subaru chockablock and draw a ragged breath.

Chase studies me from the passenger seat. Once the tilt of the world grows still, I smile at him, I engage the clutch, and we continue to creep the bumpy road that leads to Johnson Creek.

At the boat launch, the gravel single-track dead-ends. A man and a boy have set up camp beside their truck. They are concentrating on the water, casting hopeful lines in Johnson Creek.

I roll down my car window. "Any luck?" I holler, jutting an elbow out.

The father turning around to face me frowns. "Just a few squaws," he says.

Chase beside me lifts a lip. "He means squawfish," I whisper, pulling away.

I try to explain how taxonomists renamed that predatory fish a pike-minnow, how change comes slowly in these far parts, how bottom-suckers like pikeminnows are scorned as trash. The government pays bounties for them to encourage their destruction. Officials hope, by putting prices on those fish heads, to bolster slumping populations of oceangoing salmon and steelhead trout. Worse, I also explain, the word *squaw* is an ethnic and sexual slur for Indigenous women.

Chase and I are embarked on a fantasy of mine to paddle Lake Missoula. It is an exercise in creative anachronism. No one may behold that defunct water body now. Lake Missoula exists only in imagination, and inside key geological clues that verify its former life.

The dire wolves and wooly mammoths that used to roam this land have all plunged into the long night of annihilation. The invasive species humankind accelerated their Pleistocene-era extinctions, or so a growing consensus of scientists is coming to believe.

A lobe of the continental ice sheet dammed the vanished Lake Missoula. Ice froze up the lake and thawed it in cyclical successions millennia ago. Over and over its icy shores inflated with freezing, grew buoyant, and collapsed, causing floods. Those discharged waters churned to the Pacific Ocean four hundred miles away.

No one knew about the lake until J Harlen Bretz and Joseph Pardee traced its evacuation route. Those men pointed to giant ripple marks on stone, to scoured and plucked basalt that only coursing waters could have made, and to strand lines high above the town of Missoula, the area in western Montana that limned the ancient lakeshores.

Bretz floated his theory of geological catastrophe at a conference in 1927. His peers in the earth sciences sneered. They could only believe that Bretz was giving comfort to biblical literalists, that he was suggesting Noah's Flood might have had some basis in fact.

For fifty years after Bretz spoke up, scientists pored over those downstream landscapes. They explored landforms that had borne the biggest drenching ever to worry Earth. Convinced at last of the landscape-scale cataclysm, overwhelmed by all the evidence, they congratulated Bretz in a telegram that read, "We are all now catastrophists."

The Lake Missoula theory has held steady for two generations already, but it places great demands upon imaginations still today. Imagine devastating water storming across hundreds of miles as fast as railcars, eroding the epidermal soil layer with force enough to channel volcanic stone. Imagine liquefied topsoil seething south and west down the path of the present-day Columbia River. Now imagine, as if in time-lapse film, those floods occurring forty, sixty, eighty times over centuries. The ice dam at the lake's end froze, rose, broke, and froze again.

The Holocene, our present epoch, began about twelve thousand years ago. Illuminati now are dubbing our era the Anthropocene. That new locution assumes our species will continue as the major geological force for millennia. We are the weather-makers, the future-eaters, though I hold with those who doubt the planet itself is doomed. Even if we doom ourselves, the planet and its vermin are certain to outlast us, as shown when the Mount St. Helens blast zone came back.

* * *

My fourteen-year-old son occupies an awkward age and stage. I was the same way. Chase is six feet tall, leggy as a calf giraffe, his hair a mop, his voice cracking. His variable emotions may be measured by an edgy and awkward flick of his wrist.

Once we park the car at the launch spot, he feels the urge to cast a line to Johnson Creek, whose current murmurs just below us. He yearns to feel the heave of a fish and haul it writhing to the shore. I felt that same yearning earlier in life. At the put-in spot for our boat, I set the Subaru's emergency brake. Our tandem kayak rests on the roof rack, as rigid as a trophy carcass.

A car crash two years ago lacerated Chase's forehead and occasioned a brain bleed. He was riding with a family friend when someone driving the opposite direction crossed the line and caused a head-on smashup at a united speed of 90 miles per hour. Chase got knocked out cold.

In an ambulance heading to the hospital, he clung fast to life. A fractured wrist, a bruised intestine, and a battered skull propelled him in and out of hospitals for three days. Now his jagged healing brow gouge looks like Harry Potter's, inflicted by the envious Lord Voldemort.

Chase's random headaches and numbness fret his mother and me. So do fears of more concussions. One consequence of his injuries is misophonia, a revulsion to sounds. Though he says he has no memory of the crash, unexpected aural stimulation agitates him, even casual sounds like biting corn on the cob at the supper table. Experts call his condition a kind of PTSD.

And yet World of Warcraft and other raucous video games can enthrall him for hours. Summer nights till two or three, wearing bulky headphones in the darkened office, he competes with online players whom he never sees. He converses in sharp exclamations as if with ghosts.

Time spent outdoors might dampen cranial trauma, might thwart its formidable force. Or so some research claims. Meditative mindfulness outdoors might alter the makeup of the brain.

On this outing we are going to test the waters of those hopeful notions. We are going to take the first of several paddle trips that hold the promise of restructuring his cerebral cortex, reshaping his adolescent neurons. Or so I hypothesize. Time away from media might enfeeble the power of the car crash, douse the electrons that blaze like comets on his computer screen.

Chase is bending beside Johnson Creek now and extracting his fishing tackle from the hatchback of the car. He couples the halves of his rod and threads the fine line through each eye.

Fishing is a kind of magic. Fling a gaudy replica of a bug and you never know what kind of being might bite. He clips a lure to a swivel, creeps to the stream, and casts his bright enticement just shy of the far bank. The water mutters and breathes up steam. An osprey clears the line of poplars, followed by another. For such big fish hawks, they peep like barnyard chicks.

His mother labored to usher Chase into our world. He was overdue by two weeks. Hikes around the neighborhood, long massages, and cups of black cohosh tea helped the process along. The labor was painful and protracted. The breaking of her water overcame us. When Chase appeared, his skin was loose and dry, his limbs desiccated, his fingernails and toenails overlong. His chin was sharp and thin as any elder. He had spent too long a time in the womb.

The Ice Age floods that scoured our homeland were earthly births, as devastating as they were generative. Flushing off the topsoil west of here, they made our homeplace what it is today. Our language tells us landscape is land shaped. Shaped by humans in our occupied environs, by water mostly in the wild. We shape the land, and it shapes us. Imagine replaying birth's ordeal dozens of times, enduring parturition for centuries, like the battered landscapes around us did.

No pikeminnows are biting for Chase now, no trout or bass. We walk across the lot to the fishermen's camp to have a look at their catch. In five-gallon buckets their pikeminnows swim small circles. Living meat, like lobsters in tanks at upscale markets, later they'll be whacked in the head, fileted in slabs, slathered in egg and milk, dipped in breadcrumbs and deep-fried. Chain-link stringers from my childhood still clash with live trout threaded through the gills and out the mouth, stringers that clash and clink against the hulls of aluminum rowboats.

Chase and I gaze goodbye to fishermen and fish and head back to our launch. We lash dry bags on the kayak's webbed deck. Dressing for warmth, we slip into flotation vests and zip. I steady the kayak to help him creep in crabwise. Then I shove off with a wobble and leap to the stern. A lurch of current overtakes us, spinning toward the river and the lake. My old assailant vertigo recommences, the hazard and commotion of my water issues following Braden's disappearance.

The French voyageurs from two centuries ago trade words in my head. They dealt pelts with the Indigenous people. The voyageurs' bark bateaux, sturgeon-nosed prows carved to imitate those Jurassic fish, weighed three hundred to six hundred pounds. They portaged those bateaux across rapids and headlands, the ninety-pound pelt bundles off-loaded at every carry.

The bundles had to weigh exactly ninety pounds. Savvy supervisors could tell by the heft if any furs had been purloined. The beaver and muskrat pelts reeked like money, were money to come greasy-wet and flesh-rank. The voyageurs took gustatory interest in the beaver tails only.

In messy factories afield, the carcasses had to be split from the skins, abandoned where they lay, left for scavengers to have their way with. Salt pork proved to be the ideal food for the traveling trappers. Brine baths at home leached the blood and preserved the pork for weeks.

When Theodore Winthrop stormed across Washington Territory in 1853, he penned an apostrophe to pork in purple prose. "O Pork! what a creature thou art!" he warbled, "cutting neat slices of that viand with my bowie-knife, and laying them fraternally, three in a bed, in the frying-pan. 'Blessed be Moses! who forbade thee to the Jews, whereby we, of freer dispensations, heirs of all the ages, inherit also pigs more numerous and bacon cheaper. O Pork! what could campaigners do without thy fatness, thy leanness, thy saltiness, thy portableness?'"

A Boston Brahmin, heir to a Puritan heritage, Winthrop would have sniffed at a meal of beaver tail the voyageurs enjoyed. He would have sneezed at the beaver served whole in Canada to Prime Minister Wilfrid Laurier by Thompson River chiefs in 1910.

Johnson Creek merges with the Clark Fork River for Chase and me. That sterner current seizes our kayak like a fist. Murky with snowmelt and rock flour, the river is the color of clouds. This current surging from Montana will take some getting used to. Chase and I need to learn to stroke in perfect tandem to keep from clashing paddles and propel the boat on an even keel.

Three ravens high in cottonwood trees above us mark our passage. They strain, bend down, aim their faces at us, and surrender to full-throated cries. Their wings widen, their necks flatten like adders, the moving beak parts come ajar. Their tongues flick and glint like their prehistoric reptile kin. When they take wing as a single organism, their flight feathers sound as eloquent as grunts squeezed from wet lungs. The cottonwood limbs they pitched from throb. Far downstream the birds ratchet out the news of our arrival, down a chute of trees to the lake. That watery relic of Lake Missoula opens far ahead of us and reflects a patch of sky. Its enormous bowl transmits a molten blue, as if the expanse of liquid were a calming sound.

Soon we will enter the 148 square miles of Lake Pend Oreille. It is forty-three miles in length. Its name sounds like *pond-array* and translates as "pendulant ear," after the earlobe deformations from shell earrings that the Kalispel people displayed.

Lakes adorn this territory so close upon the Canadian border. French traders christened most of the lakes. To the south of us, Lake Coeur d'Alene—*core-da-lane*, "heart of an awl"—got its strange name from the piercing savvy of the Indigenous people in the ways they traded hides.

The Kalispels are nowhere in this area to be seen. They don't trade beaver pelts anymore. Their stronghold is the distant town of Cusick, Washington. They direct a small domain that specializes in casinos. Gaming on US Indian reservations generates more money than Atlantic City and Las Vegas combined. None of these Indigenous people are going to vanish, despite the forecasts made a century ago by Anglo-Americans, including Seattle photographer Edward Curtis, whose twenty volumes of portraits open with a photo he titled *Vanishing Race*. That grainy photo shows a band of several people slumped on horses, backs turned, riding away.

Like the voyageurs who poured their French words on the water, Chase slaps the gurgling surface of the river with his blade. He is *avant de bateau,* the bowsman, while I am *gouvernail de bateau,* the steersman and the rudder. Hormones surging within him make Chase moody, keen to occupy the stern where I sit, the power position of the boat. We improve our tandem pace.

*　*　*

The Anthropocene is an eponymous name bestowed to recognize our capitalist-technocratic impact on the planet. We humans, supplanting other species as top-level predators, now take on predatory functions as our own. By rifle barrel we curtail "game" animals and predators alike. The planet will outlast us, making distresses about the Anthropocene distresses for ourselves. We downplay the power of our home globe to outlast us. We belittle Earth's ability to shrug us off.

The cultural malaise encrypted in the philosophy of the Anthropocene can agitate and overwhelm the human spirit. If outright extermination of other species does not topple all of Earth's ecologies, according to that attitude, then our petrochemical exhalations surely will.

Not everyone buys into that belief. English writer Robert Macfarlane, acknowledging the proliferation of arts that explore impending doom, has written, "There are also good reasons to be skeptical of the Anthropocene's absolutism, the political presumptions it encodes, and the specific histories of power and violence that it masks." As a kind of therapy to defy the odds, I focus on planetary resilience before the onslaught of some eight billion of us technophilic beings.

Still, if one pays attention, there are plenty of reasons to be moody about our species. Chase's and my bioregion, comprising Northern Idaho and Eastern Washington, is known as the Inland Empire—a cringeworthy term that denotes imperialism. That so-called empire was built on extractive furring, logging, mining, grazing, farming, and fishing. In certain moods I catch myself bastardizing the tactless phrase as the Inbred Empire, the politics can be that retrograde.

Some of my fellow citizens incline to say, whether in gestures or in words, *If this or that belief or deed was good enough for Grandpa and Grandma, it is good enough for me.* Poet Gregory Pardlo pays satirical homage to "men claiming a hollow authority because, / simply, their fathers had claimed / a hollow authority." Filiopietistic, we may call that instinct, a phrase that I define as excessive reverence for forebears or tradition.

Philosophy gets inbred with hidebound reprise. Suspicious regard can extend to many others. Those others include citizens who move in from other states, Indigenous peoples like the Coeur d'Alene and Kalispell and Spokane Indians, and even government employees like me.

The renegades who occupied the Malheur Wildlife Refuge in Oregon in 2016, who left behind their trash and who soiled sites the Warm Springs Tribe held sacred, find camouflage in this Wild West, this land built on suspicion and disregard for regulations. Certain willful citizens regard the land itself with cut-and-run disdain. Give me the money and go away, the most entitled among them cry, demanding government handouts whenever and wherever they can.

A country squire near our home bought a plot of land where ponderosa pine saplings made good shade. The trees protected precious moisture on his acreage all year long. That squire unleashed a flock of sheep. He sheared them and ate their meat. In two years, his hoofed locusts had girdled the trees and transformed that grassy pasture into sand. Desertification is one high ransom extorted by our patterns of extraction. The culture shock of moving here, after decades spent coming of age in and around Seattle, felt like a jolt from a cattle prod.

The panhandle of North Idaho fits like a shim between Washington and Montana, on our border of the northern Rockies where Chase and I are paddling. This region is untamed, rugged, remote. Rocky crags loom here. Rivers churn, canyons lurch, and tiny tides stir massive lakes. Our adoptive homeland writhes with wildlife, even within the Spokane city limits. Our lives as humans here seem closer to humanity's primeval origins than any place I've ever visited or lived.

Far back in some ancestral past, in some collective unconscious, the recollection of Ice Age waters flowing around the globe might have inspired accounts of Noah in Genesis and Moses in Exodus. Ancient tongues transmitted tales of catastrophic floods. Edgy dreams across millennia shifted, twisted, and transformed those narratives of catastrophe into lore. As filmmaker Peter Jackson has the character Galadriel say in *Lord of the Rings*, "History became legend. Legend became myth." Blood chemicals still sculpt creation sagas in ways we can scarcely understand. Genetics, as we now name them, shape our primal memories today.

* * *

Chase and I take a break from all our paddling. We turn the kayak toward the shore and eddy out of the current. On a reed a dragonfly—translucent wings and copper body—shines like a living shred of tinsel. Chase has learned from my bedtime monologues how this creature hunts. With more control than a helicopter, it rises or tilts sidewise, it sprints rearward and forward, it races to assail other bugs. It seizes prey with six-jointed legs and dissects it with serrated jaws. Those jaws grind like saws. Oxygen-enriched Paleozoic dragonflies, propelled by wings that measured up to two feet wide, served in turn as meals for a variety of predatory others.

As entomologist Rick Moore attests, our human pressures have not diminished this well-adapted hunter known as dragonfly. Chase and I edge closer, hoping to watch its jaws work, but it is too skittish to let us approach. In a twinkling it is gone. Instances of predatory behavior take place every millisecond. These sky pilots, as I baptize the hundred-plus species of dragonflies, help to guard the flesh that coats our bones. They destroy clouds of mosquitoes and gnats attracted by our body heat. They feed on parasites we entice with our carbon-dioxide sighs.

Most killing flits beneath our notice due to its small scale. Only when it rises to human level does much bloodshed catch our care. Cats will vanish from urban yards when coyotes snatch them. A cougar near a jogging path strikes dread, as do bears in the orchard and wolves in fields grazed by cattle or sheep. Where Lake Missoula spread, fled, and filled back up, dire wolves and short-faced bears once prowled. Their descendants in predation show us how they lived. To thrive by necessity in those days made human lives precarious and brief. Adolescent Chase would be fully intact today, had he not been battered like so much cargo in that car.

The most recent Ice Age climaxed some twenty thousand years ago. After that, Earth began to heat back up, and the Lake Missoula deluges began. We read the fossil record as we do a library, but in remnant layers known as varves—deposits of dark and light sediment which layer lakebeds.

Some fifteen thousand years ago, we humans roamed forests and plains in the coming flood path. We killed big mammals with stone-tipped spears. About twelve thousand years ago, the Younger Dryas, the so-called mini-Ice Age, briefly returned the planet to glacial conditions. Some ten thousand years ago, most ancient mammals had gone extinct, including the two-horned rhino and the Hagerman horse. Deluges flushed their bones away. To find whole carcasses is rare. One farmer discovers a skull, another a vertebra. Scientists still are unsure if humans hunted them to extinction or whether other factors came into more-important play.

The origin of the word *carcass* is uncertain, lost in the fogs of time. It first called up the moribund forms of human beings. As it evolved, the word contracted to apply to animals only, never anymore to people. A whiff of sanctimony arises from the tapered semantic range of the word. It suggests our blessed bodies stay fresh better than any others, that our carcasses mandate nobler care. The word *corpse* crept in as a better fit. Humans proved so precious, they differed so much from animals, that to use *carcass* to name the remains of humans became a linguistic sacrilege. Human bodies are said to house souls the subaltern animals lack.

Is a soul a substance or attribute, I still wonder, visible or invisible? Descartes saw animals as kinds of robots destitute of sentience. "If there were such machines with the organs and shape of a monkey or of some other non-rational animal," he wrote, "we would have no way to discover that they are not the same as these animals."

Our modern languages abhor proximity to the beasts. German companion verbs suggest animals feed with greater savagery than we do. The verb *fressen*, referring to animals eating, contrasts with *essen*, referring to people. *Menschen essen; Tiere fressen.* The word *carcass* I break down to mean a case for the carne or meat, a pungent vessel for foul substances within.

Lake Missoula had its way with parts of the world's body, furrowing the flesh of our ecosphere when massive waters flowed. Stark beauty saturates the channeled scablands near Chase's and my home. Some of the planet's driest places were scraped or scaped by water. How ironic that an abundance of H_2O, three hundred feet deep in some spots, could have given way to such aridity in the Columbia Basin near where we live. John Crowe

Ransom's book *The World's Body* drove home his notion that poetry and science offer equally valid routes to knowledge, a creed that might inspire my head-injured son as he forges his own way in the world.

Chase is young and strong despite being in recovery from his car crash. It's as if he has a survivor's drive to prove a thing or two. Atop the flow he propels the kayak powerfully. He slaloms us to dodge rocks, stumps, limbs, and strainer trees that toppled from the river shore.

If science and poetry lie on opposite sides of that dynamic sphere that we name the brain, their contact points might flint up wisdom from verse, spark poetry from science. Consider *De rerum natura*, the epic poem by Roman philosopher Lucretius. As an atomist, Lucretius trusted that the entire universe consists of particles in ceaseless motion. Atoms collide and combine and shape the material world. When mortal organisms like us die, we decay and revert to random atomistic states. Unless, that is, we favor parking our carcasses in fiberglass or steel caskets that will never biodegrade. Unless overweening self-regard pays someone to ennoble our remains.

Adherents to the Gaia Hypothesis ought to question forecasts made by the most dismal prophets of the Anthropocene. Gaia is coevolving with us dependents, even if we all continue at disparate rates. Picture the moon-like scenery in the arid inland Northwest as if it bore terrestrial scars—skeletal stones protuberant, fleshy soil stripped bare by Ice Age floods. Those scabbed lands reveal a terrestrial host and the trauma it underwent. Now picture the Ice Age as that very trauma in geological time, an era of shifting and plunging temperatures that traumatized.

Now, very now, if imagination will stretch so far back in time, we can view Earth as a counterpart to our flesh and blood. Earth lives, breathes, and lies exposed to outside powers. Sixty-six million years ago, the Chicxulub Asteroid strike proved almost mortal to the planet. The asteroid almost took Earth down with it. Almost delivered a kill shot to Gaia. The planet was laid up, disabled, convalescing for an unknown time. Its flesh and respiration suffered from the wound. The atmosphere and the vegetation—the lungs of the planet and their attendant cilia—suffered tremendous harm. Whole tribes of wildlife perished in the interregnum. No wonder the Greeks originated the legends of clashing Titans, those progenitors of the pantheon of gods.

By the time the last Ice Age occurred, all those eons later, Lake Missoula had become a blister bulb, its ice dam a crust that toughened over a stubborn wound. The blister burst and drained secretions that carved the channeled scablands into wounds and scars. The planet recovered slowly. A long time in human terms, geologically a simple blip. Our region still is healing, striving still to rebuild the skin the Ice Age floods sloughed off. Images of those deluges freight my dreams and haunt my travels, recalling the loss of Chase's older brother.

*   *   *

Down the chute of cottonwoods where the croaking ravens flew, the lake mouth yawns. We have arrived. We clear the screen of trees and enter. Chase commandeers our kayak from the bow. Mountain ranges loom on every side—Bitterroots, Cabinets, Selkirks, and Green Monarch Ridge. Walls of water bear down upon my archetypal preconsciousness pervaded by this place.

Stunned on hilltops, the people feared some feral god had stirred up the fury. Torrents terrorized their homes for days. Floodwaters in the valley swept everything clean beneath. The people snagged a mastodon carcass that bobbed to the surface after one deluge. Displaced and miserable, desperate and starved, they fed on that carcass for days. They dug deep within the animal's core to get at untainted meat. Its flesh represented ready rescue from the rising waters, its bloated carcass the only deliverance they could divine. The people uttered pagan prayers to avoid the fate of the clan across the drainage engulfed by the bleeding inland sea.

A dream child born amid their peril launched thin cries at night. Tribal members bending to hush the child shoved the mother aside. They feared a predator might hear it and assail them. Those people, sick at length from eating tainted meat, turned away to other prey. Our rooted instincts still convey the wisdom of leaving old carcasses behind.

Chase has no patience for the fantastic tales I whisper each night as he is going to sleep. Blueprints for on-screen battles meet with his approval, but those characters need to emote like you and me. The people need to be seen. The ordeals of a veiled planet will not fill the imagistic bill. No matter how storytellers strive to endow and gender Mother Earth, Chase can see no face.

The closest the Mother Goose rhymes ever delivered is "Hey, diddle, diddle." That fable grants token cosmological dimension to the poetic energies that refresh our human dreams. An agile cow jumps the moon in that nonsensical children's poem I recite in the darkened hallway, between his brother Reed's and Chase's bedrooms. I place my head upon a pillow and croon.

But these are midnight matters, fantasy food, bedtime rhymes. Time to leave them behind. We are after all outdoors. An unsung boon in the big outdoors is a psyche at ease. Late afternoon on Lake Missoula has arrived. Here the wellspring of my fantasy lives. Here the ice-dam cork popped and shot froth like a champagne bottle across the whole Northwest. Here the states of Idaho and Montana merge. The waters widen, pivot, hinge, and settle. Our profiles low, our locomotion silent, Chase and I paddle faster. We propel the boat as light as a feather on the same sky-water that dizzied Henry Thoreau when he gazed into its reflective depths.

Chase spots them first, a raft of mergansers, a fish duck and her eighteen chicks. Those fluff balls scudding after the mother clamber on and off her back like pups. The hen tries to pilot them, guide them, recalling the old woman who lived in a shoe. She lifts a wing and seems prepared to swat them, school them, send them all back to the nest. The crown of her head is cinnamon red. Her feathers stream behind her crest like strands of frowzy hair. Game agents once named this species of bird a varmint and urged its destruction all year-round. The mother dives, and the panicked fledglings try to follow. Weaker of foot or lung, they surface first.

When she pops up, she bears in her beak a waterweed, its muddy roots dangling, as if she means to plant it. This harried fish duck seems to me to have become the wide world's body, a living vessel made of water. Like all of us, she serves the purposes of water by transporting it from one spot to another. Her sense of place lives within a fantastic merger of bedlam and old time. In this confluence where the river water tumbles from the mountains and curls to meet the lake, the fluids swirl to a depth of 1,100 feet. This merganser, a predator like us all, has a beak as rasped as any dragonfly. She clasps to capture slippery prey and gulp it whole.

This common merganser becomes the earth-diver of origin stories for me—the being meant to register all Earth-time for the First People. To carry out her job, she must take human form now. She must comfort us and wise us up, teach us where we came from and why.

For my family's sense of place and time, we are all catastrophists. One son capsized and vanished beneath the Salish Sea, his body nowhere to be seen. Chase found unconscious in the car crash a decade later, his essence battered like a side of beef. As a newly licensed driver four years later, Chase was smashed in another head-on. The other driver fled. No longer may we entertain much certainty of even keels on our journeys out. We have undergone rash cataclysms and survived them. We have prevailed against the gouges and scours of primordial time.

* * *

Thomas Cole made a painting in 1833 titled *The Titan's Goblet*. It hangs in the Metropolitan Museum of Art. The goblet's bowl forms a basin for a lake. Below it and upon it, a civilization teems. The goblet appears discarded, cast off. The Titan of the title its nowhere to be seen. The antlike humans would not be thriving if the goblet were in use or the Titan still afoot. So we viewers must suppose. The people who sail boats on its surface, who build vacation homes on its shore, must be incapable of viewing the entire lake, due to its colossal scale. The same incapacity applies to us, to our Earth and its processes in planetary time. We do not know how resilient this planet of our dwelling is. Earth is certainly more robust than our species, whose scrapes with viruses and plagues might be warning signs and precursor tales.

Nature is reclaiming the stone goblet made by painter Thomas Cole. A mustache of foliage furs its lip. Humans have built upon it, ignorant of its proprietor. Has the Titan perished or absconded? Been ousted by another species? Left his or her accessories behind? The painting offers us no clues. Thomas Cole might have been saying our species has pestered out the supping Titans, and all that survives of them are relics. They have retreated to their holy groves, and the only vestiges of them are artifacts that our infinitesimal scale precludes us from viewing.

Or perhaps Cole's titanic timescale, like Lake Missoula's geology, differs so far from the ways we understand it that the Titan has only paused between sips. In that sipping interim our generations come and go. Bacteria gather and reproduce on the goblet all around. We are those bacteria. Our relentless empires rise and tumble, ascend and crash. Late in life, Thomas Cole completed his *Course of Empire* series of paintings that reveal humanity's finest enterprises as in vain. If the ancients knew Earth time as titanic time, we moderns can fathom neither one.

Here on Lake Missoula, our planet's rotation makes the sun appear to slide toward the horizon. It is high time for Chase and me to scout a campsite for the night. On the river delta, where eons of river silt have settled, on an isthmus lying free of trees, we will have a 300-degree view, a line of sight to the northern lights. Our timing on the calendar is ideal for such wonders to take shape. If everything works out as I crave, Chase will enjoy a glimpse of atmospheric special effects on a screen whose grand scale far surpasses his puny computer monitor at home.

The dizziness that afflicted me at the outset of our trip has disappeared, like so much dew on grass blades in this month of June. Quiet and exposed environs always have restored me. I require open space for my imagination to rove among the plucks and crusts of geological time.

My fellow humans talk of getting away from it all. What they mean is getting away from their own species, both the detritus of our civilizations and those who most belabor and denounce them. To dwell upon the Anthropocene's wreckage will only instill a consciousness akin to original sin. It can only create a belief that our ancestors fled with all the good fruit. That they left the rest of us condemned to consume their fumes and sicken in their spew.

As the father of a young man-in-the-making, I want to trust our human efforts to improve the future. Sensible apes, we ought to be capable of learning from our mistakes and surviving this period of the Anthropocene, to be capable of overcoming this rough epoch our technology has wrought. Learn wisdom and solicitude for our fellow planetary occupants and travelers. Endure to overcome the carcasses of hidebound ideologies and leave their perishing flesh behind.

3

The Security of Dirt

On an airliner ready to head to France, the young woman beside me was nipping at her nails. We were on the tarmac at Chicago O'Hare International Airport preparing to "fly the friendly skies" our airline had advertised since 1965. Electronic chimes had begun to ping. Carbon particles showering down from overhead vents made us hyperaware of the air.

The woman nipped and gnawed and peered out the porthole and away. From the seatback tray-table clasp, her jean jacket hung. Weighted by brass snaps, that jacket slumped as a human torso might slump if all the bones were to dissolve except the spine. She turned back to the vast expanse of hardscape once again. Her neck fell to the porthole's height, as if broken. She wore a crimson football jersey, and when she swiveled to regard me her widened eyes blazed blue.

She had yet to cultivate the trick of oblivion, the surrender to technology, the flabby faith that yields its succulent bliss. She might have learned that sleight of mind from me, had she been in any mood at all to speak. Long ago I learned not to impose on strangers, though, especially women grappling with the stress of travel or occupied by books. Erica Jong titled her blockbuster of a novel *Fear of Flying*. For years I had smarted like my seatmate at the outset of a journey.

Most people relish voyages, can't wait to get out of town to lighten winter blues, but the impulse to hit the road rarely seized me. I gulped my sanity in doses close to home. Racing contemplations can cause a body to draw to a full halt. Journeys for journey's sake can unmoor a ship of state. Emerson saw the lure of tourism as a superstition, its counterpart pragmatic dread.

"I have traveled widely in Concord," Henry David Thoreau wrote, a lift of his lip curling the page. Explore "your own streams and oceans," he advised. Learn the joys of voyaging at home. He studied the patterns ice crystals made, the transits of fish in Walden Pond, the way that water offers reflection as pure as any mirror. Thoreau reveled in local joys. His friend the writer Margaret Fuller shipwrecked with her family only fifty yards from New York's Fire Island. She drowned in salty water after blundering from her homeland soil. Thoreau searched the shore for signs of her completed manuscript on the Roman Revolution of 1848. All he found were rags.

Science offers validation for Thoreau's penchants as a homebody. Recent research says common dirt harbors antidepressant microbes. *Mycobacterium vaccae* is the stuff under study. Its microbes enter us when we inhale them, absorb them through skin, or give them access to our blood through minor wounds. Such microbes can replicate the neural effect that prescription drugs like Prozac can deliver. Yes, contact with good old loam may improve human health.

Oxytocin is the chemical it generates. Oxy promotes bonding between lovers, siblings, parents, and children. The research on dirt also shows how far our bodies can communicate with our brains. How immune-system fitness can improve mental health. And how microbes stimulate serotonin—in mice and humans alike—to boost mood, memory, attention, and awareness.

Dirt is magic, after a fashion. Kids in urban bubbles must ingest too little of it. Those kids need to get out, roll around, raise some clouds of dust. Organisms that thrive without dirt are rare. Even air plants, epiphytes, need humidity as dense as soil to survive. Twice grounded, born under the Earth sign of Taurus, I cherish dirt. When I camp, I often spurn a tent. I do not mind if insects creep across me. Open air assuages primal aversions to being caged.

Barn muck, swamp mud, and chaste dirt caked the pasture and corral in my family's Seattle-area acreage. Our horses, cows, and sheep exuded vapors. From the pigeon coop, dander and feather dust eddied down. So did pollen from towering Douglas firs that shaded the acreage. When I moved away for college, though, I cut my connections to the healthful barnyard dirt.

William James, father of American psychology, separated "healthy-mindedness" from what he dubbed "soul-sickness." In his book *The Varieties of Religious Experience,* people who expect exceptional destinies, James dubbed their lot "sick souls." Their thoughts clog with concerns they have been singled out. Such souls are stalked by phantasms that behave in unpredictable ways. Phantasms that might spring upon and savage them, or lie down before and adore them, or shine a celestial light that will bring them to the admiration of all humankind.

James's "healthy-minded" study subjects did not behave at all that way. Did not fixate on the future, or brood in solitude, or bemoan past blunders and missed chances, or weep about their potential destinies as pariahs. They live openly and for the moment, as I devoutly strove to do. The acrid habit of gazing at the fantods in the brainpan had to shatter. Relinquishing touch with native terrain might help. Willingly lifting feet from this dirt-and-water body we call Earth.

Right there I found another pair of crossed hairs, a set of behaviors called travel aversion. For the travel-averse, a trip can be a foolish imprudence, a species of consumerism. Such people often find it absurd that travel broadens a body, that it fortifies the heart or mind. The recent pandemic, the invisible viruses that humankind came to fear, only bolstered such aversions.

A new vocation has arrived with the pandemic—the aviation psychologist. Erin Bowen is one such at the University of Texas-Arlington. She teaches business and was quoted in late August 2021, right when the more highly viral delta variant of COVID-19 was taking off. "In the best of times," Bowen said, "flying is stressful. In the COVID-19 environment, it's explosive."

Travel aversion at its pathological extreme can ripen into hodophobia. Or so I discovered when I found its symptoms. Greek for the word *path,* hodos (or ὁδός) is the root of *hodophobia.* Such sufferers distrust and fear paths, particularly paths tainted by humankind. Hodophobia's causes are matters of some dispute. One hypothesis holds that a key travel event can trigger the bizarre affliction. Hearing that fact cast me back to a spell I found myself locked in a car trunk.

It was a rare hot day in Seattle, and I was nine. The car, a big-finned Chevrolet. All the seats had filled with sisters, parents, and friends. I clambered in the tomblike trunk and held it shut to conform to the rules of the road. All was well until an asphalt bump slammed it closed. That was when six hands seized me and squeezed. The lungs jammed shut, I could not inhale, I hammered the lid to summon my release. Once I could catch my breath again, I felt lucky not to have mashed a finger in the latch. That damn path had bushwhacked me. The loss of Braden later bolstered my aversion, as if the cosmos itself had sent a signal.

Teach me to tolerate my quirks and faults, no confessional booth needed for that. But turn me loose on foreign paths without adequate gear, make me cling to random straws that strangers proffer, such scenarios concocted stress. My private imp was like to sidle up and hiss with glee that the wallet or the ticket was sure to be lost, street signs vanish or turn illegible, the air solidify and contrive to suffocate. I took my prompts from healthy others like my beloved when I could.

Hodophobia manufactures its own weather. Stomachs churn and gurgle from the strain of journeys. Lips grow chapped and ridden by rash. Body temperatures rise, goading sweat glands to flow. Unexpected obstacles loom large as bulging lava domes. The eyesight might even begin to blur. How find the right train, the live gate, when the world will not come fully into focus?

Captive in a German airport once, I saw a young man scan a monitor, burst into Spanish, melt into honest and open tears. I could not look away. His was the ravaged face of a stranger in a graveyard, a ghost of calamities yet to come. Agoraphobia is that disproportionate or irrational dread of being in crowds, public places, or open areas. If less than 5 percent of US adults suffer from agoraphobia, then the numbers of hodophobic sufferers must be vanishingly minute.

Mind-travel, more sustainable than going mobile across geography, may be gained by substances, by exercise, or by immersion in the arts. Artistic transport is that enviable condition I have been a lucky recipient of. Dance, literature, visual arts including sculpture, all of those have moved me mystically at times. In my late teens once, awkward to admit, I spent an hour alone in hallucinogenic meditation on one big toe. Or rather, meditating on how that toe resembled my father's, how his blood lisped in my veins, and whether I was fated to replicate his ways.

My Danish dad tousled my hair warmly and offered me the delights to be discovered out of doors. Confined indoors, though, stuck in the city or in our small rambler home, father Harold had a habit of jigging like a limberjack before the window where he stood. He jingled coins, rattled keys, and shifted his six-foot five-inch frame from heel to toe. It was as if he were performing covert recon on an alien civilization before he dared to venture there. As he aged, he grew ever fonder of his home. For her part, my mother was often late, or so he claimed. Never ruinously late, never trashing plans or missing-the-show late, just fussing with hair and clothes.

After she became a widow, my mother, Juanita, refused to budge. My beloved sisters and I took it as sheer distaste for change—some Christian inference that life may not be improved upon this earthly coil. Efforts toward advancement might only accelerate a slide toward greater decay. She seemed to believe that aging and entropy, those fusty laws of thermodynamics, might be stymied by right action. Such laws are mere scientific theories, provisional like others, fixed only till the next big notion comes along. Equilibrium itself is more than a trick of staying steady on one's feet. It is the emotional poise that may be gained from remaining connected to a place.

Bending within her hundredth decade, our mother puttered in her yard. She fussed over flowers, pets, and grandkids. She hummed. Gottfried Leibniz in his *Theodicy* claimed we live in the best of all possible worlds. A view Voltaire mocked, a view that has yet to be disproved. Stubborn Mother refused to shift, even when shoved. She declined to consider a latchkey condo, a trip to visit her California brother, turning over the care for her garden and yard. She muttered, buttressed by the enigmatic Proverbs, "A fool uttereth all his mind: but a wise man keepeth it in till afterward." She aimed to hunker in her homeplace for long ages and a day.

Some sage said genetics loads the gun and environment squeezes the trigger. That saying stuck. A product of my parents, who traveled from home by jet plane only twice, I chose to test my fate abroad more often.

To do so I had to pacify the prospects of insomnia, humidity, late planes, expired passports, unobtainable vegetarian cuisine. The jean jacket draped from the airliner seatback suffered other qualms. Terrorist seizures, pilot error, bird strikes, wind shear. My DNA transmitted my condition; at least that's how my advisory alibis played out. My parents, possessed of stolid genes, passed along my incapacity, both by example and by blood.

My motives for continuing to travel against such odds mystified me. I might have hoped to grow more at ease. Prolonged exposure therapy, the cognitive behaviorists call it. Air travel might blunt the edges of the stress, like a hamster's nails worn by an exercise wheel. But what if the cleaving that clawed my core proved to be the pleasure of some unseen deity, some foul fiend? My progress traces to my good coupling after a misguided starter marriage.

Karen and I, caught at a car-rental desk on Grand Cayman Island when the World Trade Center collapsed, gasped to see those jet-made projectiles on a TV screen. We grew weak-kneed. Afterward we could secure no flights. We could not sleep for fretting about the forsaken kids at home. Her mother had flown in from Tucson to care for them and afford us precious time away.

Airborne at last in fits and starts, we tried to doze on airport benches for two nights and get back. Homeland Security threat-level updates kept us advised of the looming likelihood of further terrorist doom. Loudspeakers fed the static stress. Airports till recently also blared mandates to wear facial coverings inside concourses and on planes. The viral kind of dirt that causes concern today is more insidious. Many more people today have become hodophobes.

Once air travel grew more affordable, we humans more willing to go mobile, we lined up like lowing livestock. Rustling and shoving, vying to be first in line, so many compliant bovines bred to become pink slime. "Where did it all go wrong?" stricken poet John Berryman asked.

These are first-world problems, I remind myself. People in developing nations rarely get to fret about the rigors of air travel. They rarely can afford it. Woe is me, we entitled types cry. Coach-class passengers used to enjoy finger bowls, hot food, and formal attire. But emotions recollected in tranquility might always be benign. From the plateau of midlife, the child's mind's eye might always revise. Then, too, some Homo sapiens grow pricklier with age.

If a tinge of claustrophobia afflicts a traveler, she must cringe when flights get overtaxed by cranky children, tiny seats, outsized passengers, pretzels for meals. Viruses party in airliner confinement. Jet cabins breed like Petri dishes. The cold medicine Airborne is well named. Air travel might be simpler were pure dirt circulating instead of human-vectored sneeze-borne bugs. One can hope that vaccine mandates in rational countries keep antivaxxers out of circulation.

Lice do it, mites do it, even lusty sucking fleas do it. But moving faster than one can self-propel has to qualify as the most Promethean feat of hubris ever. Groundless extrapolation can make it a stunning global wonder that any being of sound mind should risk the act of flight.

More people die in cars than by any other unnatural cause. Yet my fellow humans find it a rush to storm down a highway in two-ton pods of metal and glass. The 1996 film *Crash* proved spooky for its premise that auto smashups can arouse aberrant instincts. The film's protagonists, bruised and bloody in the aftermath of car wrecks, want nothing other than to get it on. Electric vehicles might begin to cleanse the atmosphere by slow degrees, but technology will never soften the sad statistics on smashups. The 36,107 fatal motor vehicle crashes in the US in 2019 rose to 42,060 in 2020, an increase in fatalities that occurred even as the COVID-19 pandemic decreased the number of miles traveled via motor vehicle by 13 percent from the previous year.

The fluids of the cinema today—semen, blood, and gasoline—make a tricky mix when they condition us to partner them with one another. Let us bleed, let us come with a raw explosion, let us drive superfast and cinematize it. The rocket ship on which Jeff Bezos blasted into space has been likened to a phallus. For many travelers, thanks to the industries that glamorize travel's fleet machines, speed is an aphrodisiac. The wildness and athleticism of sex might achieve a certain dignity at times, but not when exhaust fumes complicate the coupling.

In the Greek pantheon, Antaeus possessed a legendary strength. A giant sprung from the loins of Poseidon and Gaia, born of water and soil, he kept vigor intact by constant contact with the planet Earth. Hefted by Hercules, disengaged from his home globe, his brute power bled out. That legend can seem intuitive to planetary refugees and hodophobes. Chances for vast disasters ratchet up, it's plain to see, the more we strain to raise ourselves above the security of dirt.

Connectedness to Earth yields sensory calm. A lakeside view of water can tranquilize. But in the air or on the road, peace comes passing rare. The inner eye apprehends its speed. Telephone poles viewed from a car, bus, or train snick past like slats on a picket fence. River drainages, laced by creeks and swamps and viewed from a heavenly altitude, startle for their resemblance to our circulatory systems at work, our hidden arteries and capillaries made plain.

In a car or on a jet, the air goes rushing past so fast it becomes audible, it comes alive, it jeopardizes travelers if a door or window fails. When harm arises from our own trajectory as we rocket through the air, it is high time to sit upon the ground and spin sad tales of nirvanas lost.

Rapid travel used to make me skittish as a fart on a skillet. Now I've learned to subdue those crotchety instincts and socialize my fears. I have learned to play it cool. Even if I am my mother's son, my father's restless emanation, stalking the castle ramparts like King Hamlet after his murderous brother felled him. Today I have abandoned myself to confidence that a plain path through air or asphalt can bear no devious design.

My angst about travel has evolved into a numb trust. Surely nothing disturbing will occur. Trial and error have taught me the trick of deactivating the door chime, disabling the switch. My spine stays stiff, even when I am winging nine hundred kilometers an hour.

4

Shrub-Steppe, Pothole, Ponderosa Pine

My outings as a child began harmlessly enough. As often as our schedules allowed, my father and I packed up our camping gear and threw it in the pickup truck. We chugged across Snoqualmie Pass from our family acreage in Seattle for outdoor excursions. On those road trips we overnighted in the Taneum drainage, Colockum Pass, Crab Creek, or Clover Springs. We traveled to those parched climes to get fresher air, to spread our wings, watch wildlife, and hike.

On our hikes his every stride equaled two of mine. His proper province was the clouds. Sage-green moss swayed from pines and seemed to wreath his head. Bark chips, fallen needles, and twigs beneath our feet made a spongy duff. Our same Ford pickup served us as our bed.

Both of us needed relief from the population crush at home. We found our sanctuary in the arid Columbia Basin and Plateau. My father and I shared an unspoken contract, a tacit rapture that emanated from the land itself. We favored the dry side of Washington State so much that we came to call those inland pine and fir forests home. My mother and sisters mostly stayed behind.

The coastal interstate can become an asphalt hell for those who love the Big Outside, as activist and writer Dave Foreman once dubbed it. The I-5 corridor—that great transportation artery of the West—brooded over my bent world when I was young. Even out of earshot, the highway hatched drizzly days and honking nights. As if electromagnetic radiation had found a way to colonize my blood. Traffic racket as lymphoma. Particulates seen and heard and smelt.

Some people always chase frontiers. They find them wherever they are able—on fresh continents, on high seas, in outer space. My forebears, who emigrated from Denmark by way of Chicago, hit the Pacific. I bounced back inland. My intention was to reoccupy the intermountain West, reclaim those sparsely populated spaces that others had abandoned for the coast.

My Washington home lies by the Idaho border now. Low-rainfall natural grassland, like much of the eastern two-thirds of Washington, mixed shrub-steppe and conifers. Some moisture, mostly snowmelt, distinguishes it from sheer desert. Shrubs struggle to thrive on the Columbia Plateau. So do the many tree species in its higher reaches. Wildfires are a growing problem.

From my home, I bicycle an old railway, the Fish Lake Trail. Converted to a paved path, it links the towns of Cheney and Spokane. Wild beings throng along it. Because I hold attention to be a species of devotion, I slow to ogle creatures near me. Magpies, hawks, eagles, ravens. Smaller sorts, also, that can prove invisible—lizards, snakes, mantises, and walking sticks. On other days I blur by. I opt for speed. Music churning in my earphones, I leave the wild beings be.

A freeing sport, this bicycling. It opens us riders to aromas both pleasant and rank. Even at speed I detect leaf mold, pungent forbs, alkali water, a carrion heap. The asphalt I pedal on is a petroleum product. So are the skinny snakes of my tires, the hand grips, the cable casings. Such petrochemical reminders subdue the self-congratulation that might otherwise arise from my nonpolluting ride. I never post my distances or times on a biking app for other riders to see.

Sometimes I rack up the bicycle on a city bus and transport it to the office. After work, I cleat into pedals for the fifteen-mile ride home. Speeding stealthy as the breeze, I power past milkweed and massive ponderosa pines, past animals sunning or ambling on the path. Flocks of turkeys cause me to wonder which of us would suffer most if we smashed up. Bald eagles above Queen Lucas Lake sometimes eye me at eye level from low branches where they fish. Bull snakes, lizards, and the occasional rattlesnake soak up the heat radiated by the pavement's black.

On the west side of Spokane where we live, moose have sometimes spooked us. They stand at shoulders six feet high. We almost collide on bicycle rides or backroad scrapes. At night they have outsized our compact cars. Woe to the motorist who slams into one. Approaching them on foot is risky. Moose injure unwary citizens every year. They tower over witless wanderers and strike like horses with the forefeet. We surrender our domestic spaces to them without being told. We lavish them with gratitude for the wildness they typify so nearby.

Living beside the largest city park, like my family and I do, means moose are frequent visitors to our gardens and yards. They feed on our landscaping and linger in the leaves. During the peak of the pandemic, when most people were isolating, moose strolled our streets. Complete attention extends our utmost devotion to them, to their size and power. One cow moose I've seen during my rides wears a blond chest and a forehead blaze. Other moose are chewed bald in spots by ticks—parasites that overwinter these days due to climate change.

From within our Spokane home a decade ago, I watched a young bull moose nibble at the leaves of a river birch I had planted as a sapling. The animal shoved its considerable weight into that top-heavy tree. It bent the whole birch to the horizontal and ransacked it leaf by leaf. Farther up the trunk it heaved itself and chewed. In its formidable power and determination, it appeared to me monstrous. It straddled the trunk and bent the sapling back to Earth, much like Robert Frost's youthful swinger of birches did for sheer sport in his poem titled "Birches." When that tree sprang back up between the moose's hind legs, it must have been a rush. Next year the leaves sprouted again like revelation. In succeeding years that tree grew too sturdy to subdue.

Moose are ruminants. They chew cud like cattle do. Their stomachs divide into four chambers. Each chamber successively helps to digest the woody biomass they feed upon.

A coyote hunting along the Cheney end of the bike path got a big surprise. Close upon it I pedaled and whistled a shrill hands-free alarm between my lips and teeth, aiming only to keep it alert and alive. It flashed a glance my way, leapt a stream, and bolted up the twelve-foot berm. Railway laborers had built the berm when they excavated rock to level a path for the railway more than a century ago. Overgrown heaps of basalt cobbles tower along the Fish Lake Trail.

The leavings of the railway laborers remind me they were more than machines. A century after Italian immigrants swung sledgehammers and picks to flatten the grade, their rock ovens still stand. I stumbled on the ruins of one while stalking redhead ducks in a pothole pond.

Waterfowl forgotten for the moment, I focused down on the crumbled dome beneath my feet. Crafted by hand, gray and overgrown by lichens, the mud mortar that cemented the stones long washed away—it wore a tumbled igloo shape. It also began to resemble a human visage the longer I gazed, a heap of fallen facial features. In that jumble it reminded me how people's mouths cave in and wither with old age. How our gums shrink and we grow long of tooth.

Using stones of local basalt, the laborers made shift to bake themselves dense loaves of bread. Think of wood-fired pizza today. A slate slab toted from site to site served as oven floor. Wood burnt inside the oven super-heated the whole dome. The baker then raked out the spent coals, sprinkled meal on the slate slab, molded the dough, and sealed the door. To bake those loaves from start to finish, I have it on excellent authority, took a mere quarter hour.

The barely visible aperture of the oven door became the tooth-shaken laborer's mumbling mouth. The stone oven also put me in mind of a kiva, a subterranean chamber Indigenous people in the Southwest built, its shape thought to replicate the arrival of kachinas, those ancestors from former environs or lives. For the émigré laborers who laid our transcontinental railbeds, Europe might have resembled a stained and tainted netherworld. America became the promised land.

History lies closer to the surface in this arid landscape than it does on the coastal third of the state. Soils are shallower, scrubbed bare by Ice Age floods. The potholes, where I stalk ducks with my binoculars, were formed when Pleistocene-era vortexes or eddies plucked and scoured the rock. Geologists know those vortexes as kolks. Bodies may not be buried deep here due to all the stone. In the complicated historical exchanges between settler-colonists and Indigenous people, place-names continue as blunt reminders of our ancestors' legacy of conquest.

Col. George Wright hanged members of the Yakama and Spokane Tribes. He slaughtered hundreds of their horses to weaken their ability to fight. His name now memorializes a fort, a cemetery, and until recently an arterial drive. His most well-known victim, Qualchan, involuntarily lent his name to a real-estate development, a golf course, and a footrace.

Onomastics, the study of proper names, has stirred my imagination since I settled here. The name *Spokane* looks as if it ought to be enunciated like *cane* at the end—and I hear it said that way in airports and on phone calls. But the Indigenous name *Spokane* has been given a midrange second vowel, in a syllable enunciated like *can*. The creek where Qualchan was hanged appears on state maps as *Latah*, Salish for fish, but as *Hangman* on the national records. Federal cartographers seem unwilling to let the state forget its treacherous bit of regional history.

Like our history itself, a tool I found along the Columbia River also lay upon the surface. With Karen and some other friends, I paddled on the Hanford Reach of the Columbia River. Before we launched, I read online, "Radioactive ants, flies and gnats have been found at the Hanford nuclear complex, bringing to mind those Cold-War-era 'B' horror movies in which giant mutant insects are the awful price paid for mankind's entry into the Atomic Age." Plutonium at Hanford helped to manufacture the Fat Man bomb the US dropped on Nagasaki in 1945. If paddling past a nuclear reactor on a river seems counterintuitive, we did not worry about it at the time. We were moving fast and were new to the area. On an island opposite the Hanford Nuclear Reservation, we pulled out our kayak to stretch our legs and take a break.

We had come to experience that last free-flowing stretch of the Columbia River. By the grace of its fifty-one miles of fast-moving water, Chinook salmon still spawn there. Every other ample part of the river has been dammed. On that sandy island formed by sediment before the dams went in, a stone tool from the First People lay in plain sight, as if crying aloud be found.

In my cultural naïveté, I pocketed that three-inch tool. Carried it to my office and placed it on a shelf, little knowing that the legal protocol for such artifacts is to let them lie, leave them behind, make a big museum of the Big Outside. From black basalt, a fine-grained igneous rock, the tool was made by knapping, my archeologist colleague Stan Gough said. To knap is to shape stone by striking at it with another stone to fabricate an implement. Stan named this one a flensing or skinning tool. I made sure to repatriate it to the Yakama Tribe of Indians.

The beauty of that tool lives in its simplicity. In the heft of its antiquity. And for the way it manages to shave the imagination. Its value lies in an absence of utilitarian worth today. We assign undue merit to technological artifacts that surround us—to smartphones and microwaves, smart speakers and autonomous cars. The man or woman who knapped the skinning tool focused his or her attention with a keen devotion. A devotion that would have been more Earth-centered than most other forms of reverence that flourish today. Less otherworldly and more this-worldly.

All this futile beauty lies far beneath the surface of the landscape for my kind. Inside our jaded gaze, natural splendor seems to drain like so much topsoil during an Ice Age flood. While museums draw millions of visitors, and paintings command hundreds of millions in appreciation, the arid landscapes of the American West abide in silence, in dire need of federal funds to rectify their decades of neglect. Such landscapes might be acquired tastes. Only certain sensibilities might find their desires mirrored in the stark and spartan geography of my adoptive home.

My father was never a collector of artifacts, a Wild West reenactor, or a practitioner of creative anachronisms. My father, Harold, was a modern man from Seattle who often needed to get away from the city. The last time he visited me from Seattle, we motored out to open range, that quaint space where grated cattle guards keep stock from breaking away.

An Angus steer trotting along the roadside tickled him. It was "out for a morning jog," he joked. The cow really looked the part. Tail raised, hoofs clopping, dust puffs settling behind.

5

The Trumpets of Solitude

Travel can be hazardous, as the disappearance of my oldest son showed. It can also be healing, as I hope kayak outings with son Chase reveal. My challenge was to find a balance between getting out, taking chances, and curling in the cocoon of home. To be committed to an outdoor education means shoving the downy fledglings out of the nest to flex their wings.

Computers and televisions offer alluring alternatives to firsthand experience. To press a remote control, to slide a mouse on a track pad, takes so much less effort than packing gear and facing gnarly elements in the out-of-doors. On-screen entertainments prove accessible even from the comforts of bed. Media studies show more folks prefer to consume nature at a distance than at firsthand. The open air presents distresses to contend with—heat, cold, snakes, bugs, and mud.

Not only did I have to overcome the multiple enchantments of the entertainment industry to get my offspring outside. I had to compromise and let go my own doubts about television. At home I finally caved. I bought a TV, DVD player, and cable service. My boys wanted to watch videos and shows. They wanted to see the whole world shining in its savagery and glee. They had been badgering me to get with the program. After clashes with TV's freeze frames, fast cuts, implausible plots, and sensational effects, I rolled over and agreed to try my hand at relaxing in front of the TV's flat screen. I would regard it as a penance for being resistant for so long.

My childhood experiences with TV had left me offended. It promised entertainment, education, even art, but it delivered so much less. All the same, I grew habituated. My habits included Johnny Weissmuller as Tarzan at 4:00 p.m. on Sundays, *The Wonderful World of Disney* at 7:00 p.m. the same day, *Daniel Boone* at 8:00 p.m. on Thursdays, *Lassie* at 2:00 p.m. on Saturdays. Those shows honed my tastes for natural spaces I could not see at home. TV's vivid simulacra lured me from the wider world, from that massive screen with no ads where I preferred to spend my time in swamps and trees.

The marshy acres of my Seattle borough cultivated auditory dream fodder for a modern child. Wild spots stirred with the rhythms of water, wind, and birds. Natural noises filled the interstices between civilization's dissonance, as if tape loops were undergoing overdubs. The moment a temperate wind would lift me to its lips and whisper, cymbals from the city would crash, horns roar, every intimacy shattered. I yearned to be in earshot of water all the time.

As my domain I claimed the seam of airport, wetland, highway, and woodlot on Seattle's south side. My homestead's acreage had become a noisy place. Escape proved difficult without obsessing on plants and bugs, without retreating far into the apertures of the imagination.

The whistling of widgeons turned nervous when a neighbor's hammer rang on a post. Those ducks took wing when a country squire's pent-up Labrador tore from its kennel door and raced their way, choke chain jangling. Jet planes drowned out coughs, curses, even gunshots, swallowing the innuendoes of birdsongs whole. Finches feeding upside down on thistle seed heads ceased when a car on the highway flung a clattering hubcap. Rock doves cooing on roosts grew grave in the wake of sonic booms military planes made. Classes in my school fell silent for twenty fragmented minutes every day to wait out passenger planes that roared by overhead.

Something in television's white noise seemed to assuage the busy growth and change in my environs. Curled before the TV, I could believe in being lulled to sleep beside still waters.

* * *

My mentor in this meditation on television is poet Wallace Stevens. He "explored exotic verbal words in his poetry while working as a claims lawyer for the Hartford Insurance Group," a *New York Times* writer noted. His poetry plumbs the pleasing prospects of an aestheticism TV lacks. In "Notes Toward a Supreme Fiction," Stevens rhapsodized: "In solitude the trumpets of solitude / Are not of another solitude resounding; / A little string speaks for a crowd of voices."

Solitude may resound like a noise, Stevens implies. Those for whom solitude is fraught or appalling may silence that clamor with the sounds and sights the television provides. Such proxies might not still the din, but they can supplant it by distracting the listener who—to recall Stevens in another context—"nothing himself, beholds / Nothing that is not there and the nothing that is." The volume of our trumpets can assess our inner wealth. We may watch TV to distract our imaginations from the frightening silence that we imagine preceding and following oblivion.

One night I was feverish, or had simply burned a few too many images on my retinas, when I woke with a groan from a terrifying dream. My nightmare-nation had mandated a ritual sacrifice, and at random I was named. The TV broadcast the news of my nomination to the nation and to me. That same polystyrene box glared and prepared to cast the death ray that would do me in. Before it I lay transfixed, the culmination of my martyrdom at hand.

On my birthday the year before, Ohio National Guardsmen had shot to death four Kent State University students, an ordeal broadcast into living rooms around the nation. I accepted that event as a dark gift from my government, the same government to use the TV to market the war on Iraq following 9/11. Whether I was awake or asleep, I had become an edgy habitué of the TV.

As a college student, I grew more skittish about watching. For years I withdrew myself from any TV whatsoever, even shunning a room where one was playing. Still, I never lifted an eyebrow over others who indulged. Their carefree faces even edged me into envy. Rejecting the medium kept me from being drawn in, co-opted, self-betrayed. If environmentalists were pushing for no compromise in defense of Mother Earth, I held that no TV was good TV.

When my college friends tuned in to *Saturday Night Live,* I crept away to read books or listen to live music at downtown beer bars. *All in the Family* and *MASH* had absorbed me in high school, both shows rich in social commentary. Then, in the decade after college, I responded to *Northern Exposure*, a Shakespearean show produced and filmed in my beloved Northwest landscapes. But I always felt antsy before the screen, as if its commerce were programming me.

Even public TV, I noticed, captured funds from companies that needed to cleanse their trade in petrochemicals, wood products, agriculture, and more. Bad corporate actors exploited TV to greenwash their behaviors. Sponsorship imparted a lustre of midday to corporations benighted by malfeasance or greed. Sponsorship of public programming bought cheap PR in the same market segment that historically had been skeptical of corporate messaging. If the elites could not suss out television's impostures, what hope remained for us eaters of pork and beans?

Enhanced sponsor credits on nonprofit networks became de facto commercials. They transmitted logos, slogans, promises, pledges, names, phone numbers, and websites. Ever since Congress began to gun for PBS hosts like Bill Moyers, alleging that they push liberal agendas, PBS has become blander and more circumspect. Taking the principle of balanced coverage to extremes, its producers beat the bushes to flush divergent points of view out into the open. If I had come of age in a democratic socialist nation, in Scandinavia like my paternal ancestors did, commercialism might not have dominated my society and irritated me so much.

An image of my father entering retirement still pulverizes me. When the Sunday paper delivered the weekly guide to the network listings, he mapped out the evenings of his week. He studied the network grids and circled his favorite shows in pen, rarely straying from that script. Toward the end of each evening's canned laughs and ham-handed humor, he treated himself to a bowl of ice cream topped with maple syrup—gustatory treacle topping off the optical stuff.

Bonds falter, conventional bets erode, but lockstep programming dispenses constancy. In TV Land, everything works out. The same characters appear week after week, foibles on display.

The comic strip *Calvin and Hobbes* bashed TV often. Calvin made watching "a complete forfeiture of experience." He drooled, mouth open, "eyes half-focused." Naïve Calvin yearned to "take a passive entertainment and extend the passivity" to his "entire being." He invited inertia to set in. He welcomed the sensation of his "neural transmitters shutting down." His wise tiger, Hobbes, excused himself and vacated the premises before Calvin could begin "attracting flies."

From the pen of comic artist Bill Watterson, a thundering herd of *Calvin and Hobbes* strips gored the sacred ox of America's favorite form of relaxation. Having taken the comic as far into a cultural criticism as newspapers and their corporate owners could oblige, Watterson retired early from public life. Too bad corporate television can't assess itself as well as he did.

Were Karl Marx alive, he might say TV overtops religion as the opiate of the masses.

Following college, I discovered the book *Four Arguments for the Elimination of Television* by former ad executive Jerry Mander. "At first, I was amused by TV's power," Mander wrote, "then dazzled and fascinated with how it worked. Later, I tried to use mass media for what seemed worthwhile purposes, only to find it resistant and limited." Mander's view affirmed me in my trepidation against the unholy alliance of Madison Avenue and the tube.

Mander also gained my respect by coining the term *ecopornography*. It caught on as the perfect word to name the ways that industry came to exploit and manipulate the natural world.

When writer Edward Abbey posed for photos beside a television screen he'd shattered with a rifle slug, a boss of mine threw a private party and invited me to join him. We blasted his old TV and watched it shatter. The antique vacuum picture tube made a fine and lively implosion when it went. Few deeds satisfied more than to take up arms against a babbling box of discord. Symbolic action, I reasoned, might prove more satisfying than no action whatsoever.

In the movie *Being There*, Peter Sellers played Chauncey Gardiner, a witless victim of TV. Television holds his attention and helps to keep him tranquil. His culture ironically mistakes him for a prophet. The catchphrase used by Mr. Gardiner is "I like to watch." Jerzy Kosinski, who wrote the novel and cowrote the screenplay, depicted television viewers as passive conduits of frothy nonsense. Interviewed about the film, Kosinski warned, "Imagining groups of solitary individuals watching their private, remote-controlled TV sets is the ultimate future terror: a nation of videots." The trumpets of solitude sounded louder and louder for me as time went on.

In my first years as a teacher, I found myself allied with other souls distrustful of the TV. By unplugging, we hoped to weaken corporate control. We hoped to revive our creative lives, reanimate our imaginations, and shape our opinions and ourselves on our own terms and time. In the words of old Ralph Waldo Emerson, we hoped to enact a "self-culture" against the odds.

Some colleagues turn to TV now with claims of touting a cultural literacy. One colleague published a book titled *Who Is Who? The Philosophy of Dr. Who.* Nor is that colleague the only one who appears bedazzled and entranced. Rutgers University Press issued a study, *Look Closer: Suburban Narratives and American Values in Film and Television.* The assumption is television can teach us who we are and gauge our cultural currents. On the contrary, my inner curmudgeon mumbles, TV fabricates those currents and then convinces us we all are eddying there.

Several years ago, I met a German American named Hart Rink. On the face of it, we have little in common. Hart loves to hunt and fish; I gave up those sports long ago. He retired from the US military; I never served. After he retired, Hart kicked off an encore career. He wrote soap operas. For a decade he made some thirty thousand surplus dollars every year. He intrigued me because he disdained the medium in which he had been complicit. "TV dumbs us down to our basest instincts," Hart said to me in the health-club locker room where we met. For Marshall McLuhan as for my friend Hart, the unseen broth of the televisual medium bathes us every day.

A similar message came to me at a presentation by Barry Lopez, the nonfiction National Book Award recipient for *Arctic Dreams.* Once before I had heard Lopez speak. He liked to keep it real. One shred of that public presentation still itches in me, like so much embedded shrapnel. TV manufactures both products and consumers, Lopez said—hardly a blinding insight. But TV programs are not the products, he said, nor are we the consumers. *We* are the products of TV's manufacture, whom corporate sponsors devour from the inside out. We are food for industries that have discovered ways to graze upon us, like so much aphid nectar for the overlording ants.

Barry Lopez reminded me of statements by communication professor Sut Jhally, who has produced dozens of videos that document the sad status of American media literacy. One of those videos, *Advertising and the End of the World*, reported the average American consumer—just by traveling from home, to work, to grocery stores, other errands, and back—is exposed each day to some 1,500 commercial "impressions," a number TV watching certainly augments.

Despite all these data in hand, these biases in mind, I needed to try to make nice with the new family TV. As a father and a husband, I had to soften my ideals. My society is imperfect, I know in spades. Nor have I greater claim to decency than any other people whom I know. If politics is the art of compromise, so are parenting and marriage. A favorite line of mine out of Shakespeare's many plays comes from *Twelfth Night.* Sir Toby Belch utters the question, "Dost thou think, because thou art virtuous, there shall be no more cakes and ale?" To paraphrase those lines by the Bard, it is unwise to impose one's values, no matter how virtuous they be, on others.

No longer do I refuse to linger in rooms where TVs are playing, a strict aversion that would be perverse to keep, a fundamentalism that would shame. We are all complicit in this TV nation—in the affliction that some wise soul named "affluenza." My family and I consume a ton of stuff sold by multinational corporations. We fill a city garbage bin to heaping every week.

And so, I crouched on the couch at home, my knees beneath my chin, and watched a TV show from start to finish with my children on the new set—an imported flat-screen 48-inch light-emitting-diode television. We watched a show on the Animal Planet Network. In that episode on that network, African wildebeests were being herded and captured, driven toward chutes and pens, baffled by shouts, funneled by fabric screens, and shunted brusquely into trucks.

All except a few of the wildebeests grew captive in the trap. Those few escapees began to behave less like herd animals than like independent creatures. Seeing through the ruse, they vaulted the screens the humans had erected and stampeded back to the vanishing savanna.

* * *

TV celebrity Steve Irwin died in 2006, pierced by a stingray's tail. He was filming an episode for a commissioned TV series. His widow says the footage of his ordeal will never be released. Starring as the *Crocodile Hunter* for twenty years, he educated first-world audiences about untamed critters and their habitats. He hunted crocodiles. In Sanskrit *chaturanga*, which for yoga practitioners means the crocodile pose, is one that proves difficult to hold for long.

The auburn-haired Aussie mugged for the screen. He tutored us by acting goofy, fearless, even rash before the predatory megafauna he seemed so fond of. He took over his family's destination corporation, named Australia Zoo, and built it into a multibillion-dollar enterprise. That zoo includes a 5,500-seat amphitheater. Like other TV celebrities, he gave his audiences what they never dreamed they'd want. He manufactured their consent. Now his widow, Terri, and his daughter, Bindi, carry on his legacy by massaging his interlocking animal products.

His signature cry, "Crikey!"—exhaled as ersatz aftershock from the most premeditated scrapes—aimed to give a voice to everything that proves primeval and rare. He positioned himself as a junkie for the rush that comes when brushes with the abstract wild become concrete.

Viewers became adrenaline junkies right along with him. Witnessing his crazy capers, viewers reveled less in the ecological or educational value of his forays than in the entertainment function of his cunning stunts. Irwin helped originate, even perfect, one of the few extreme sports to demand that humans tangle with formidable species minus the tools of technology. For that reason alone, I doff my Australian slouch hat to Steve Irwin's barehanded daring.

If hunters and anglers were to compete with their bare hands, those nominal sports would dry up fast. Even bull riders in rodeo rings are wearing helmets, face masks, and Kevlar vests. For viewers who prefer their hunting at secondhand—think Outdoor Life Network and other pseudosports programs, not to mention "reality" shows like *Survivor*—the rush may have come from seeing how closely Irwin's artful escapades could exempt him from agony or death.

Some say he should have taken greater care, even worn a Kevlar vest, when he gave chase to short-tail stingrays. After the eight-foot ray stabbed him, he kept swimming. He tried to survive it. That act of bravado alone may secure him entry to some televisual pantheon. Resisting mortality, he cried out in body language akin to Saint Paul in Corinthians, "O death, where is thy sting? O grave, where is thy victory?"

Whether his heart was pierced outright, or poison from the barb traveled through his bloodstream, even his most unwholesome fans might never have a need to know. Irwin's deathly ordeal generated a species of mythology. Online commentators swapped stories that he had yanked the detached stingray barb from his chest before he died.

Controversy shadows his legacy today. His cameraman and diving partner, Justin Lyons, in an interview on Australian TV, said the ray "attacked" him, killing him with "hundreds of strikes." The water filled with blood. He knew he was dying. Strict rules had guided taping, though. He told his support people to keep the cameras turning no matter what went down.

The videotape of Irwin's final moments must be lurking in some vault—painful, instructive, never to be aired, if Terri has her say. Meantime his daughter, Bindi, agreed to be youth ambassador for the harried SeaWorld, a career move with which her own grandfather disagrees. SeaWorld's profits fell 84 percent in 2014 after the animal-abuse allegations and accusations exposed by the documentary film *Blackfish* that Netflix made available briefly.

On several levels photographer Justin Lyons's account resists reason. There are no records of stingrays premeditating attacks on humans. Like millions of tourists, I have swum among their sundry species, often at close range, and never felt the slightest danger or faced a threat display. The claim that Irwin suffered hundreds of strikes is also unlikely. Unless the ray had pinned him against a rock or bank of coral, there is no way. Nor did Lyons add such mitigating details. Steve Irwin must have made a dire mistake, menaced the ray, and placed himself in inescapable peril.

Decades before Steve Irwin came out to play, the avuncular Marlin Perkins, a zoologist of the experiential school, helped create *Wild Kingdom*. Sidekick Jim Fowler played the man's man in snug shorts and khaki shirts and hairy chest, a wrestler down and dirty with the animals. Fowler and Perkins invited viewers, beginning in 1963, to take part vicariously in encounters with nature red in tooth and claw. *Vicarious* is the operative term.

Perkins was bitten offstage by a rattlesnake and had to recover for several weeks. A bit of folklore combusted spontaneously—an urban legend that foreshadowed Steve Irwin's followers in their belief the stingray barb detached from the animal and that he pulled it from his chest. Viewers of Perkins's earlier *Zoo Parade* television show swore they saw the fangs hit him on-screen, so far were their imaginations enmeshed in his venturesome celebrity.

Who says TV disengages the mind's eye? Those viewers' flammable imaginations call up accounts of true believers who have seen the face of Jesus take shape in pastry dough or tree bark. In 2004, a decade-old cheese sandwich said to bear an image of the Virgin Mary fetched twenty-eight thousand dollars on eBay. If Perkins turned off some viewers with a bland *naïveté*, he meant well, at least by my lights. Marlin Perkins intended to edify, but he was over a corporate barrel of sorts.

Mutual of Omaha, an insurance company, sponsored *Wild Kingdom*. It seemed just and right. Something causes us to clamor for coverage when reminded that danger lies just around the corner; that nature strives so steadily to clasp us to its breast. It was a shrewd device for selling new policies—stir us up, calm us down, urge us on to buy. One writer for the program had no other job but plugging in commercial segues, usually spoken by Perkins in voice-over.

"Just as the mother lion protects her cubs," went one segue, "you can protect your family with Mutual of Omaha." Product placement strategies these days most often dump such clunky disruptions and plant brands more subtly. We organic products have gotten shrewder. Travel influencers in this century accommodate the greater sophistication of viewers who have come to hone their tastes on mediating screens. We no longer know that we are being sold.

Steve Irwin, when he was in his late teens, chose to go off into the Australian Bush alone, according to Australia's *Daily Telegraph*: "Irwin flew the family nest and went to find himself in the North Queensland wilderness. There he stayed for five years, conversing mostly with his dog." Like Athena launching from the head of Zeus, celebrity mythologies spring fully formed.

Irwin entered a naturalist pantheon. If John the Baptist fed on locusts, and Thoreau killed a woodchuck for its flesh, Steve Irwin hunted crocodiles. His entertainment become his destiny. Significantly, the *Daily Telegraph* story about Steve's leaving "the family nest" has vanished.

As he presented himself on the screen, he shared a bent with Timothy Treadwell, the hero of the documentary film *Grizzly Man*. As a champion of brown bears, Treadwell claimed that he could communicate with the bears and save them. After filming hundreds of hours of his jaunts, chiefly in Katmai National Park where he camped, he died by brown bear jaws in 2003.

Before each filming session, Treadwell combed his hair with care. He hoped to parlay his videotapes into a TV series one day. He claimed he had been passed over for the bartending job on *Cheers* that Woody Harrelson got. He also claimed he was protecting bears from poachers, which are slaughtered for their gall bladders sold as potency enhancers in Asian nations. Nature became a device for Treadwell to gain his rightful destiny as an entrepreneurial celebrity.

As with Irwin, Treadwell's final moments are documented. An audiotape is on record of the ordeal he shared with his girlfriend, Amy Huguenard, whom the bear fed on also. The attack occurred so fast that his habit of scrupulous videotaping fell apart. The ordeal must have taken place at night. In the documentary film *Grizzly Man*, director Werner Herzog warns Treadwell's former girlfriend that she ought not afflict herself by listening to the tape. One wonders if Terri Irwin had the stomach to watch the video that documented her husband's final moments.

Irwin and Treadwell shared a kind of hubris, a sanctimonious belief that they would be spared. Such complacency often manifests as macho jeering in the face of all known natural law. It has killed off people for millennia. Katherine Anne Porter's character Granny Weatherall believes she enjoys an "understanding with a few favorite saints who cleared a straight road to God for her." When those favorite saints do not pull through, and God reneges as well, she bends and blows her candle out. In much the same way, TV's fair-haired performers-cum-naturalists cultivated a belief that Nature, the Mother Almighty, had chosen them to sit on Her right side.

Jimi Izrael, a blogger and self-styled hip-hop journalist, judged Steve Irwin more harshly than most, but his accusation bears repeating, if only to moderate the lavish praise. "You and I were expecting him to die like this," he wrote. Then Izrael's tone gains apocalyptic trajectory: "Irwin made his living agitating and teasing wild animals. He sealed his fate long days ago."

What role might television have played in the sealing of Steve Irwin's fate? How did he paint a pattern for other gonzo performers and extreme-sports buffs? One outcome of our TV viewing, and I include myself, is the social creation of nature. The intelligent designs of corporations, all of them bent on consuming us as media products, inflect what we think we know about outdoor adventuring. Irwin as a media product had a reckless courage, a loopy sense of derring-do.

* * *

After a one-year trial with cable TV at home, I canceled the service. My kids at first were disappointed, but they made the switch just fine. The boys watched movies on DVDs and played video games. They subscribed to a commercial service that let them "stream," a locution which positions TV as one of the four elements, its electrons akin to water. No man steps in the same river twice, Heraclitus said, because it's not the same river and he's not the same man. Nor are television shows the same as they were in the so-named Golden Age, those early days when hour-long anthologies, roundtable discussions, and probing talk shows dominated the airwaves.

Groomed by prime-time viewing, my kids have grown more media-literate, I pray. Early on, their tastes tended to the fantastic and the gladiatorial, toward animated battles and fiendish plots by villains ambitious to master a yielding universe. When I say "their tastes tended," a trumpet inside my head reminds me of the industries engaged in shaping those tastes for them.

All the same, their palates have evolved. At the age of eight, Reed sat absorbed with me for more than four hours before Kenneth Branagh's *Hamlet*. It fed his attention that the ghost of Hamlet's father proves so spectacular, supernatural, fantastic. Burrowing underground like a hulking mole, the ghost erupts at just those times when too much talk threatens to bog the plot.

Overseeing what they choose to rent and view, I try to be hands-off. I try to keep an open mind. A verbal mutt learning visual tricks, I grate in the face of every rational instinct cultivated by my decades of biased likings. I grind imaginary teeth and clack them. Whenever I spend much time before the tube, my fingers flex instinctively to grab hold of the remote.

6

Ecstasy, Euphoria, Transport

A Russian ballerina, asked what she meant by a dance, answered with ex-asperation, "If I could say it in words, do you think I would take the very great trouble of dancing it?"

Marriage, like politics, is the art of compromise. I have compromised for decades in my marriage. I have compromised by taking junkets abroad with my beloved. I have compromised against my better instincts about hazards to ecologies and Indigenous people when we travel.

My partner for her part has compromised as well. She has camped in farm fields with me when night has overtaken us on road trips. She has seen a coyote besiege us when we erected a tent too near its den. She agreed to marry me when I was unemployed. For a milestone birthday of mine not long ago, she proposed we take a trip someplace special to celebrate. We could count eagle rays in the Caribbean, sea lions in California, glaciers calving in Alaska.

I declined. Better, I decided, to attend an ecstatic dance and journey in sustainable ways; get all goofy and sweaty a ten-minute drive from home. No bags to check, no cars to rent, no frenzy, rush, or fuss. We had attended ecstatic dances arranged by friends in previous years. Those uncommon dances are wonder-working revels whose delights I hope to make more widely known. Come to think of it, we met at a dance hall long ago, and soon after we two got ecstatic.

My lowbrow birthday outing transported me back to a formative phase when the art of dance first spoke to me, when I found its raw ability to stimulate the primal. In the 1980s in a Pike Place theater in Seattle I rose. A supple puppet tugged by hidden strings, I juddered to the concert documentary *Stop Making Sense,* my limbs like appendages on a jig doll. Later I learned that going to dance concerts could be more gratifying than getting sozzled and feigning animation in loud crowds. Dance afforded me a form of transport superior to geographical travel.

* * *

Seattle choreographer Mark Morris had the audacious ingenuity to choreograph literary texts that ranged from an essay by French critic Roland Barthes to sketches by cartoonist Charles Burns. The production that caught most notice, though, was his adaptation of two early verse works by John Milton, "L'Allegro" and "Il Penseroso." What does dance have to do with poetry? I asked. Those poems apply the notion of medieval humors to elucidate human moods. They juxtapose cheery daytime lives with more contemplative moods at night. Handel set the Milton poems to restful music. Mark Morris choreographed them both in a large-ensemble dance show.

From my seat in a heated auditorium, I experienced pure elation. Time slipped its gears and spun to a tangible standstill. Elation took me to a state that has no name. I call that condition transport today. It is the euphoric trance William Faulkner conjured to blast me back to 1850s Mississippi, the same altered state that galvanized a sculpture to life in the Musée d'Orsay.

A marble nude before my bench in Paris began to shimmer at that museum. The statue rose to life. The cold stone transformed into warm flesh. All awareness of time ceased, and the sculpture breathed. That grand circumstance is enviable now, an extraordinary state at any age.

The fusion of music, movement, and endorphins created the Seattle magic. It generated moments of artistic transport that were worthy of the Dionysian Mysteries. If classifying dance as sport sounds strange, consider the competitive televisual spectacle *Dancing with the Stars.* Consider the outlet that people gyrating to live music find in pubs and honkytonks. Endorphins are those happy chemicals within us. They are miracles of animal physiology, the hormones we all need. Endorphins generate feelings of well-being. They help to keep melancholia at bay.

The word *endorphin* is a contraction of the words *endogenous* and *morphine*. Everything that is endogenous arises from within our cores. Those natural opioids called endorphins calm or modulate our central nervous systems. They support mental balance. As every athlete knows, too, endorphins generate a comforting buzz after a good workout. Lives too indolent, though, must stunt the greatest opportunities for endorphins to generate cheer and uplift drooping moods.

No exertion is needed to view marble or read Faulkner. Nor can physiology alone explain every nuance of transport that ensues from a sport or art. Mental and emotional stimulation took me out of myself to inhabit both the world of the novel *Absalom, Absalom!* and the lifelike contours of that marble sculpture. I am eager to regain the rush, even if I cannot fully explain it.

Dance, the artistic dedication to human movement, became the surest route to transport I could find. Dance, less far-fetched than the *Star Trek* transporter that dematerializes human bodies, might not beam anyone up. It might not move humans to remote locations on the surfaces of planets. But some dancers do report feeling as if their molecules have been scrambled.

The endorphins generated by movement on a dance floor, the sensory overload of music and motion, can conjure out-of-body experiences of sorts. Such transport became a model way for me to journey vertically close to home. Dancers like to travel inwardly in efforts to move out.

* * *

Acting impulsively my first year in college, I enrolled in a ballet class. I jammed my size 13s into slippers. My feet slapped like seal flippers. My knees gnarly in burgundy tights, my turnout crooked, my *grand jeté* earthbound, I gutted out those dance lessons all the same. The medium of ballet had a sensual dimension. Eros staged at arm's length to match the AIDS era. Abstracted, dissociated, and rarified Eros minus love's vulnerability. Dancers' lives peak early enough, without the worry of transmitting a virus or becoming undue objects of desire. A woeful awareness that dance careers prove risky, ruthless, and brief afflicted the dancing friends I made.

If the athletic women whom I danced with rarely questioned my enthusiasm, some of my male friends did. They considered dancing to be sissy at best, fruity at its worst. Some of those manly friends, buff fellow students, spun on the edges of cliffs and ice fields. They skin-dived, rock-climbed, tested themselves in the open air. At that time in the Northwest, lug-soled boots and nylon parkas were standard-issue garb. Dances that included mellow tunes, dances without a squishy partner to squeeze, often got lumped in with onanism. Such crude inconsideration could harsh the most robust buzz. Then again, I consorted with hunters and fishermen at that time.

Long male hair, a facile signature of cool, could grant a body access to certain hip peer groups. Straight or curly locks worn to shoulder were flashed like union cards, shaken like hands.

My astonishment still resonates from a shaggy thug whose bad behavior I saw. He rear-ended a Seattle driver who dared to stop too fast. Then he leapt from his car, left the door ajar, hauled the other driver from his seat, and punched him in the face. In cities where I came of age, navigating my wobbly route in starts and fits, encounters too often rolled that way. Dance as an outlet, as a metrosexual way of dodging the fray, rescued me from certain masculine fates.

I found myself on the margins of a fringe of women who were exercising for elegance and physical rhythms, whose limbs took cues from their vivacious cores. For one would-be lover I sampled jazz dance, for another, modern. Neither set of lessons managed to sustain relations.

Those self-sufficient women traveled paths of physical articulation and artful awareness. Normal language cannot frame the corporeal inflections and innuendoes of their athletic sport. Their movements proved poignant, radical, and ecstatic at their best—rapturous gestures that lay outside the realm of sexual love but could replicate it safely. There it was, the substance and draw of the dance scene, that it might approximate the twitches and turns of private intimacies.

Some years later, as a footloose graduate student, I joined a drum-and-dance troupe. We romped at festivals and parades. We blew steam one could see on autumn evenings. Our group leader—a percussionist named James who labored in a laboratory all day, conspicuous among us in his game leg and thick spectacles—named our motley ensemble Choda. His was an inside gag alluding to private portions of the human anatomy, a coinage that would perish everywhere except in urban dictionaries. We painted our faces in Day-Glo shades. We dressed in tie-dye clothes. We stamped, sweated, and astonished children who gaped at us from sidewalk safety.

My spotty knowledge of the avenues of dance reached a peak near Bellingham in a farm field. A dozen of us churning to live music on a baking summer day made a kind of gestalt. We freed dust from its earthbound confines. The dust rose head-high. It settled over our sweat, caking our arms and legs. Dust rimmed our ears and eyelids as if we had dyed our faces in smoky guises. Dust became an emanation of the infinite for me that day, the ecstatic spirit of the global dance momenta made manifest at last. Elvis Costello asked listeners in a lyric, "If dust could only talk, what would we hear it say? / Before it's brushed aside, just as it's swept away?"

* * *

Ecstatic dances began in San Francisco. One goal was to build community, to fellowship in secular ways. Another goal for ecstatic dancers was to gain a trancelike state. Print and online sources spell out how rule-guided it can be: no alcohol, photos, shoes, speech, or cologne. Those public celebrations venerate private impulses. Ecstatic dancers share their idiosyncratic whims. All those good group energies, of course, fell away in the era of social distancing from the virus.

Ecstatic dances are commonly held in yoga studios for the smooth wood floors. Shoes are prohibited, as in yoga classes, thus giving rein to a special kind of reverence. In larger cities like San Francisco, the dances take place in ballrooms. The feet can slide. The acoustics prove ideal.

Tom Robbins, that literary wild man in La Conner, which is a seaside town between Bellingham and Seattle, contemplated ecstasy in *Another Roadside Attraction*. That novel took the top of my head off, to cop Emily Dickinson's definition of good poetry. A passage from it memorized itself in me. "Amnesia is not knowing who one is and wanting desperately to find out," Robbins wrote. "Euphoria is not knowing who one is and not caring. Ecstasy is knowing exactly who one is—and still not caring." Ecstasy is a state of abandonment and surrender and willful oblivion, a determination to float free, a disposition of spontaneity, celebration, and cheer.

Relationships at ecstatic dances can develop without words. People-watching ought never to intrude or overwhelm, though. It's uncool to stare, just as it is to offer "unwanted physical contact," in the words of Donkey to the smitten Dragon in *Shrek*. Some dancers groove mildly on margins. Others, wildly in the middle of the floor—ranging across space, going with the flow.

Dancers shift as the spirit moves them. They hunker, leap, plunge, or flail. They articulate unbridled bodily joy. Fans of Grateful Dead shows, where melty-swirly colors and improvisation reign, put a finger on the pulse of ecstatic dances long ago. Stable outlandishness can claim its time and place. Occasions to behave in stately ways proliferate in abundance enough already.

* * *

The dance I attended on my birthday was an old-school throwback, a fit gift to myself. One fellow in dreadlocks named Logan rolled on the floor. He left a smudge of sweat and no one begrudged him. No one rushed in with a mop like they do at basketball games. No one cared. His partner, Annie, struck challenging yoga poses on the margins for long moments. There she could keep from getting in the paths of others. Later in the evening she tumbled with her perspiring partner on the floor. Their limbs entwining, they resembled a pair of puppies locked in a knot.

Those twenty-something faces were the most youthful in the crowd. Others creaked within late middle age. One bearded friend, some seventy-five years old, a child psychologist of national renown, crouched dramatically and waved to an interlocutor we could not see. He raised and lowered his arms in hoops, as if lifting and dropping a ponderous ball. In another dramatic gesture, covering eyes, grinning and grimacing, he summoned inner visions and blocked out disagreeable scenes. His consciousness was traveling in those spaces, transporting him far away.

An elder woman at our dance gave her name as Eulalia. She stood rooted for a solid hour—eyes closed, arms held forty-five degrees at her sides, palms facing toward the circle, as if to absorb a collective vibe. She was a resident deity making certain we stayed safe. For the last half hour she moved with us just a little. Afterward, she confided to me that one of her aims in dancing is to summon a venerated virgin martyr saint who hailed from ancient Spain.

Eulalia, a name of luscious consonants and vowels, was already memorable for me. Wallace Stevens has a character Eulalia in the poem "Certain Phenomena of Sound": "Then I, Semiramide, dark-syllabled, / Contrasting our two names, considered speech," Stevens wrote. Dance and poetry are kindred art forms. Formal verse is measured by its feet. Poetic meter (trochees, spondees, iambs, anapests, and dactyls) resembles the taps of heels and toes on a floor.

For our ecstatic dance event, the tunes that organizer Frederick recorded were some jazz, some soft rock, but chiefly world music, wordless and rhythmic ethnic beats that transported dancers to a tribal space or a desired rite of passage. Frederick's partner, Cheryl, claimed to have whispered her myeloma into remission several years before. Yoga and ecstatic dance, she said, helped her to engender a medical recovery. Physicians used to scorn such claims as unscientific bunk. Now the conventional wisdom is changing, a change some pundits find long overdue.

The dancers during our evening split evenly between women and men. The ecstatic way is not to couple up, though, as on most dance floors. It is free-form, extemporaneous. As in yoga, no one will speak. No one will cry out for "Stairway to Heaven." During one jazz ballad, some people did couple, both hetero and same-sex pairs. A tacit practice of ecstatic dance is to break down the standards of heteronormativity. Such breakdowns help explain the lavish touching and rubbing that take place, if the receiver invites it or arrives with someone open to the exchange.

A man I will name Happy sported a batik print shirt with a cartoon guitar on the front. He had a ton of unembarrassed fun. At one point he waylaid my winded partner, flared a hand like a splash of paint before her widened eyes, and whispered "Boo!" That move threw both of us back to times of high psychedelia. It was a reliable trick, a device to surprise and delight without doing any harm. During one long song, I found a seat to rest my knees and catch my breath. Happy slid past, as if on greased rails, his face twelve inches from mine, blasting a massive grin.

Another dancer, Avery, proved so keen to move that he got underway before the music. We did not recognize him at first glance; he had cropped his shoulder-length hair and wore ballet slippers. A blond thread of a man, an arborist by trade, he broke a foot several years before when he fell out of a tree. From the way he plunged, you'd never know he had spent time mending. A trained dancer in his youth, he embodies a code of open sweetness and kindly concentration now.

* * *

Some altered states are induced by exercise and sensory input from music. Other such states derive from inside, thanks to biological good fortune or ingested substances. The festival in the Nevada desert named Burning Man is rife with every kind. The hot sun baking heads on the alkali of the playa adds to an altered state where euphoria reigns. Euphoria is that state, Tom Robbins wrote, within which you do not fully know who you are and do not care. Religious fervor, sexual excitation, psychopathology, or recreational remedies can activate euphoric states.

At a time when many Americans seem ready to write off chemical experiments from past decades as botched social research, Michael Pollan arrived with his book *How to Change Your Mind*. That book recounts solemn and ongoing psychological experiments and therapies that integrate psychoactive substances such as LSD, psilocybin, and even extracts from a venomous toad that inhabits the Sonoran Desert. At this moment, the legislature in my native Washington State is entertaining a bill to decriminalize psilocybin. One of my interests in artistic transport, particularly in the art of dance, is the way that human movement might change the mind.

Greek *ekstasis* denotes a condition of being beside oneself or rapt out of oneself. For the ancients, it necessitated neither bodily progress nor the production of endorphins or sweat. Those wakened ancients believed the soul leaves the body during meditation. Participants sometimes entered trances. Attempts to wake them failed. A winged creature was said to creep or fly from the mouth. At length that bee, bird, or butterfly returned, and the communicants came to. Such a winged creature is known cross-culturally to stand for the soul on an out-of-body excursion.

In some seventeenth-century poems, *ekstasis* encourages the so-named soul to venture beyond all physical bounds. The out-of-doors often activates the state. "Casting the body's vest aside, / My soul into the boughs does glide," wrote Andrew Marvell in his poem "The Garden."

People are transported out of their time, place, and even personality by absorption in a piece of art, by a reverie that arises from words, paint, gestures, or sounds. Some like to dub the encounter transpersonalization, a term too polysyllabic to suit. Visual artists deploy color and texture as their media. Poets summon words. A fresh phrase or sentence can excite a writer, a verbal gesture invigorate her surprise. Physicians manipulate bodily humors or tempers, while dancers can claim physical movement as a gateway to transport. Creativity can be healing. Dance is a lively alternative to commercial tourism, a vertical balm for the itch of the horizontal bug.

"Ecstasy is knowing exactly who one is—and still not caring." It is the liberty to be a bit of a freak or anomaly without fear of judgment, reprisal, gossip in the workplace, or questions at home. It is impulsiveness without the drugs, spirituality minus religion. The dopamine enhancer MDMA, the Ecstasy associated with rave dances, has all but eclipsed the original in name today. To linguistically relinquish the ecstatic state to a chemical would be to impoverish humankind.

To be or to stand outside oneself—the goal of natural ecstasy—is not easy to achieve. I aspire to chase that state more often. Through the arts, through exercise, meditation, yoga, social activism, and love. Mind-travel is too rarely acknowledged, except for a so-called trip on LSD.

Followers of some faiths discover ecstasy to be an enviable unself-consciousness, a frame of mind akin to that condition before their biblical ancestors chose to attach leaves as modest clothing, a circumstance humankind enjoyed in total innocence before the curse came down.

among
the predatory

7

Broncos in the Salon

On three occasions Karen and I took trips to France. Academic colloquia drew us all three times. We were dreamy newlyweds on our first trip there. She had lived in Paris for several months and knew the City of Light well enough to be my guide. At the Sorbonne Université we got free lodgings, thanks to colloquium organizer Pierre Lagayette, who was a professor there.

Our second night in that ancient monastery, thumps on the landing told us company had come. We were sitting in the kitchen over *eaux gazeuses*, fizzy waters. From hallway shadows a green jacket, a green necktie, and a pair of green jodhpurs appeared—all of it draped on a chap who looked as if he had straight dismounted from a horse. It was Roger Scruton, the keynote speaker at my American studies symposium, his curly red-gray hair windblown. He announced right off that he was a foxhunting man, a note that set Karen's animal-welfare nerves to jangling. Affection for animals and environments had brought her and me together several years before.

Roger harbored such strong opinions about the sport of foxhunting that he wrote a book to recommend it. That monograph, which I later bought and read, is titled *On Hunting*. With surprise I realized that our symposium theme of "Loisir et Liberté"—Leisure and Liberty—would be wider open than I had dreamt. My research abstract had landed in Roger's hands, and though he disagreed with me that rodeo enacts a quaint imperialism, he favored the cowboy's inspiration and proposed we kick off the two-day symposium with a strong brown drink.

From a kitchen cabinet he scavenged a bottle of whisky, and we began to sip. The social fire of booze can forge strange bedfellows. We made small talk for a while, comparing our two nations, and soon I was reciting my favorite Wallace Stevens verse with a deviant zeal. "Two things of opposite natures seem to depend / On one another," Stevens had written amid World War II. For the next hour, swapping opinions with gusto in that petite cuisine, Roger and I discovered we agreed on precious little. He leaned against a kitchen counter all the while we talked, cradling his ambered glass in his right hand. Only later did I learn his formidable status as an ethicist, a philosopher, a public intellectual, and an author of some twenty books.

Roger long had stood for a vanguard in conservative thought. He wrote for *Forbes, Wall Street Journal, National Review,* and the Heritage Foundation. He enjoyed visiting stints at Cambridge and Princeton Universities. Prof. Pierre Lagayette had taken a course from him at L'Université de Pau some decades before. One of Roger's more recent books when we met was *The Soul of the World,* "a defence of the sacred against today's fashionable forms of atheism."

Roger was nostalgic for the way the world once was. Society was fast going to hell in a handbasket, morals abandoned, and he hoped to slow it down. His fondness for leisure outlets like foxhunting owes its ardor, he claimed, to an "experience of membership that crosses the barriers of class." That clever phrase reversed the course of a historically elitist sport to nip at the heels of anyone who described foxhunting as either animal cruelty or human degradation.

Hunters from adjoining English shires, Roger wrote in his slim book, engage in chasing and hounding the fox. The death of the animal is swift, he said, sure. It may even be considered a mercy. If the fox takes to a cowardly burrow, the hunters must labor with spades to unearth it.

English author T. H. White watched as a fox, which had gone to ground, got dug up and tossed to hounds. A circle of hunters "screeched them on," he noted with disapproval. American hunting, Roger sniffed in our French kitchen, that is "mere shooting," not at all the same. The hairs on Karen's neck were standing up like a guard dog's amid a home invasion. When she raised her voice to contradict him, Roger cautioned coolly, "You know you're taking off now."

Roger had not read William Faulkner's novella "The Bear," which I recommended as an instance of American ritual, American chase. Like Roger's beloved foxhunting, the bear and deer in the Faulkner story are chased by hounds. Briefly I thought also to broach English bearbaiting, discredited in civilized nations for centuries, but then I remembered historian Thomas Macaulay, an English writer like Roger, who had noted with a superior smirk in 1849, "The puritan hated bear baiting, not because it gave pain to the bear, but because it gave pleasure to the spectators."

I had swilled my fill of bourbon, and jet lag had me by the short hairs after our thirteen-hour flight. To honor the late hour, I pledged I would sidestep further controversy. To make nice with Roger, I tried to shift the conversation into neutral territory. Gazing out the window, I noted that the Eiffel Tower was sporting a novel set of sparkly lights. Sharply Roger pronounced such ornamentation a modern device of which he could never approve. We headed to our separate sleeping chambers, to resume disputes the next day in symposium. Leisure and liberty indeed. How naive of me to assume that every intellectual might be affable and kind.

Two weeks after we got back, Roger sent me a letter—a bit of a bitter missive: England had banned foxhunting. He hoped and planned to move to the USA. He and his wife owned real estate in Virginia; he was bending toward a stateside lectureship. There must be family money, I guessed about him, after learning that he and Sophie owned farms on both sides of the Atlantic, one in Montpelier and another in Wiltshire. Like Karen and me at that time, the couple had two small children. Pricing Virginia boarding schools, Roger averred that private institutes were superior forms of education. He seemed to be displaying an ability to fall upright on his feet.

His letter brought our French connection flooding back. Nicolas Sarkozy, president of France when we met, tried to quell the African Muslims who protested his election. In a flex of militant muscle, he ordered riot police to fire tear gas at the rowdy crowds of Paris protestors who gathered in the streets. To newspaper reporters he dismissed those protestors as "scum." Like-minded protests and reprisals came to the streets in the wake of Donald Trump's election as president in the US. Sarkozy later was convicted of campaign finance violations and given a one-year sentence. In 2020, sadly, I read that Sir Roger Scruton had died at the age of seventy-five.

AN INSTITUTIONAL CHILL

Our transit to Paris had been an ordeal. Following a day and night of plane failures and layovers, sprawling in lobbies and shuttling to hotels, we travelers were feeling as inert as lumps of flesh. Twice we trundled ourselves and our gear on and off jets at Chicago's O'Hare airport without catching any air. Transportation Safety Administration officials, patting us down, never cracked their plaster with the faintest smiles. A sturdy quartet of French musicians trooped on and off the planes beside us. The mandolin player, unshaven and longhaired, got flagged at each pass for the most detailed electronic scans.

Traveling musicians must find time to practice. In the airport concourse, the mandolin player and his mates on fiddle and guitar tuned up, then began a mix of Franco-Gaelic shanties and reels. We airport auditors sat agape, grateful for distraction from the hurry-up-and-wait routine. Swinging into tunes from Cape Breton, the harmonica player sprung up front, faint without a microphone to amplify his notes, grooving and bending from the waist all the same. Our low-tech respite knit some gooseflesh on my neck. Karen and I were tempted to levitate beside those players and swing our shanks on that cold tile floor.

At the University of Paris-Sorbonne, I had been promised lodgings. That monastery-cum-academy was the site for my symposium. Other choosier and wealthier symposium participants reserved their own hotel rooms. I had proposed to speak on rodeo. My speech on broncos, bulls, clowns, and queens would impart some grit to the haute couture of Paris. My herd of creatures and cowboys would rouse productive conversation. Seesawing between extremes has always steadied me. Where the cultural fulcrums glide and totter, there I try to balance and ride.

The call for papers for the symposium had emphasized the theoretical. Organizer Pierre Lagayette urged participants to crack open the topics of

"Loisir et Liberté." My goal was to guide my comers around the rodeo arena from the point of view of one who had lived long in rural lands. My research showed me Indigenous people had capitulated to the cockeyed canons of frontier rodeo chiefly to beat out white competitors at their own game. I had seen those competitors in the Eastern Washington town of Omak, at its Suicide Race, the deadliest horse contest in the world, one that has injured countless riders and their steeds across the decades.

A conscientious objector to the sport, I had shelled out to huddle among the flag-wavers, the country-music fans, buckle bunnies, and lanolin wranglers back home. Born among horses, my sisters Diane and Jill and I rode a fair bit as kids. Horses were bred on our family acreage. Then and now, my abiding preference for animals over their big-hat handlers colored all I saw.

AN IVORY-TOWER SEVERANCE

Uniformed *vigiles* confronted us at the gates of the Sorbonne when we tried to enter, as if the university were working as a monastic fortress still today. Had *vigiles* been on guard when terrorists attacked Le Bataclan club in 2015, fewer people might have died. In cracked French I convinced them we had a room. Head upstairs, they pointed. See the president to get a key.

Up flights of marble risers we schlepped our cumbersome valises. If work expands to fill time available for its completion, unsavvy travelers overpack to fill the bulk of their big bags. Once we arrived at the president's office, we found it locked—like the Sorbonne itself. Weary and dismayed, we rang a doorbell twice, trying to recall what day of the week we had arrived.

A silk cravat opened a crack. Then swiftly, like the castle keeper in *The Wizard of Oz*, he relocked the door and left us in the hall. After two days on planes and subways, we had already done our dreamy duty—evaded the flying monkeys, slain the witch, and fetched back her broom.

Admitted at last, we watched three *fonctionnaires* flutter. *Tu veux du jus, Perrier, fromage?* We accepted two bottles of water and stood to carry them out. Too soon one was opened and poured, though, and too late we discovered our blunder as we watched the server bend to hammer the cap back on. To make amends we sat back and chatted, grateful for reprieve from the Western Laconic we both knew too well. Appreciative of the welcome respite from the blunted manner of the Marlboro Man and the contrived languor of the Great Basin states.

To find our way to the university's fourth floor, we wound around another set of echoing marble stairs and along an old-growth oak-paneled corridor. Our wheeled bags fell hush. We stood before an elevator with whose punch-code we had been entrusted. We tapped in the numbers, we breathed relief, we entered the creaky elevator and rose to another floor. Panting before Les Appartements des Professeurs, we plied our precious key and flung open the door.

The wainscoted hallway wound past scant monastic panes. Through those windows the lighted Eiffel Tower shone. The hallway gave out to a marbled parlor with built-in bookcases, to an indoor phone booth, or *cabine téléphonique*, to a set of ornate chairs and a cut-glass armoire, and finally to a furnished kitchen we were meant to share with three other symposium speakers.

Woozy, jetlagged, we flopped on the bed and breathed deep. My travel aversion faded. My adrenal saturation drained. The tension from our journey flowed away like water from a rooftop gargoyle's throat. I pulled aside Karen's long hair and nuzzled her neck with a stubbly chin. Paris for us would be a second honeymoon, several years after we coupled up.

We slept in late the next day, waking only when musical notes began to pour through the floor beneath our room. A practicing pianist was gentling us awake. The music shivered softly at first, then with greater ardor once the pianist's blood grew warm, the coffee kicked in, the passion built, and the day grew bright. Were we earwigging Brahms, Berlioz, Debussy? To be embedded within a building where scholars kept their studios and offices was altogether novel.

Robert Sorbon, the King's Chaplain, founded Sorbonne Université in 1257. He believed that scholars living and studying in ensemble like monks would flourish best. Soon the school became synonymous with the doctrinal practices that shot through other medieval universities. Church fathers led interpretive studies of texts. They practiced patristic exegeses on their pupils. Traces of that tradition still imbued the building's towers and spires, its passages echoing like gangways on a ship, its broad brass handrails, and the iconography of hollow-cheeked saints.

Cigarette smoke on posters and wallpaper made common areas musty. The toilet stalls were so cramped we had to turn our slim selves sideways to enter. And for all this, the Sorbonne managed to cultivate a studied composure, an ivory-tower severance from the burly world below.

A SURROGATE FOR DIRT

Once the hour for my presentation arrived, I set up my slideshow of snaps from rodeos and began to speak. From the front row Roger leaned in keenly to see the animals on the screen.

I trotted through rodeo's key events: steer wrestling, bronc riding, barrel racing, bull riding, steer roping. All told, those peppercorn sports typify a conflicted desire for bygone times. Rodeo as a leisure outlet fulfills an "imperialist nostalgia," a term sociologist Renato Rosaldo coined to characterize the complex and unconscious ways imperialism plays out. Rodeo is a belated sort of settler-colonialism, I said. Rodeo participants romanticize both the Old West of strapping heroes like John Wayne and the Indigenous cultures those heroes set out to subdue.

Such an intricate wistfulness allows rodeo participants to contend with guilt stemming from economic benefits after a century of occupation. Renegades like those who occupied the Malheur Wildlife Refuge in 2016, near the town of Burns in the US state of Oregon, believe a centralized government is infringing on their rights, as if public benefits and privileges have become entitlements. They wax nostalgic for a lawless past. They demand the public's lands. A leader of that protest, Ammon Bundy, ran for Idaho governor in 2022, despite his conviction for trespassing, resisting, and obstructing police in the Idaho statehouse during a coronavirus protest.

The notion of nostalgia arose in the seventeenth century. A Swiss physician fused the Greek words *nostos* (a return home) with *algos* (a painful state). That mix typified the strain of melancholy experienced by the nation's mercenaries. Soldiers paid to engage in combat far from their birthplaces felt homesick. True to such nostalgia, reenactments in rodeo events carry a pathological smack. Audiences and participants yearn for a golden age when ancestors lived on ranches and farms instead of in cities. *Heimat*, a German word for home or homeland, signifies a similar romantic longing for the security of nationhood, region, and ethnic solidarity.

Some rodeos outfit donkeys, cattle, goats, sheep, and horses in hats, skirts, and frilly shirts. Dressed like dolls, some are even trained to act out skits. Such humanizing of animals is the complicated behavior of people inventing novel ways to overtop more-powerful beasts. The control freak Torvald Helmer, in the Henrik Ibsen play *A Doll's House*, regulates his wife in much the same way. He dresses Nora in Romanian garb and has her dance a frenzied tarantella.

Rodeo participants might mourn, without acknowledging it, the absence of those qualities and objects that they have altered or destroyed. Norwegian patriarch Helmer yearns for the wild woman he loved before they married, the carefree wife-child. Rodeo's events can conjure the cattle that roamed open range, the Indigenous people who lived freely before reservations were mandated. Feral and wild beasts alike strayed unconfined by brands, barbwire, rifles, and knives.

Renato Rosaldo also assessed the ways that "someone deliberately alters a form of life, and then regrets that things have not remained as they were prior to the intervention. At one more remove, people destroy their environment, and then they worship nature." We see that pattern in the custom and culture of the northern Rockies where we recreate and make our home.

I had pitched my research project to Paris in part to please my partner. She loves France. The strain of the occasion was compounding my time warp, though. So was my hangover, my relative poverty, and my inborn reluctance as a tourist. Speaking at the Sorbonne, my podium began to wobble. Top-flight scholars filling the room caused me to question my own authority.

Investors eying markets, I asserted, help to bring about the end of nature. Cars and shoes and office parks bear names that memorialize those razed places, lost species, and demoted beings. When I drive highways, I see them as they pass. *Cougar, Cherokee, Mustang, Apache.*

It bewilders still today—that process of yearning for what we have subjugated. Rodeo as a cultural event had to be invented, though. Even if the frontier has folded, rodeo still may stun. It can bring to light the hopeful opening that a borderline wildness might still thrive inside desire. That costumes, drama, and animal dander might replicate the shuttered frontier's unruly past.

The sport draws massive crowds. Tourists in cities eat it up. They find solace within the rodeo by paying witness to the dirt and disorder from a distance. Riders enter arenas, and hoofs raise clouds. When bull riders tumble, when ropers bulldog a calf, dust haloes them. The quest to subdue massive mammals, if only for the eight seconds aboard a bucking bronco or pinwheeling bull, confirms the rider's identity. It bestows on him or her the powers of those bareback beasts.

If some hunters commune with their prey by stalking and eating it, the rodeo rider might aim to gain an interspecies merger with her horse, like my former student Naomie Peasley did as a member of the Colville Confederated Tribes. I paused and let my slideshow work its juju.

Objections to my talk were clamorous afterward, but so were my supporters. One prof from the University of Calgary protested that we should not have to turn ranchers off the land, and I agreed. Another asserted that the risks to humans from rodeo were perceived risks only, negligible when held up against other extreme sports and transports. Perceived risks, I responded with conviction, become actual risks on a bareback bull whose weight can run to a full ton.

Roger used the question-and-answer session to tout foxhunting, letting the other scholars know his antique views about animals. He also took the opportunity to accuse me of class prejudice, of snobbery and opposition to rural people. Woozy after our whisky-sodden soiree, I kept feet flat and held my ground, thanks to several in attendance who had attended rodeos and had my back, people like Virginia Scharff from the University of New Mexico. No fop in jodhpurs, I muttered under my breath, was going to school me about the America I knew. Roger rankled me in several ways—as an unoriginal conservative, a hunter, and as an ideological bully.

CITY OF LIGHT, CITY OF SCENTS

"Time to go," Karen tugged my sleeve. My part of the symposium was over, my obligation shut and done. We gathered up and headed across the university courtyard. Statues framed the quad, Victor Hugo on one side, Louis

Pasteur on the other. Like so much of old Paris, cobbles pave it, three-foot stones rounded at the corners, uneven enough to turn an ankle on. How did she do it, Juliet Binoche, when she high-heeled her way across those cobblestones in the movie *Bleu?*

Le Marché aux Puces de Saint-Ouen was summoning us, the largest flea market in the world. Before we arrived, we had read about its lowbrow charm. I had suggested it to Karen as a cure for the tourism that tainted my views of worldwide travel. I could not wait to see the fleas. We would travel vertically. On our way to the flea market, the funk of a cheese shop seeped into the cobbled street. Standing in line to buy some fromage, we overheard an adolescent French boy behind us ask his parents, "*Sont-ils Americains?*" Are they Americans? His mother shushed him.

Then in a whisper he remarked, "*Elle est tres grande, et il a une barbe.*" She is very tall, and he has a beard. Karen played college basketball and is more than six feet tall. We found it cute and unusual to be on display that way, so far away from Oz. Proving rube enough to buy a wedge of sharp outdated cheese, I gnawed it as we strolled and felt my tongue welt up.

At Le Marché aux Puces, translated as the Market of the Fleas, we cast our eyes across all its fifteen acres. It was like the garage sales I had patronized to afford my bootstrap college education. But this conglomeration outsized any rummage sale at home by a thousandfold. Here was a network of warehouses, alleys, and two thousand covered and open shanties and stalls. Gauntlets of geegaws reached out to seize our euros. Awnings gaped. Colored crafts crowded cardboard stands. African vendors hawked hand-craft wares. Wisps of incense squiggled to reggae rhythms.

We were ingesting soil of a sort that was alien to me. Urban dirt, less familiar and more aromatic than the swamp mud and barn muck on the acreage where I grew up. City paths carved in hardscape have often estranged me. My ideal pathways meander, roam, and stray. The dirt routes and game trails I preferred to embrace all trace the capricious curves of Mother Earth.

At an art-print shop where we browsed, waist-high racks cached jewelry and engravings. Illustrations of New World nature radiated the peaches and penumbras that poet Allen Ginsberg praised. *Les Indiens* by Theodore de Bry mesmerized, *oiseaux* by Mark Catesby and Alexander Wilson, and *plantes* by William Bartram. Karen untucked hair from her new French scarf.

One anonymous engraving titled *Les Indiens d'Amérique du Nord à la chasse* showed a troop of pinto ponies, their noses arrowing after bison thundering on the plains. Atop the horses, a band of monstrous Indian riders thrashed them to the chase. The surprise came in the riders' facial shapes—the thick lips, dark skins, heavy brows, and kinky hair. The artist had imagined those Indigenous Americans as Africans. Pondering a low-ball bid on the oddball picture, I decided it held only archival value and carried only antiquarian appeal. It would never do for display in an office or a home. Nor did I care for the burden of keepsakes or curios that would make me a collector of picture-postcard charms, as Joni Mitchell branded them in her "Amelia."

Jet lag, Jack Daniels, strong espresso, and ideological conflict had teamed up to bust my rusty French and wring my tongue dry. Like a saddle blanket from the rodeos whose images still filled my head, I felt rode hard and hung up wet. A greengrocer's cry of "Un euro!"—used to attract buyers to the purple flesh of figs at his sidewalk stand—carried past the streets to scramble and mash reality's candor. Beyond all words I was grateful that Karen knew the city so well. She guided me, blind and bumbling like my childhood avatar Mr. Magoo, till I began to relax into our French sojourn. Gradually I found myself fall into a kind of Parisian swoon.

For hours we walked and talked. The farther we strayed from the Sorbonne, the more the sensations pleased me. The dishing out of coins and bills, the exchange of words while buying a scarf or a drink, made it seem as if my lover-partner and I were scarcely parting air. Never had I felt so wonderfully insubstantial. The process of traversing the streets gained a surreal edge. The tremors of my inborn aversion to horizontal travel fell away. We would make two later trips to France where I would speak again, one to medieval-era Perpignan. Each trip proved more fun.

We were sightseers no one noticed till commercial promise gave us shape, till we entered zones where the loss of euros made us lighter. The cauldron of time's disorder and sundry liquids had so far decentered me, I could pass through glass and suffer no grief. We gained substance when we lost it, and those losses themselves invited courtesies. *Bonjour, Merci, Au revoir!*

Fellow symposium-goer and poet Alan Michael Parker materialized to lead us to a men's boutique. There he hailed a familiar tailor. Tugging on the vest he'd bought the day before, Alan piped, *C'est bon!* Smiles creased each visage in the store. *Un euro!* the greengrocer cried, his voice carrying down the street—a calf bawling to summon a mother, an udder, some warm milk.

Through entrances of galleries and stores we slipped without notice. We tripped the crowded markets door to door, as if finger food alone could carry us throughout the day. Spectral in the city, I found the illusion of immateriality broken only when $3.80 euro left our pockets, when we two shared the airy baguette baked around a bed of calamata olives and olive oil, when our teeth tore the bread, scuttled the vessel, and made the pond of sliced olives swim.

Gnashing in tandem, we became a pair of characters in a comic drama surviving on street food. We dripped on the sidewalks and our hands. We strolled, wiped, laughed, gawped, chewed. Far from being Americans of substance, we were light enough in pocket and heart to float upon the notes of cathedral bells and the Mediterranean spices that had no certain origins or source.

Ours were substances we could abuse—our American bearing, our indigent ways, the intoxication of financial exchange, the salivation triggered by ornate window displays. It was like waking from some hibernation to find ourselves, we steadfast vegetarians, salivating after the salts on smoked and hanging shanks of hogs. Fogging up a shop window, we saw our own reflections bending toward delicate powdered sugar frosting the berries on fresh-baked tarts.

8

My Climate Change

On a hot August day, stripped to a short-sleeve tee, I was throttling my motorcycle across the Columbia Plateau. The twisty road unreeled beneath me, the cheatgrass a bleached hair on the shoulder, potholes and chain lakes showing and going as the roadway rose and fell.

Chancing a glance to the east, I spotted a column of smoke ten miles away. Smoke lifting from the hilltop where we live! Adrenaline kicked in, a cortisol I would taste. Wheeling my wayward horse of a motorcycle in a sudden hairpin turn, I goaded it toward home. By the time I drew a halt in our driveway, the viewshed had grown opaque. The odd thought fogged me that calamities ought to have an auditory accompaniment—timpani, trumpets, a rain of chorus frogs.

My pocket stung me like an electric current, jolting my hands from handlebars to unsnap the helmet and extract the phone. My friend Robin was shouting from it: "The fire looks close to you! Can you see it? Will you have to evacuate?" I had no answer for her. My greatest worry arose for those who live closer to the column of smoke. If a wind whipped flames their way, the electronic gate that guards the neighborhood of Erika and Andrea Zaman would do them no good. Fires grow legs in windy weather. Those legs can vault rivers, roads, and lakes.

Helmeting back up, I throttled north toward the fire until a barricade stopped me. A traffic-control car catawampus in the road held back local natives from going home. Trailers full of stamping horses filed behind the barricade. Horsetails draped over trailer gates and dogs clouded the windows of SUVs, smearing glass and peering out. Homeowners shuffled and scanned the sky for a sign. One rancher in Carhartt canvas pants shrugged when I asked how the fire began. His smartphone showed the ordeal being dubbed the Houston Fire, its hot heart pumping where Grove and Houston Roads converge. Six years later, in 2021, officials would get wiser and throw open fairgrounds so that evacuated people could shelter animals there.

Through the view afforded by the straight-arrow roadway, we could watch the fire. It crept like a glow-worm through the understory. Crept, glowed, and smoldered. When the fire hit a tree, it nibbled the lowest needles then crowned it in a feast of flames. A small plane began to whine above the dog-hair pines. I had seen planes douse wildfires in Central Idaho twenty years before. This one dipped low, dropped a rooster-tail of orange slurry, and banked in a wide turn.

Planes were aiming to check the fire before it spread to the seven hundred adjacent acres of Palisades Park to the east. There the fire might rampage unimpeded and gain speed. No roads inside the park would give the firefighters access. It would burn. Some of us had bought homes nearby to enjoy access to park paths for running, biking, horseback riding, and watching wildlife.

When brisk winds whip branches in the tall pines of our yard, my jaw tightens at the prospect the flames might gallop through our trees. There'd be little to do but clamber the roof with a garden hose and sprinkler, drench the structure top and sides, hope for the best, and flee.

* * *

Climate disruption is changing western landscapes and lives. For several summers on my native Washington State's dry side, wildfires have seethed around us, smudging our horizons for weeks at a stretch, blackening a thousand square miles. Fires make shut-ins of unlucky breathers born to struggle with their lungs. Those of us who opt for lives in the provinces—subsistence types, country squires, and suburban malingerers alike—pay close heed to smoke in our airshed. Others take themselves away, they crash with friends, they find safe shelter from the flames.

Record-busting years of wildfires have frazzled everyone in our Far West. In Spokane, where the Houston Fire sent up gusts, the three months from June 1 through August 31, 2015, proved to be the hottest, the driest, and the fiercest on record. The city received only 0.44 inch of rain that summer at its airport, the official weather-monitoring site nearby. The average for June through August is 2.48 inches. No one among the civic leaders wants this news to leak out.

The city is in a boom phase now, with real estate values jumping 72 percent in three years, record heat waves drying arid forests further. In July 2021, more than 517 human-caused nearby wildfires in Washington were seething. Refugees from the coast, escapees from the built-up freeway corridors, are moving here all the same, clogging up the byways and highways. Pandemic telework has taught many companies how easily employees can produce from home.

In mammalian heads like ours, smell and taste entwine so far, we ingest the smoke. Pine resins lodge in nostrils. Tar from burnt pitch won't wash out. To gain relief we take to the water. We rinse in lakes. A nasal-irrigation remedy can help. Several years of summer fires have caused throats to catch, eyes to stream, lungs to cough up stuff. Clear mountain air turns to murk for days, reducing visibility to a couple hundred yards. "Apocalyptic," my friends sigh, peering out their windows and paying grim witness to a gloom they can frame only as the end of the world.

Wood smoke, invisible aerosols loaded with carbon in tandem with nitrogen particles suspended by the billions, seeps through screens and panes. It settles as a film indoors. Friends in rural Winthrop north and west of us watched hillside flames creep near for several days. When embers began to drift down from cloudless skies, they bundled their favorite artworks and pets before motoring from their wood-frame home and embedding themselves in Spokane far away.

Weltschmerz and low-grade stress sweep in with smoky weather. Smoldering horizons call to mind humidity's murk in the Smoky Mountains, but our limited vistas prove dusty-dry, not sultry and humid. Bitter skies are the new norm, in a phrase by now outworn. Smoke-birds are those who migrate for clearer views, if and where they can find them, in July and August.

Sometimes I motorcycle north to try to get a reprieve from it all. Passing Kettle Falls and Republic, I veer toward the Spokane Indian Reservation and the town of Keller. As one who turns to internal combustion for recreation, I add to the carbon clangor I decry. Farther north, I might cross the international border into British Columbia and reel beside its glacier-fed lakes and streams. That border was closed for most of two viral years, due to fears of travelers who would not vaccinate. One sign on a red minivan read, "Vaccinated in the Blood of Christ."

More than seven hundred Northwest glaciers are shrinking fast, says scientist Mauri Pelto of Massachusetts. Each summer's drought cycle erodes 5 to 10 percent of ice-field volumes. Pelto studied glaciation for three decades on the slopes of Mt. Rainier, the most heavily glaciated peak in the Lower 48 states, and on ice fields in Glacier National Park in Montana nearby. He reports climate change has made the signature glaciers of the Pacific Northwest punier than any time in the last four thousand years. Glaciers are ecologically essential. They balance out droughts. They act as storage reservoirs for in-stream river flows during the hottest parts of the year, when sea-run fish are most at risk, most in need of chilly water to fin up streams and spawn.

Our industries and transport systems exhale carbon particles and gas. Buried ancient forests come into view when ice pulls back. Our industrial vapors make us planetary raiders.

The late University of Washington researcher Wendell Tangborn dubbed glaciers "the canaries in the climate-change coalmine." He tied them to droughts and fires. Glaciers' so-called mass balance, a measure of their health, compares yearly growth from new snow against yearly shrinkage from ongoing thaw. That balance is tipping to the negative for the first time in history.

Human-vectored climate disruption is an ice age in reverse. As the planet warms and polar ice caps melt at faster rates, weird weather becomes the rule. Industrial emissions, our technological outbreaths, corrode every crevice and rivet in the voyaging spaceship Earth and diminish the remaining regions unscathed by humankind. Microplastics pollution is being discovered, we now know, from high on the slopes of Everest down to the trenches of deep seas.

When the Houston Fire began to flare across Grove Road, our neighbors Andrea and Erika had their sitter caring for two of their kids. Erika was working her job as a drug rep in Seattle, an hour's jet flight away. Andrea, busy fetching older son Noah from the airport, managed to blast back home and scoop up the sitter and the two youngest. Authorities brushed aside the chance the fire could jump the road—until it did. Along with fifty-some other residents, they evacuated. They waited for helicopters, boots, bulldozers, and planes to dispatch the flames.

The sitter's mom fixed them dinner. They were luckier than many have been. No houses or lives were lost on their street. They breathed their deep relief, offered firefighters their sincere and public thanks, ran the AC, kept the windows tightly closed, and tried to get some sleep.

* * *

Climate-change skeptics claim such weather events are normal. They point to ocean oscillations, volcanic eruptions, to the planet's wobble on its axis, even to sunspots as probable causes. They point to anything outside of human-brewed pollution as a cause. Science is the enemy's refuge for such skeptics. Cockeyed counterscience becomes a creed. To deny the planet is suffering anthropogenic global warming often means blaming environmentalists. Four years of "alternative facts" from the White House only emboldened climate deniers to dig in.

Craziness has gone mainstream, climate-change skeptics say. It began in 2006 with *An Inconvenient Truth*. The Academy of Motion Picture Arts and Sciences gave that documentary film two awards. Hollywood liberals suckered the public by politicizing science, the skeptics say. Such liberalism encourages culture warriors to fashion crises from thin air. Greens are bent on crippling rural America. Enviros demand set-asides for spotted owls, shelters for torrent salamanders, entitlements for the Bruneau hot springsnail that sucks mud near Boise.

Shielding such creatures is insane. Nature has always intended for some dumb beasts to vanish like the dodo. Nature kicks the weakest to the curb, as even the most casual disciple of natural selection knows. Watermelons, those reds who find shelter inside green rinds, would like to limit carbon and cut off business at its knees, all in the interest of stymying climate change.

Some industrialists and climate-denying legislators announce that ranchers and loggers have the answer. Grazing and logging forests would keep wildfires from stoking up so hot and often. Cows eat browse that serves as tinder for big fires. Billboards in my region have been hired to read "Public Land: Log It, Graze It or Watch It Burn." That equation creates an either-or fallacy as superficial as it sounds. Old-school lawmakers approve. Federal largesse will come into play, they say, when industrialists are granted rightful seats at the forest-policy table.

If only the Endangered Species Act were not being misapplied to lock up natural resources. If only Al Gore and his technocratic carnival could be refuted once and for all.

Thunderous bombast often echoes heat lightning in our western resource wars. Richard Pombo of California, who served in the US House from 1993 to 2007, is still a force. He ridiculed claims of rising extinction rates in his book *This Land Is Our Land*. Fallaciously he argued about species protections: "Some of these species may carry organisms or bacteria that could be extremely harmful to humans or other life. Maybe their extinction will save us!" Pombo claimed that dreamy love for bunnies and bugs has burdened public lands with flammable stuff.

Extractive interests hope they can cruise into wild set-asides and get the cut out, instead of hemorrhaging precious federal treasure to snuff out wildfires resulting from undermanaged forests. Such reasoning leads to more truck traffic hauling timber to sawmills and public lands being harvested as if the trees had grown in rows. It causes lands to be pruned back like massive orchards rather than being curated diligently for public use and wildlife habitat.

In revisionary economic policies like these, a flaw prospers. Rock-ribbed traditionalists often invest in forested lots on the urban-rural interface. They build cabins and vacation homes on the margins of flammable forests. Those homes and cabins mean trees can't be toppled and hauled away without voluble squawks from rank-and-file ratepayers. Nor are controlled burns going to be authorized if they might blight somebody's viewshed for an hour, a day, or a week.

Prescribed or controlled burns, a kind of medicine for overloaded forests, have been used to good advantage in refuges and parklands. Indigenous peoples deployed fire as a management tool for millennia. Controlled burns work by clearing the underbrush safely in wet weather. But NIMBY values often trump ecological necessity in the picturesque backcountry. Not in My Back Yard, some monied interests will say, no matter how that backyard serves a greater public good.

Loggers and ecologists have gone head-to-head for decades in the Inland Northwest where I live. More than custom and culture is at stake here. Lives are too—the lives of breathers disabled by respiratory problems. The lives of people who cannot readily flee when the next fire comes by. The lives of myriad other species that are rarely factored into the equations.

Carbon sequestration provides an answer, but it is complex. Carbon dioxide, a substance that is hazardous to all living creatures, can be captured or sequestered. The goal of sequestering CO_2 is to curtail or compound it, like the atmospheric renegade it is. Such impoundments can be natural or artificial. Forests sequester carbon, just as oceans do; sequester it and make oxygen.

Oceanic phytoplankton produces two-thirds of the planet's oxygen, while trees and other leafy vegetation generate the other third. Photosynthesis ought to be fostered, and the creation of carbon dioxide stalled, in the interest of augmenting planetary health. The wildfires afflicting air quality in the entire United States generate the compound CO_2. How far tourist travel adds to the growing climate crisis is difficult but essential for public-policy experts to quantify these days.

Think of forests as absorption organs. Instead of doing the job of sponging or absorbing CO_2, they are turning into ash as wildfires grow more commonplace. Western wildfires in this millennium start earlier, burn hotter, last longer, and increase in acreage every year. If spent fuels from polluting industries including travel are heating up the planet, as environmentalists divine, if they are driving regional droughts and causing ever-hotter fires that destroy more trees, then the causes are reciprocal. Pollution causes more wildfires, and wildfires cause more pollution.

Federal oversight of national forests has become an exercise in backward-looking guesswork. In recent years the US Forest Service has spent more than half its entire annual budget fighting wildfires—an unprecedented outlay that says much about these crisis times. The only solution might be for undermanaged coniferous forests to burn up—just plain flame away.

* * *

The anthropogenic argument on climate change, by contrast with the views of its deniers, holds that petrochemicals are the chief source of planetary grief. We mine oil and gas beneath the planet's surface. We destroy the cleansing vegetation that grows atop those fuels. We refine crude oil and fabricate more flammable stuff in districts called cancer alleys. We contaminate when we combust that stuff. Carbon pollution spreads misery beyond the rural-urban interface, where wildfires take the greatest toll. We are the weather-makers, the future-eaters, in phrases Tim Flannery has taken as titles for his books. Leisure travel is a consequential cause.

The headache of global warming leaves citizens few opportunities to act locally. All of us, sometimes for the first time, need to think and act in global terms. Such long odds can cause even the most optimistic global folks to despair. One easy fix is to drive and fly responsibly. Again, the clear skies afforded by our held-back industries and travel, during high coronavirus times, gave us a baseline from which to view the anthropogenic impacts on weather day to day.

In my region, plans are afoot to triple rail traffic hauling crude oil from North Dakota and coal from Montana and Wyoming. Transported in closed cars, the heavy oil gets loaded on crude tankers and floated to refineries in coastal ports like Louisiana's. The federal ban on exporting crude oil, repealed in 2015, means crude may now be shipped anywhere. That change has boosted drilling and rail traffic in the long term, contributing ever more carbon particulates. The push is all the greater since Russian oil was embargoed after that nation's invasion of Ukraine.

The coal gets heaped on open train cars. Exposed to the elements, available to foul water and air along thousands of miles, it eventually gets boated to Asian nations and burnt to energize the industries there. China's GDP now is set to overtake that of the US. Free-floating coal smoke erodes the ozone in greater proportions than ever before, deteriorating already-vile air in such cities as Xingtai and Beijing. Everyone gets whacked in the global village we inhabit.

In an irony of energy production, Americans are breathing air fouled by the same goods we ship abroad. Elevated emissions from Asian industries drift across the Pacific, like so much invisible tsunami debris, to worsen baseline ozone levels in the US. The 2021 megafires in the American West socked in cities in states far away as New York, New Jersey, and Pennsylvania.

International climate activists strive to curtail carbon generation in every way. They labor to slow the coal being transported by trains and burnt to make electricity. They work to curtail the highly combustible oil being pumped from Midwest American fields. They lobby to limit the sprawl of homes that call for long commutes from urban cores. They aim to devise incentives for automakers to manufacture cars that increase miles-per-gallon fleet averages. Such bad patterns generate particulates and erode atmospheric protections on the planet. It is a wise awakening for climate activists to have begun to factor tourist travel into that diversity of equations.

Elizabeth Kolbert names the problems "business as usual," or B.A.U. Another phrase for such obstacles is status-quo bias. Few of us are eager to bring about the changes demanded by a needy planet if those changes impinge upon our perceived entitlements, or upon our status. The Biden administration promises with the Inflation Reduction Act to incentivize electric vehicles. How well any administration can parley with a Congress that has historically been intractable on energy policy remains to be seen. The energy industry holds great lobbying power. It is one of the few industries that rival the reach of the international tourist economy. In ways that need to be investigated fully, the two industries are silent partners in a range of ecological misbehavior.

Some companies finally are feeling the heat. The Volkswagen Group lost market share and cash for defrauding buyers with the mileage claims it made, both for individual models and for its corporate average fuel-efficiency standards. VW swindled consumers and governments through clandestine software designed to dupe regulators. It was not just the work of a few rogue engineers. Renegade fumes the cars put out, intensifying under the hot feet of blameless buyers, increased climate change and warming. The corporate culture conspired to hide the deception.

ExxonMobil is also being called to account, finally, for closeting four decades of research that showed global warming as a dire threat. ExxonMobil hid the evidence that everyone around the globe was being made to suffer in the interest of continuing to grow its bottom line.

In a peep of progress here in Washington State, Spokane-area climate activists got a victory. The Rev. George Taylor trespassed in 2016 on Burlington Northern Santa Fe tracks to register his concern about the hazardous transport of coal and oil through cities and over waterways. He and several others blocked a train. The other activists accepted pleas and bowed out, but Taylor stuck with it. His arguments, denied locally, were appealed to the state Supreme Court, which ruled in his favor in 2021. His case was scheduled to go to a jury trial, where Taylor would present the "necessity defense" as a rationale for his activism. It was necessary, in other words, for him to blockade the train because he had exhausted all legal remedies. At the last minute the railway withdrew its charge, fearing a dangerous activist precedent would be set.

* * *

Two weeks after the Houston Fire calmed down, I motorcycled out on Grove Road to the sixty-acre burn site. The scent of ash and phosphates fouled the air. One barn was now cinders. Another stood scorched. Bulldozer-carved fire-lines scarred the land. Fallen barbed wire fencing resembled a guitar neck widowed of everything but strings, the cedar posts of fretwork having all gone up in smoke. Orange-clad convicts bussed in to mop up the mess stamped on grass clumps and tree roots. They deployed their big boots to guarantee the embers all went dead.

Blighted trees and grasslands stretched far. On both sides of rural Grove Road, chemicals from the phosphate flame retardant, dropped by planes, painted the gravel and the fields dull red. Invasive weeds and grasses, wakened by the shock of flames, fed on the phosphates that fertilize fresh vegetation. New green shoots stabbed through the ash to rally stronger than before.

Catastrophic climate change is ours to avert, but it will take more than a little political will. In 2020 in my native Washington State, eight hundred thousand acres of land burned in more than 1,600 fires. We residents have struggled to catch our breaths for six summers. We have hoped for rain.

When it came, raindrops atomized the dust and flung it in the air like miniature atomic bombs. Cooling rainstorms pelted down. The parched and thirsty pungent vegetation proved grateful to the nose. Tender scents lifted from the herbs and forbs, and weary dwellers on the land spun with a bliss we did not know we had been missing.

9

Survivor Tree

First week of November and already it's freezing. In the largest park in my homeplace, the same wild stretch named Palisades that the Houston Fire threatened, snow fell this week. Some rain followed, then more snow. Together they made for a penetrating chill. Dampness in the air and on the ground. The wild cherry trees have lost their leaves. A few shriveled stone fruits, overlooked by finches and waxwings, have become easier to view and soon will be gleaned.

Last spring a grapevine reared near a fir tree and found it could use that rough trunk as a trellis. The vine volunteered from domestic stock left behind by Anglo pioneers. Grape fronds laddered up the bark all summer. Out and down from the branch ends, they sent fresh tendrils that reached to soak up sun. The corkscrew shoots of that probing grapevine colonized the tips of the limbs. Three-lobed lime-green leaves shone pale against the fir tree's bluish needles.

November now, those grape leaves have turned autumn yellow. I duck under a fir branch, squint up into the canopy, and find several grape clusters still hanging. Frozen globes, the same pale gold as the leaves, a pigment that protects them from squirrels and birds. If these were wine grapes ripened after the first hard freeze, their sugar content would be ideal for making ice wine. And if foxes lived in this region, they might jump to grab the grapes, as one did in Aesop's fable that made for the saying "sour grapes." The fox was sour because it could not reach them.

A two-foot maple tree beside the trail has held my attention all this year. Its red leaves are shrinking, curling, losing juice. Soon they'll crisp off in a wind. As a four-foot sapling a year ago, its trunk ruptured. The tree's top half dangled like a broken arm. Come winter, that fractured bit detached. Twenty years of living and traipsing here, and I'm glad my local postage stamp of soil still holds mysteries. I hope to discover what force it was that shattered the trunk of that vine maple—whether animal, bird, stout boot, stiff wind, or fallen branch. To discover what caused that limb to shatter will take some doing. Such mysteries are part of the charm of having safe access to public lands. If the mysteries were all explained away, we would be the poorer.

At our house nearby, five cats have vanished from our lives in the score of years we've lived there. They slipped outdoors when we were unwatchful, and their vanishing's not hard to fathom. Great gray and great horned owls cry at night. They rule winter pines around us and trade muted calls. Reading by the fire indoors, I catch their aural drift. Our chimney functions like a hearing trumpet. Their hoots drift down to our hearth and fill the living room.

My late father taught me how to imitate the horned owls' three deep notes, in the same way he taught me so many other traits and innovations that stem from nature. Out to the porch I creep after dark, cup hands before my mouth, and blow rough between the thumbs. The owls answer back. Their hearing is so keen they must be heeding every indoor sneeze.

One cat came in blood-crusted on its head. The scrapes and punctures bore the talon-signatures of an owl. The tabby, Chester, acted skittish ever after that. He cowered when he saw a ceiling fan rotate, ducked when we switched on lights or lifted a broom. A sudden blow must have concussed him—before the silent five-foot spread of feathers overhead began to thrash.

Coyotes occupy Palisades Park. They bully me with threat displays if I come too near a spring den. One coyote almost nipped my heels. Skulking behind me, it zigzagged and turned its top lip inside out when I stopped. Others yap in joyous packs at night. A swing-shift worker saw a cat dangling from a coyote's mouth in his headlight glare. They stray our way even by day. They skip with impunity up the center of our street. They lay claim to our environs as their own.

We do our best to keep our cats indoors, but cats are natural-born predators. Coyotes coevolving with us in our suburban streets will seize our pampered pets whenever folly and opportunity provide. Outdoor cats in turn take a toll on billions of songbirds every year.

The clamor of one ambush of a cat in our yard will never fade. It was 1:05 a.m. when the yipping woke us. Two separate coyote voices sounded out. My best guess is our straying Maine coon cat had holed up in a shrub to keep from being caught. The yips were meant to unnerve him, flush him out, and the meager evidence says they did. The ordeal took less than five seconds. The upshot of that waylaying was one sharp squall then silence.

The cat had been content indoors for the year after its rescue from a shelter. Once it found an opening, though, it got a taste of the great outdoors and reverted to a feral state. There was little we could do. Bell the cat and predators can only detect him better. Anglo immigrants in the early American colonies were said to have "gone native" when they took up with the locals.

Neither owls nor coyotes would have had cause to injure this small maple. Skunks haunt our yards and parks, they leak vapors and make their presence known, but no skunk would ever have cracked this maple sapling. Porcupines savor the bark of cone-bearing trees over leafy trees, and anyway this deciduous maple trunk is too flimsy for a quill pig to climb. Porcupines can weigh up to forty pounds, their ponderous guts the millers of their being. Moose move in and out, they chomp on twigs, but never have I known a moose to shatter entire limbs or boles. I ticked through the list of critters that circulate around us, but no other species came to mind.

We suburbanites on the receiving end of unwanted attention from wild animals and birds can feel harassed. Some of us think we have earned and deserve first privilege and priority, just as colonizers among the colonized believed, and as destination resort developers believe today.

We invade their home domains, we occupy their historical quarters, but when they nibble at our fringes, we feel put out, injured, outraged. Rudyard Kipling was on the wrong side of the equation when he wrote "Rikki-Tikki-Tavi." In that short story, his cobra coiled in the bathtub proves unduly vengeful. Kipling forgot how snakes and "coolies," as he named the locals, preceded Britain in India by millennia and rarely proved adversarial. Laws governing US water allotments follow the rule "First in time, first in right."

Those who occupied the region first, that is, deserve to be the first in line to get the drink. Our laws have codified privilege and priority.

Last year at this time, I thought for sure the maple tree was dead, but when April came it greened up once again. As trees will do when they get topped, it sent out new growth at the horizontal only. More shrub-stubby now than tree-tall, it hugs the duff like a timid creature crouching. It lies low to Earth. It huddles near the security of dirt, less apt either to snap from an ice storm's weight or to fracture if or when the ponderous pine that towers above it sheds a limb. Lightning always strikes the tallest structures. This modest maple will be safer going low.

From one angle of vision, the maple appears crippled, gnarled, twisted like a bristlecone pine. Those pine trees are said to be the oldest nonclonal creatures in the world. Trees that are honored in their antiquity with the unmistakable name *Pinus longeava*. From another angle of vision, my maple has taken on the shape of a bonsai sculpture. One pleasure of the bonsai craft is contemplation for the viewer, followed closely by the exercise of ingenuity for the grower. I am no grower, but I find contemplative serenity at the sight of this survivor tree in the environs where I bike and hike. This tree that has exerted persistence and resilience against all odds.

Columns of basalt gave our wildland park the name of Palisades. The name pertains to the word *palings*, those sharp security stakes buried around frontier forts, those palings capable of impaling an intruder. In the eyes of some old settler-colonists, I would guess, the cliff columns of vertical stacked basalt resembled wooden guard stakes that made them feel secure at home. In our park stony game trails lace cliff-breaks. Those trails link growths of ninebark, oceanspray, and saskatoon growing below stands of ponderosa pines on the plateau up above.

Climate change is making wild areas like Palisades more vulnerable than ever. The drying that arises from climate warming worsens wildfires. The resulting wildfires worsen changes in the atmosphere in turn. Wildfires unleash carbon particles that abrade Earth's protective layer. The ripple effects of wildfires are enormous. Habitats are destroyed. Topsoil can come to be sterilized outright by the abnormal intensity of burns today. From our homeplace on a precipice a mile from the park, we watch warily for smoke and flames throughout the summer.

In this penetrating wet November, though, any wildfires have snuffed out. A decorative fringe of frost rime envelops the vegetation in the park. After a grind of a hike over frozen mud ruts, I sat down on a rock to catch my breath. My head and neck were steaming. Pennants of perspiration climbed the hill. It is one of the charms of outdoor silence—the focus on minutiae, the twinkling of small things.

Most of us humans congregate within doors. We ruminate, if at all, in social circles. We concentrate collective wills toward one shared goal. Even our classrooms are set up on the model of group-directed learning. For me, it has always been best to plunk down someplace all alone. Winter or summer, spring or fall, I welcome the ambient air to wash over me.

Poet Jean de La Fontaine was sculpted during an outdoor contemplation. The Duchess of Bouillon delivered the image. She reported seeing him seated against a tree one morning, then in the same spot and posture come evening. In that place all day he sat, just reflecting. Sculptor Pierre Julien immortalized La Fontaine that way in a marble statue. Longhaired, musing, clad in a cloak, manuscript on one crossed knee. At his feet a fox pauses, gazing up at his face. Its paw rests on a book the poet brought along. Both book and fox allude to his fable *Le renard et les raisins,* or "The Fox and the Grapes." Poet and predator mirror one another in the lifelike statue. Foxy features contour the poet's stone visage.

On the hillside where I steamed, my mental chatter fell still. I readied myself to enter a practiced meditative phase. I sat motionless, intending to get some contemplation done. Several minutes in, though, a rattle rose from a thicket far below. The clatter sounded as if a half-full quiver of arrows was being shaken. I froze in close expectation, I arrested my breath, I tuned in as well as my shotgun-damaged ears could manage. The time of year, and the stories I had read in sporting magazines when I was a kid, gave me some foreknowledge of what I was hearing.

Seizing a fallen branch within reach, I made bold and rattled back. Clashing the stalks of an elderberry cluster that grew beside me, I tried my best to imitate a mammal toxified by hormones, an ungulate spoiling for a fight. The season's penetrating chill carried the sound far and clear. My rattling was not prolonged. I knew enough about silence not to overplay my hand.

In the brush far below, twigs twitched. No, antlers. Bony tines took shape, materialized, then disappeared again. That was when I had my answer. Why hadn't I thought of it before? The maple that survived the cracking in half must have been battered by a white-tailed deer in the rut.

Bucks rub velvet from their antlers on trees and bushes in the spring. They vent sexual aggressions on foliage in the fall. Quaking aspens in Palisades Park bear fractured branches and scarred trunks. Antler-tine wounds on their white bark heal back black. I held my breath and waited, but the buck must have seen me. Roan deer can hide in the shrubbiest of cover. I kept still for another quarter hour on the chance he would circle around. Again I found myself alone.

In the novel *As I Lay Dying*, William Faulkner has a character named Jewel Bundren. A head higher than his sibs, he's the offspring of his mother Addie's extramarital affair. He mopes alongside his Mississippi family while she is dying. One brother recalls how Jewel snuck out every night, all night, at age fifteen. His siblings surmised that he was rutting, a cognate noun for *roaring* that signifies a seasonal state of sexual excitation. Some speakers favor *tomcatting*.

Nobody in the family witnesses Jewel's tryst. One brother gibes that he admires the imagined lover's stamina. Another brother muses that Jewel is being so sly, the woman must be married. Such surmises and conjectures make for subtle humor and prove tantamount to gossip.

It turns out instead that Jewel's been busy plowing at night. Plowing a cotton field and not some secret mistress as they guess. He's been laboring overtime in a neighbor's field to buy a high-spirited horse he adores. Everyone is wrong about him. Perceptive Faulkner saw how many animals prowl within us. Also, how we as an oversocialized species often rush to judgment.

Anse Bundren, the brothers' hawk-like father, compounds the whole ordeal. In an act of underhanded exploitation, the father covertly trades Jewel's prize horse for a team of mules.

Deeds of predation swarm like so many wasp hives. They catch at my attention all around. Magpies plunder nests and nestlings. Parasitic wasps stun spiders and caterpillars, then lay eggs that hatch as larvae and eat their living hosts from the outside in. Our own pets fall prey when we place them in harm's way. Deeds of predation are seething inside human communities just as sure. The thug who picked my pocket on the Paris Metro did not wound me. He was only benefiting parasitically from my negligence. So were the coyotes that hauled away our gone-feral pet. They left a smear of fur in Palisades Park, a fibrous pile of scat.

Predatory behavior takes so many forms. One day I saw a bull elk sling its urine and bend its antlered head to gouge a nearby calf. Hormones crazed that rutting elk. The blameless calf distracted the bull by standing too close. Savvy capitalists view raw opportunity and seize it. Mostly they make away, escape unscathed. Sexual predators freeboot among us. They cultivate a sixth sense for the vulnerable, for the quarry they might most easily seduce or betray.

One must wonder whether bloodthirsty wildings—hawks and coyotes and street thugs—get turned on, get physically off, from the rush that accompanies their successful plunders.

Walking through a city rose garden on an April day, I saw a woman in front of me get seized. A husky male came from behind her, threw her caveman-style over his shoulder, and began to steal away. I shouted and made a run at him. He dropped her, unaware that anyone had been watching or nearby. He cast a dark glance back at me and fled. Like a hawk upon a starling that thug stooped to surprise the woman and scoop her up. In falconry and ornithology, the word *stoop* comes to describe the sudden dive or plunge of a raptor on its target mammal or bird.

The woman's fear paralyzed her, made her unable to struggle in his grasp or even to cry out. After he turned her loose, she toppled, lay limp for a time till she could find her legs and rise. Neither of us wanted to guess at the extent of his intentions. Reluctant to approach her too closely, powerless to trail the thug or chase him down, I kept a proper distance. Nor could I produce any consolation or wisdom to confer. Walking her to her car, I telephoned in a police report—a futile and token deed to hinder such an incident from taking place again.

A metaphysical fear prompted William Blake to write "The Tyger." His five-hundred-pound feline proves formidable in its symmetry. Its eyes burn with fire enough to scorch any hand audacious enough to touch it. The poem's fluent meters belie a deep anxiety on Blake's part. If the animal is terrifying—and here is Blake's point—its creator proves even more so. The design must be devious, the intention dire. If we made the god that made a predator so ornate, we made the god in our own shape. Milder and nearer home, what chemicals flooded the deer's hypothalamus and drove it to ransack a four-foot tree? I wish I had been a witness to that act.

Did the buck paw the dirt first, a cartoon bull in a Spanish arena? Did it rear like bighorn sheep do, in advance of a head-clash to win an admiring ewe? Or maybe the deer "took a run at" the tree, a pet figure of speech since a friend used it to describe a despotic boss's bitter conduct.

In my mind's eye, the white-tailed deer was more impulsive than calculating. As if brandishing multiple blades in its antler tines, the buck rehearsed the moment for an opponent. It twisted and turned its antlers in the sapling till it heard a satisfying crack. It practiced how it might carve up some competing venison that had yet to enter the field. In William Blake's freakish metaphysic, the creator took a run at humankind by contriving the predatory tiger.

Once I decided the maple tree had outlasted a mangling by a white-tail, the ground around that tree began to gather to a magnitude. From where I sat behind the elderberry bush, the dirt writhed from centuries of toil. Radiating tensions, the landscapes groaned. My homeplace has endured conflicts far more monumental than a broken trunk. It has seen great floods blast out of Lake Missoula and scour it for millennia. Prehistoric reptiles and mammals have risen to dominance and died. Outdoor place is fundamental within Indigenous songs and stories because so much has taken place here. Places are as full of stories as our libraries are of books.

Within the elderberry bush that I had rattled, a few mute fruits, dusky blue, hung where varied thrushes and flickers had not gleaned them. Songbirds sometimes hanker so hard for a berry they will hover and beak aside a branch to seize it. During one baking September day, a hungry waxwing gave a Cooper's hawk the opportunity to slam it to an elderberry's crotch. That blow, like the owl's that almost took out our cat Chester, concussed the cedar waxwing. It lay insensible in a tangle of twigs. The hawk could not breach the bush and carry the waxwing away.

That songbird lived to learn from its carelessness and haste. For ten minutes I watched to see if it would revive and fly. It shuddered, then slit open its eyes and gazed straight ahead. It was as if the bird were reflecting on what had taken place. Or so I personified it from ten feet away. Foregathered instinct might remind it not to replicate the negligence that caused its head to ache today. Once I stood up and entered its vision, it unrolled its feathers and made away.

And so, I have come to believe that a white-tailed buck in rut ruptured the sapling vine maple. I recognize the sundry shapes predation can take, the bloody scrapes and striations that take physical time to heal, the assaults that throb and bother beings all their days. So many creatures around me—people, birds, and trees—have been pummeled, punctured, or torn. Some forever crouch, anticipating another blow to arrive from overhead with no warning and no sign. Such survivors, conditioned by other species or by their own kind, come to fear the approach of the abstract unknown. I hope my son Chase is not among them, and that he can fully heal.

Some concussion might befall me like it did that showy maple tree. A driver who does not see me on my motorcycle, a slip and fall on granite scree, an unforeseeable medical surprise. The death of another loved one. Anxiety might tempt me to play it safe, duck and cover, send out new growth at the horizontal only. May I instead snap back, revive fast, prove persistent and resilient against all odds. Experiences like these make me wonder why we respond one way and not another. It seems idle to worry and wonder what might next transpire. The best we can do is bear witness to all such encounters that surround us.

10

Shooters and the Tools They Use

Not only have I seen predation, but I have taken part in it. Not only do I know what drives nonhumans as predators; I know also how my own species often gratifies its lust for blood.

Autumn means hunting season in the rural environs of these United States. Outdoor fun in the autumn risks those folks who don't wear orange or pack a gun. Stray as I often do around the rural West—on a bicycle, in a kayak, on skis, or on foot—and you had better be prepared to yield ground to *los hombres armados,* the men with guns. Like my wise advisor Henry Thoreau, I reveled in the chase at an early age, until such desires began to pass me by. Still today, a rabbit or a marmot that scurries across my path can spark those dormant passions into flames.

My misgivings about the chase might seem petty when compared to human-rights abuses across the globe. A bird or animal killed for sport or food bears scant comparison to the great totalitarian evils of the twentieth century. In case I need to say it plain, the US is a splendid place to live. To try to raise a family among drug cartels or in the thick of an insurgency would be far worse than living in earshot of provinces where gun racks on pickups prove more the rule than the exception. Still, it bugged the spit out of me one sunny October day to watch my young sons fall to crawling along a muddy trail when the guns of autumn began to boom nearby.

In the interest of full disclosure, I am a born-again nonhunter. Like a renegade priest with his fuming censer, I swung my guns and drew a lethal bead for twenty years. Then I began to give away the family "shooting irons," as Daddy dubbed them—my father who taught me the risky ropes and manly rewards of guns. My pet weapon, a 12-gauge shotgun with 30-inch barrel and battered walnut stock, issued puffs of smoke and ordered nature to obey. Squirrels, doves, pigeons, partridges, ruffed and dusky grouse, quail, pheasants, ducks, and geese—some of them now protected under the Endangered Species Act—tumbled to the yellow eye of that long gun.

During my spell as a hunter, habitats shriveled or crashed, an upshot of the human-population stressors brought to bear on habitats in Washington State, where I came of age. Under the tutelage of my friends and elders, I tore the flesh of hundreds of animals and birds. I was good at it. In the end, my heart began to grate and brim over with tender empathy for the dead. In the end, my pastime felt as if it were fraying the planet's fabric. Shooters decimated the dodos, passenger pigeons, prairie chickens, sharp-tailed grouse, sage grouse, bison, and so many more.

A whiff of the confessional arises when I speak of hunting and shooting now. On my chest I've borne a load of stones as dire as those old Giles Corey bore in Salem. I began to ask myself some questions about my family and my culture. Is hunting chiefly a sport, or a game? A way more honestly to produce food? An exercise of those primal drives that keep us healthy and sane? An alibi for escaping to the outdoors and keeping alive a withering reverence for nature? Depending on whom you ask, all these answers might rise to hunting's absolution. If one is going to eat meat, I agree, then seeing or taking part in the killing is the most honest way to go.

Our language tells us much about our regard for this sport. One meaning of *game* is "wild animals, including birds and fishes, such as are hunted for food or taken for sport or profit." Implicit in the meaning of *game* is the notion that the contest needs to have a winner and a loser. Contrary to other games, this one's stakes are high. The loser usually loses all, while the winner, in our technologized day and age, risks little. Discerning diners describe the meat of some wild birds and animals dressed and brought to the table as gamy—"having the tangy flavor of game," or "having the flavor and odor of game or other meat kept uncooked until slightly tainted." *Game,* it is sport and prey and tang all bundled up in complex sets of associations.

Some priests can scent sin right through the confession grate. If venery denotes both "the practice or sport of hunting game animals" and "the practice or pursuit of sexual pleasure, or the indulgences of sexual desire," then our language seems to yearn to tell us that the lust for hunting is analogous to other lusts. Like sexual athletes, hunters who shoot their deer or kill their limit of birds are said to score. The kill shot afield equates to the money shot in porn. Aristotle notes, in his *Nichomachean Ethics,* "As well as plain, unthinking brutishness and vice, which are the opposite of virtue, people may also do wrong through incontinence, or a lack of self-control."

There lies the nub of a conundrum: some hunters have too little self-control. Such hunters become gunners, poachers, butchers, and worse. In the novel *Main Street* by Sinclair Lewis, the middle-class husband Will Kennicott obsesses so often about hunting that his wife doubts she can ever compete with that desire. If hunting has historically been the sport of kings, shooting is a pursuit of the privileged too. Add essential travel to the sport of hunting, and it becomes exotic.

As a young man of college age, I shot and hung wild ducks on the porch of an apartment. Wire hooks pierced the soft palates of the lower beaks. The mallard's orange feet dangled down; their bodies stiffened in the autumn chill. Visitors to my apartment regarded those carcasses at eye level. Hanging them for a week was meant to age and tenderize the stringy flesh. It worked. I could cook a duck like no one else. In truth, there was not a lot of competition for that honor in Bellingham. Even my pacifist friends gathered for duck dinners. For those occasions I split the skinned carcasses, seasoned them high, and broiled them hot and fast. Some chichi restaurants age prime beef for as long as a month before they serve it. That culinary practice proved good enough for me. Blood from the gutted ducks on my porch blackened the concrete path.

Hunting was fun. My German shorthaired pointer and I got exercise in fields, ponds, and sloughs. Unsporting hunters, though, became the disappointment for me. In a more or less exacting term that circulates among those who endorse and enforce the sport, "slob hunters" are those who flout the law. They pillage, plunder, and generate a tragedy of the commons. The public lands, or commons, make up 48 percent of the eleven western states. They enrich us in our communal land tenure. But such shooters and slob hunters blight our radical national experiment.

The distinction I draw between hunters and shooters rests on the reverence one extends toward the prey. True hunters, Indigenous or otherwise, honor prey in various ways. They obey the laws, care for the meat, enhance game habitats in the behavior they practice and the fees they pay. They might even whisper a prayer or benediction before or after making a kill. Shooters, by contrast, care more about rocking the world off its axis by the firepower they wield. They will travel thousands of miles—indeed, to other continents—to pacify their innate predatory urge.

The distinction is different in Britain, as Roger Scruton reminded me in our exchange. Shooters mostly take part in drives. They sit and wait for the birds or animals to be driven toward them by dogs or people beating bushes or fields. Then they shoot. Drives historically took place on country estates, sometimes with planted animals or birds as prey. Some British lords reported shooting a thousand or more birds in one day, the carcasses piled for underlings to dress.

Every month, in my region, a story hits the press about a bull moose or cow elk that has been poached out of season and left for dead. What possesses shooters to do that? Aldo Leopold characterized it as "trigger itch"— that craving to blast, no matter the quarry or the target. Leopold regretted his own trigger itch when he opened fire downslope in New Mexico and wounded a female wolf with pups. As he approached his fallen prey in those mountains, he became unwitting witness to the "fierce green fire" that died in her eyes. His honesty in that account has endeared him to readers since his *Sand County Almanac* was published in 1949.

Had Leopold competed with a spear or club, we know who would have won that game. And while Leopold was no slob or simpleminded shooter, only doing what his times considered right, his rifle gave him a distinct advantage over the faraway wolf.

Shooters who utilize advanced technology repudiate the stakes of "fair chase." Hunters and government officials alike are recognizing poaching as a problem that too often squanders ecological sustainability. At the same time, manufacturers are enhancing the chances that shooters can score in spades in the fields, forests, and swamps. High-tech inventions have grown more inviting in recent decades. Corporations are undercutting the best efforts of the states, the nation, and ethical hunters. Business products make it easier to succumb to the slob impulse.

On a logging road in Pennsylvania decades ago, I met an old boy who claimed he had jumped from a rolling truck, chased down a deer, and expertly knifed it dead. He did not offer any evidence. A steep slope slowed the deer and leveled the killing field, he said. Back then, I believed technology and hunting have little in common. Even today, conventional wisdom about hunting says it pits human wits against beastly wiles to concoct a contest either one can win.

Browsing through a catalogue of Nebraska-based Cabela's, the "World's Foremost Outfitter" of hunting and fishing gear, I could see how far the stakes of the contest have changed. High-tech gadgetry threatens to transform hunting sports beyond recognition. As hundreds of businesses line up to seize market share, fair chase is becoming an antique fable.

The Cabela's catalogue incites its trusting buyers to keep up technologically: "If you're like most hunters, your pockets are already bulging with shotshells, pocketknives, calls, and about a hundred other accouterments you can't possibly live without. That's where the FS-50A Free Spirit Field Dog Trainer comes in handy." The Free Spirit zaps the dog ("provides seven different levels of stimulation") into submission. If the dog roams too far, barks too loud, or threatens to fight another dog—zzzap! Like an unruly child, a high-spirited pointer or setter needs correction, or so the ethic of the Cabela's catalogue suggests. Technology affords the means.

Unless the dog exceeds the range of the technology, that is, like the hound I found high atop Lolo Pass in Montana at the peak of one spring bear season. Panting, spent, the antenna on her collar bent, the dog wore a tracking device that allowed her master to trace her. The antenna on her collar was intended to undercut and govern her free spirit.

Collars as devices of control and domination tie shooting sports to slavery. Errant slaves wore muzzles, tongue suppressors, and other devices redolent of medieval torment. "A state of bondage, so far from doing violence to the law of nature, develops and perfects it," lawyer and Confederate colonel R. R. Cobb wrote in 1858. Some enterprising criminologists, some penal professionals right now, are wondering if shock collars might be just the thing for managing drunks, sexual offenders, or meth cooks on the loose. Ankle-bracelet are already a thing. What an outcry might arise if one were to propose granting animals the same rights as our fellow humans who commit the baser crimes.

Military-style laser sights are revolutionizing shooting sports. The military excels in developing technologies that corporations may co-opt to create civilian needs and satisfy them. The huge US defense budget helps corporations to profit, and shooters to shoot, with the greatest of ease. Binoculars, monoculars, spotting scopes, and riflescopes are available now with the Night Vision feature, formerly available only for military use. Poachers of animals, it stands to reason, need all the after-hours ocular assistance they can get. The Yardage Pro Laser Rangefinder, likewise, "can make you a better hunter, no matter what kind of hunting you do."

Walker's Game Ear II helps the clever hunter to "detect and amplify sounds that would otherwise go unnoticed." Every snap of a twig, chirp of a bird, every curse and cough will be technologically augmented. If I were a robo-hunter today, I would worry the "safety shut-off device" on my Game Ear might fail and deafen me with the amplified blast of my own gun.

Even hunters with enhanced eyes, ears, and firepower can gain from robotic duck decoys. Motorized wings on remote-controlled decoys are proving so effectual that some states have banned them. A&M Waterfowl commands hundreds of dollars for each flapping unit. Robotic duck wings can spin at 500 RPMs, guaranteeing to deceive the sharpest eyes.

Wildlife feeders available from Cabela's mail-order include a "high-torque motor, electronic microprocessor, memory back-up," and a "quartz clock that ensures accurate, dependable feeding times." One may habituate a favorite prey to free lunch before lowering the crosshairs. And when feeding after dusk, the Game Call Spotlight might be just the ticket.

If jacklighting disappoints, the Electronic Game Caller features "20 Hrs. of Continuous Calling." Picture a stakeout (I mean a stand) where your microprocessor is spewing food, your speaker is playing calls to gather, and your laser-sighted rifle is seeking heat. There are, of course, also programmable Global Positioning Systems, used by cops and shooters alike, to find the way back to that salt lick discovered before the season began, back to that flocking duck pond in a secret spot. Just call up those stored coordinates and go.

Enough already. Some travelers might be growing cross with my topic and tone. Some might suppose me an animal-rights radical sneering at the tradition of Davy Crockett and Daniel Boone, Teddy Roosevelt and Ted Nugent. Even Aldo Leopold, a father of ecology, he who saw the fierce green fire die in the eyes of the wolf he'd shot, kept on slinging lead. Never would I claim all or even most hunters wallow in the technocratic gadgetry the sporting catalogues offer.

Some throwback sports today use black-powder guns or bows, even longbows like Robin Hood shot. State regulations reward these throwback hunters by affording them special districts and seasons earlier in the year, before cracks and booms have warned the animals and birds that gamy humans are in pursuit. The vestige of a hunter that still itches in me applauds archery and commends archers for the sporting spirit they bring to the field. Most folks would applaud, except for those who hold that any sort of hunting is yielding to base and brutish impulses. Still, all hunting aficionados today enjoy a technological supremacy their fathers never knew.

In my local newspaper a story appeared on a robotic deer that wildlife officials are seeing the need to deploy. The deer decoys poachers and scofflaws. It wags its tail and twitches its head. Like an undercover female detective, it utters visual come-hither plaints. It traps shooters who shoot out of season, on private lands, from roads, or after legal shooting hours close. Cosmic justice allows the shooter to become the hunted and get bagged. How dangerous it must be to work that deer, to invent fresh ways to bust the shooters and the slobs, armed to the teeth as they always are, angry about being duped, often hateful of government overregulation to boot.

One trait of the shooter is firing from paved roads—a practice now illegal in every state. Pickup trucks moving slowly and stopping often on rural routes can be a dead giveaway. Another tipoff is a spotlight sweeping a field after dark. Public lands, private lands, highways, gravel roads, pastures, even residential yards become the prowling grounds of that subspecies of shooter too lazy to walk. A convenient form of travel for the shooter is the ATV, the all-terrain vehicle, a four-wheel hybrid of a motorcycle and a jeep. Whether shooting illegally from a roadway or throttling down upon a herd to get a shot one ought to earn, the driver of an internal-combustion machine has taken his or her technological advantage to an unfair extreme.

In the interest of full disclosure again, I recall more than once when my beloved father shot at prey from roads and encouraged me to do the same. That helps to explain my antipathy, though the laws in those benighted times were much more forgiving than they are today. One incident still hurts my ears. My dad had bought a .300 Weatherby rifle and was eager to try it. My buddy Darryl and I were riding with him near dawn on Interstate 90 between Cle Elum and Ellensburg. Darryl and I were fourteen years of age, full of hormones and bloodlust. Beyond all reason we loved guns and firepower, and we knew my father was a crack shot.

A coyote ahead of us scattered gravel and took off across a farm field at the approach of our truck. We were driving on a freeway, mind you. Without out a word my father slid the vehicle to the roadside, pulled his loaded rifle from behind the seat, and rested it on the hood of the truck. At full tilt the coyote tumbled before the blast of the gun could echo off the windshield. We stood beside my dad and cheered. Then we ran out to the field where the coyote lay, its head all but severed at the neck by the impact of that big slug. Its amputated tail became a token trophy.

Coyotes even today, like wolves for Aldo Leopold forty years before, were considered varmints, never subject to seasons or to laws. Shooters could make free use of them as moving targets anywhere they showed. The mythology back then was that coyotes took away the game. Shooters were encouraged by the game laws to become de facto wildlife managers. In my office today, a coyote skull rests alongside other mementoes of times gone by. The entrance wound of the .22 slug at the top of the head is tiny, the exit wound conspicuously large, like all such wounds after the lead slug has mushroomed. That skull narrates a story. A hunter wounded the coyote, then descended on it from a godlike height to administer the kill shot.

There are other subspecies of shooter besides the motorized type. One kind shoots road signs. Folks who have traveled often in the provinces have seen bullet holes pocking the thick aluminum of state and county highway signs. In counties where aluminum is too precious to afford, wooden road signs will be peppered by shotgun blasts, splintered by rifle and pistol slugs.

The signs are trashed because they make for ready marks. The shooter is also registering his rejection of laws. By vandalizing signs, shooters pass on replacement costs. Hunting and travel again combine. Others shoot illegally out of state, kill more than laws allow, gun down protected species, or lean on the crutch of military technology to make odds the more lopsided.

The story about the mechanical deer in my local newspaper, titled "Bogus Buck Targets Road Hunters," told how hunting and wildlife groups are so focused on the growing need to arrest shooters that they are buying and donating expensive equipment, including devices like robotic deer, to try to slow the slob trend. Rangefinders, GPSs, metal detectors, and surveillance cameras are also being brought to bear on those who kill without license, cause, or law.

My local article missed an opportunity to entangle the upward trajectory of illicit shooters with the downward trajectory of legal hunting in the United States. Licensed hunters are becoming fewer and fewer, a statistic that causes anxiety for those who advocate for the sport. The ranks of hunters in the US have fallen, even as the estimated number of guns has boomed past one for every man, woman, and child in the nation. Some fifteen million people were hunting in 2020, a drop of four hundred thousand from 2010, when the nation had twenty-two million fewer people.

Other numbers are difficult to obtain—much like numbers for the impact and ubiquity of commercial tourism. The downward trajectory of hunters is not difficult to puzzle out, though, especially if one has much experience afield. The rising cost of gas, shells, licenses, tags, and guns compounds the other obstacles that confront fans of hunting and shooting sports today. Supply-chain shortfalls amid the pandemic raised the price of shells and made them hard to get.

Another problem facing hunters is the lack of access to prime wildlife habitat. Reciprocal causes might be involved there as well. The rise of illicit shooters causes fewer acres of private lands to be open and accessible. Who wants to enable poaching or suffer property damage?

Diminished hunting opportunities tempt some hunters to cross the line into poaching, first by firing a few minutes before legal hours at dawn, or a few minutes after legal hours at dusk. Once they cross those lines and see no punishment forthcoming, no legal reckoning, then the disgruntled hunter might slide the slippery slope and become cheat, poacher, shooter, slob.

Some shooters jacklight. They deploy lights sporting tens of thousands of candlepower and often bolted to vehicles to hypnotize reflecting eyes at night. Such shooters turn away the outstanding ethical hunters in bitter disgust from the accessible fields, forests, and streams.

Fred Zitterkopf of the Inland Northwest Wildlife Council is a Vietnam veteran, a retired military engineer, a volunteer for a variety of good causes in my region. One in every three hunters, I said to Fred, is a shooter, a scofflaw. Fred took exception to my claim. He found my numbers inflated, and I was willing to yield to him. He is a hunter whereas I am long lapsed. So lapsed, in fact, it sounds dead wrong to attach the epithet of *sport* to the ancient chase today.

Fred's solution for the crossing lines—the upward line of shooters and the downward line of licensed hunters—is to get away from others into remote rural counties like Pend Oreille in Eastern Washington, a massive pocket of undeveloped lands that borders vast tracts of British Columbia to the north and the wilds of North Idaho to the east. I bit my tongue and silenced my view that his getaway fix is a fix for him alone. Out of sight and out of mind popped right into my mind. If Fred does not have to have to see shooters in action, it is easy to imagine all is well.

The same faulty logic applies to influencers and travel promoters who presume to tell you how to escape the crowds. The travel trade often claims to offer secrets on how to avoid others. Once more, that secret spot is soon to be spotted by the spoor of fellow tourists. The planet's beaches, parks, and peaks are finite—all to be found out and overrun as populations grow.

Near Fred's favorite stomping grounds in Pend Oreille County, Washington, I went for a hike with my wife and kids on a striking stretch of Lake Pend Oreille in North Idaho. Chase and I would paddle that same lake two years later. It was a sunny Saturday afternoon in October.

Several American grebes were feeding in an inlet where the public enjoys rare lakeside access. Hunters and birders can recognize grebes—the long necks like snakeheads, the pointed beaks like a heron, the red eyes. When grebes dive, they vault straight up, arch those necks, and let the momentum of the vaulting carry them far underwater where they fish. Any decent hunter would not mistake a grebe for a duck. Nor are grebes legal to shoot in any of our United States.

The quaking aspens had drawn us to this shore. In his poem "Spring and Fall," Gerard Manley Hopkins has a pastoral counselor addressing questions to a young girl. The pastor asks, "Margaret, are you grieving / Over Goldengrove unleaving?" Hopkins was writing about a species of tree that is close kindred to our aspens. The pastor and speaker of the poem asks if sorrows find their origin in nature, in empathy with the seasonal cycles and the annual leaf-fall.

My family and I had come to that shore for color, for the freedom the public commons afford us. The boys hoped to catch some fish. They were carrying their poles and planning to cast for the perch and smallmouth bass the massive lake sustains. They would catch and release the fish, ideally still oblivious to the grief that Hopkins's poetic speaker found in autumn's loss. The quaking aspens, *Populus tremuloides,* trembled at every leaf and blazed bright gold.

But this grove of aspens shielded a hunter. Water flanked his makeshift blind on three sides. He was calling from that blind for ducks and geese, blowing on a commercial reed, hoping to veer distant flocks toward his hidden spot. His calling sounded to me like a pastoral throwback to shepherds of olden days. His manufactured reed made wild music like those that summoned a flock of sheep. Poets celebrated piping shepherds for their rejection of the city's conflicts.

Just when we thought we might enjoy the scene despite the hunter, just when the primal chase had taken on a classical tang, a pickup halted on the levee we had just hiked from. The doors of the truck flew open. Two men bailed out, shotguns blazing. From the road they fired at the feeding grebes and in our direction. Their pellets raked the water right before us and before the hunter in his blind. The grebes never tried to fly. In the jargon of such shooters themselves, the men *ground-sluiced* that protected species of waterfowl. Ethical hunters wait for fowl to fly.

My boys fell to their hands and knees on the trail. Their mother ducked and prepared to run with them. I whistled to let the poachers know we were there. The booms of their shotguns carried on, as more grebes rose to the surface for air. Then a flock of geese, some one hundred yards high, far out of range, drew their fire. Ethical hunters call this bad practice *sky-busting*. It only wounds the birds and makes them too skittish for other hunters to call in. The spent shot from those shooters rained down around us. Their pellets pelted the quaking aspen leaves.

That did it for the hunter in the blind. He bellowed from his covert. He loosened a stream of curses and threatened to perform impromptu jack-knife castration on the shooters if he got the chance. They vanished, but our autumn outing had turned sour. We traced our path back to the car, wary to keep our heads low and our opinions about the *los hombres armados* to ourselves.

Never would I claim most hunters wallow in the technocratic gadgetry and stunted ethics that infect illicit shooters. My friend Darryl, he who saw the coyote beheaded with me, packs a black-powder rifle and hunts from high up in a tree stand. He sips coffee, cradles a blunderbuss, and waits for the elk or deer to approach close enough to make his one shot count. A throwback to a simpler life and time, Darryl gets away from it all. He escapes the shooters like those who sluiced the grebes. Other hunters, those who have shifted from ethical hunting to illicit shooting, often exploit a technological supremacy their fathers never knew.

Reed, our oldest surviving son, has shown an interest in hunting. He has been practicing in the backyard with his bow. At fifteen years of age, he enrolled on his own and passed a firearm-safety class online. I agreed to outfit him with a shotgun and take him out in the fields and forests someday, show him the ropes, even if his choice of pastimes wings some hearts.

11

Hawk Watching

Like a lot of born-again nonhunters, my interest in the outdoors has evolved into bird-watching. With the same determination as those who kill for sport, bird-watchers watch birds. With the same pleasure that others derive from watching television, some of us wander fields and streams. Before COVID-19 rebooted travel's ambitions, I crossed paths with ornithologists who have the wherewithal to spend big on German optics to help them zoom in on their quarry. One need not buy pricey binoculars or spotting scopes, though, to keep track of backyard birds.

From my bedroom last year, I saw a hawk catch a starling, and now I know how many ways predation can go wrong. It was early spring and the dry stalks rattling beside her put the Cooper's hawk on edge. To worsen her windy earthbound perch, a chain-link fence blocked her escape route on one side, a serviceberry or saskatoon bush hemmed her on the other side, and lines of electrical wires congested the sky. She had blazed down a utility easement and surprised the starling as it pecked at shriveled serviceberries fallen from the bush. The prostrate starling lay upside down beneath one clenched set of talons, writhing and entirely alive.

The hawk stretched and craned to see if she was safe. Her eyes shone. My bedroom window hid me from her view. I say *her* because females are larger than the males. Cooper's hawks display one of the largest size differences of any bird of prey. So large, even experts mistake the male Cooper's for the female sharp-shinned hawk. Had she already laid a clutch of eggs, she would have been incubating on the nest, the male on the hunt and scouring for food.

She rose atop the starling, nineteen inches tall, the size of a large crow, to get a clearer view of her environs. She loomed bigger than any hawk I'd ever come across in our woodland neighborhood. But all I could see from the bedroom window was squeezed by scale—her broad and checkered breast looming over the throttled starling in her grasp. Then she relaxed, her outline fell. She bent her head to her talons and her task. She began to pluck her prey.

English poet Alfred Tennyson recoiled from what he saw as a cycle of eating, breeding, and dying that prevents transcendence. His friend Arthur Hallam had just entered the carbon cycle, and the poet felt ill enough at heart to censure "nature red in tooth and claw." Decades after his friend's death, Tennyson got decorated with a lordship. Predation, like its companion death, cares nothing for societal dictates. No matter what Parliament decides, it will have its way.

From my bedroom I was stooping and peering out, keeping my silhouette low, keen to watch the talons flex and the preying game play out. I trained my eyes on the female hawk's every move. Her presence in my backyard fascinated me and began to feel transcendent.

When I was a child on my family's Seattle acreage, Cooper's hawks had orbited our pigeon coop. That massive wooden rookery looked like a peaked ark, fifteen feet long by six feet wide. A high hatchway allowed the homing birds to wing in and out at will. Coops like ours were known as dovecotes in Europe and the Middle East. They produced eggs, flesh, and dung. Ours produced visual pleasure only, a vestige of a backward plan to send the pigeons out as carriers. In those days we knew the Cooper's hawk only as a pigeon hawk, squaring it against an inherited philosophy that human civilization was the ultima Thule of the universe.

My parents had moved there from the city before I was born. They had drained the marsh, cleared the alders and cedars, and established pastures for a hobby farm. One of my after-school chores was to fill the water and grain troughs in the pigeon coop. A flock of pigeons proved to be a sore temptation to other predators besides hawks. Raccoons caught squabs when they could. Brown rats—aka sewer rats, the great *Rattus norvegicus* from Norway—slipped through cracks in the door and floor of the coop, scaled the walls, and crept along the bird roosts six feet above the ground. There they tried to pick off feathered fruit. A rat and its scaled tail could stretch a foot and a half—a thrilling sight to stare you down when you're eight years of age. Those brown rats, mostly nocturnal, burrowed underground where daytime hawks could never see to seize them. Rats naturalized and thrived in Seattle's tender weather, a temperate coastal rainforest that stretches from California to Alaska.

The native hawks had preceded humankind by millennia. Even so, they seemed to us to be the invaders. They infringed on our exceptional rights to "rule over the fish of the sea, the birds of the air, and over every living creature that moved upon the ground." The hawks that orbited our pigeon coop and sometimes assailed a pigeon, we could view as nothing less than predators of our livelihoods and pleasures, aerial invaders whose goal was to rob us of our husbandry and harvests. Armed with better understanding of ecology today, we can view humans as the invasive species, the exotic imports that encroached on local privileges of every sort.

Falcons fall like feathered lightning bolts delivered by the sky. They strike prey from above at speeds that can exceed two hundred miles per hour. The smaller accipiter hawks that include the Cooper's will slip in just above the ground to astonish witless and ignorant victims from the side or from behind. The flat trajectory of the accipiter plays stable bass beneath the falcon's high ballistics. Postmortems show a quarter of all hawks suffer breastbone fractures from such sudden rushes. As a dazzled kid, I watched one hawk knock a pigeon to the turf, lift it to a branch, flex and squeeze until the pigeon ceased to breathe. The hawk faced into the wind atop its prey and preened, before it plucked the pigeon and wafted feathers across our farm pond.

Songbirds often collide with windows. They lie concussed on dirt or deck. Some revive in time to fly, but not with a watchful accipiter around. Goshawks, sharp-shinned, and Cooper's hawks ravage feeders. They haunt our backyards, half-hopping and half-flying as they prowl for songbirds inside suburban shrubs and lawns. Their long tails enable them to steer and veer in flight. They search for stunned lumps of feathers beneath our wounding windowpanes.

Ancestors of that hawk crouching in our garden have been feeding on songbirds for centuries. Now, naturally, their descendants strive to shackle the starling flocks we introduced to this soft continent a century ago. They plunder those exotic relatives of ravens and crows. Eugene Schieffelin of the New York Zoological Society brought the starling to Central Park in 1890. He wanted North America to harbor all the birds in Shakespeare's plays. The starling, that messy cognate of the blackbird clan, took hold like no other. Attractive up close, clad in iridescent feathers, the exotic squawker can be taught to speak. Even so, its noisy scientific name, *Sturnus vulgaris*, replicates its foul behavior.

Flocks of starlings and other birds can down jets. US Airways flight 1549 had to land on the Hudson River in New York on January 15, 2009, because shortly after takeoff it hit a flock of Canada geese that destroyed the engines on the Airbus A320. Our thirst for travel takes a heavy toll on the natural world. Forensic ornithologist Carla Dove and others name it *snarge*—the goo scraped from inside jet engines following bird strikes. Carla Dove works to avoid disasters. For the record, birds do not strike planes. Jet-engine intakes suck birds from the air.

The native Cooper's hawk has had to cope with a host of invasive imports to North America—rats, starlings, Homo sapiens, and now our jet planes. The rats and starlings it can eat, but our human species consumes the hawk's habitat, competes for airspace, and commoditizes its historical home. The bird's haunts are vanishing, shoving the species to the urban-rural interface. That's why the hawk in our backyard had hazarded a capture so close to our suburban dwelling.

Songbirds feed on openings afforded by our domesticated spaces, our leafy yards and gardens that used to grow meadows and groves. In some ancestral memory, those groves still grow. The native Cooper's hawk is evolving today to adapt to our environs. Urban Raptor Conservancy, a Seattle volunteer group, banded fifty-four Cooper's hawks in 2020 and discovered sixty-one nests in and around the city. Within those nests, 191 youngsters fledged and flew. Those Seattle volunteers curate the birds.

In our woody neighborhood of ponderosa pines, the Cooper's hawk in flight proves hard to set apart from the smaller sharp-shinned hawk. To my untrained eyes, both species strobe as gray shapes through shady clearings before they vanish into branchy tangles. Look fast or they'll be gone. Both species feed on other birds. The same branches that afford nesting habitat for songbirds will camouflage the rapid accipiter hawks. The same yards and gardens that attract starlings to berries, seeds, and beetles give fair advantage to their fleet predators.

One morning a hawk on a winter branch outside our kitchen window made the yard a staging ground for a hunt. Statue-still it perched and gave me opportunity to view it. Back within the shadows of the house I stood, each of us petrified as stone. Among the snowy pine limbs stubbed above it and below, the only moving thing was that hawk's eye. For all I know it was the same hawk that was plucking the starling under the saskatoon bush, the same bird trembling with anxiety in the confinement of the chain-link fence beside it and the strands of power lines above.

I was lucky to have binoculars nearby when she stooped. Otherwise, I would have needed to press to the glass and risk disturbing her more than her tight environs and the wind already did. With my handy field-glasses, I could perch on our bed and visually pierce two layers of glass, the bedroom window and the tempered panes of the deck. The word *stoop* from falconry describes the dive of a hawk on its prey. A kindred image applies the word to a fit athlete on the run, leaning to seize or swat a low ball on a court or field. Among hawks the stoop happens so fast, the viewer might see nothing more than a sudden puff of feathers lofting down.

The Cooper's hawk, governed by human rule like every talon-bearing bird on Earth, is subdued and trained to fly on demand. We name such recreation falconry. It is the habituation of any bird of prey, from minuscule kestrel to golden eagle, to hunt from a human handler. When we draw on gauntlets and teach those birds to rest on our fists, a trifling form of rewilding might ensue. The handler holding her winged surrogate partakes in a savage world from which our civilization shields us. When I watched the hawk capture and subdue the starling in my yard, my pulse rose as if on cue. For a short spell, I could set aside the human distractions that threaten to abrade awareness. In that moment I could be fully aware. Eagles in Mongolia are raised from chicks, trained to wing out from riders on horseback to take down deer and wolves.

We first-world peoples practice a more specialized falconry. Radio telemetry allows the handler to trace the bird with receivers. Those antennae devices, held like crossbows, track the errant flyer. The master chases down the mastered if it tries to fly away. The handler becomes a technocrat. Batteries and electronics help him or her to check the bird. Cooper's hawks, human-imprinted, fed by hand, are outfitted with electrodes and wired into thralldom.

A paradox ensues. Hoping to engage with whatever forces we like because they are so wild, we curb that outer wildness and ourselves. Rick Bass, in his book *The Ninemile Wolves,* points out how "wolf technocracy can run amok"; Bass reviles radio collars when they attach to wolves and other species in the wild. "Just behind the collar are trappers, helicopters, computers—*knowledge,* instead of mystery." Technological implements taint our experience of wild animals and birds. We might as well be watching them on screens. We *do* watch them on screens, untold millions of us, huddled behind keyboards, rarely venturing outdoors. Instead, we might try learning to appreciate the environs where we live, vertically traveling through our actual or nearby backyards.

In my former life as a hunter, I shadowed my bloodstained elders through woods, fields, mountains, and streams. I shot BBs when I still counted my years in single digits, commanded firepower when I entered my teens, scored great accomplishments of carnage once I became a man. Still today it gratifies me to narrow the gap between a wild creature and me. After the hawk landed on the starling and pinioned it, I felt as if the three of us were somehow mingling. Predator and prey, hunter and hunted, observer and observed.

English poet Jon Silkin wrote about a notional gland that excretes our compassion and our spite, much like adrenaline or bile. If that spectral gland does a poor job, then medicinal fixes might need to come into play and regulate the human subject's functions. Never have I exuded much empathy on behalf of raucous starlings. But seeing an individual bird pinioned upside down and plucked alive caused an odd sensation akin to pain. Compassion leaked inside me, compounded by the penetrating sense that I was seeing a predator red in beak and claw. To clean their beaks of blood, hawks wipe sideways on grass, on moss, on bark, even on the squirming prey. The action resembles a chef caressing a whetstone, a butcher stropping a blade.

In some lovers and friends, I have seen empathy degenerate into rank anger and despair. Observed shouting matches between gunners and animal-rights people at readings and lectures. Watched votaries so seething with righteousness that their chemicals could foul a room. My Scandinavian ancestors did their best to stave off the curse of overcooked empathy. And yet I could not simmer down my imagination from its boil in that backyard, could not cool the predatory drama. It was a head-rush as if I were the one being held down—my chest soon to be flayed, my oppressor preparing herself to pluck me and smear my blood upon my clothes.

Something in the raw scene conjured up the Old Testament deity, a vengeful and erratic lord whose first instinct was to impose dictates and lash out. That lord instructed humans to replenish and subdue Earth, claim dominion over lesser species and one another, and behave in the face of the world like an imperious bird of prey. My adolescent training in the Lutheran catechism, the mental calisthenics led by one Pastor Bretheim, imprinted on me.

The unfolding garden drama gave me my own godlike prospect and advantage. In our private backyard space, a hawk had seized upon a starling, and I had the power to regulate the exchange. I could fling open the sliding glass door and overturn the odds, release a housecat to chase them off. If we chose to do so, Karen and I could uproot the saskatoons, plow the turf and plant grass seeds, then install sprinklers armed with timers to shoot off on the clock.

The former owners of our home had kept pets and kids secure by erecting the chain-link fence, much like old the colonists and militiamen once bordered their forts with palings or stakes. Such fences and stakes keep humans and other intruders at bay. They force the howling wilderness to skulk outside the pale.

What absorbed me most in the backyard predatory performance was that a bird had broached the confines of our property, the man-made barriers of fence and power line. She had claimed a brief piece of our bounded domain. A wild flyer bold enough to impinge on our environs had habituated herself to us and our dwellings. Filling a vacant ecological niche, she was curbing the starling flocks that humankind had launched.

Imagine it all from a hawk's-eye angle of vision. A feathered bit of food beneath you flutters and a switch within you flips. Hormones flood you, and you plunge before you assess the situation as well as self-preservation requires. Your inner being locks onto the yielding flesh. That fraught piece of meat differs little from sexual acquiescence in its longed-for surrender. It is as if one were to tap the pumping jugular of the wide world's frame. The blood that you beak up will sustain you, will link you to the life force and fuel the moment's reckless necessity.

Accipiter hawks, monogamous, take their mates for life. The two had learned to trust in one another, to feed from the same sensuous trencher. They knew compliant flesh equates to the survival of their genomes, that blood on the beak and meat in the gullet could see them through another week. Her mate watched her mantle her wings, bow above her prey and shade it.

Hawks need to take in some 12 percent of their weight each day. If the carcass is large enough, they return and feed hour after hour until it is gone, in much the same way that cougars will camouflage a kill and return to drive off scavengers as needs be. The starling beneath the female hawk would be a single meal for the two of them, and a scant one at that.

Ranging far from her treetop sanctuary, frazzled by her narrow confines and the starling's stout resistance, the Cooper's hawk was anxious. In the capture she had behaved in impetuous ways. The eggs of the season swelling already, she was craving protein. She was also feeling vulnerable. Hawks tumble to predators like other animals do, even as near the top of the food chain as they are. They suffer mortality from coyotes, housecats, eagles, and owls.

From a nearby pine, the male hawk unfolded. He dropped down the passageway between the chain-link fence and the saskatoon to join her. He might have been overanxious for the meal. He might have meant to deliver the kill stroke that was so long in coming. His mate was bent—gripping, plucking, ready to feed and be gone. When his shadow crossed her line of sight, she lost her nerve, she freaked, unwilling to take a chance the shadow signified anything but risk.

Instinct seized her and she vanished. Her thrash of wings made the male in turn believe that a predator was near, and he too flapped off. The starling, undressed and ready to be plucked, likewise fled. All three scattered before they could piece together what had taken place. Her capture of the starling had not stabbed it to its vitals. Its breast feathers would fill in, the talon punctures heal. Future flocks would feed the hawk, her mate, and her offspring.

In *H Is for Hawk* the writer Helen Macdonald asks, "Have you ever seen a hawk catch a bird in your back garden?" I have seen such an event, and now I know how many ways predation can go wrong. The moment wrote itself like a sprinkle of blood on saskatoon leaves, a scatter of feathers underneath a pine tree, a patch of matted grass where watching wild hawks paid off.

12

Tidings from the Virus

Isolated by COVID-19 for two years, many members of humankind felt the walls close in. To get away became a challenge like never before. Only the greatest economic privilege allowed some people to lift off and fly to warmer climes. Others of us could not drive the roads without feeling we had violated guidelines. Signboards on US state highways displayed STAY HOME / LIMIT TRAVEL / SAVE LIVES. Printouts at trailheads enforced closures.

Such directives cramped the style of many people accustomed to carefree outings. Travel will be transformed forever because of the COVID-19 pandemic. Awareness of overcrowding and overtourism will worry many of us Homo sapiens forever. In time, though, this period of large-scale global shutdown might be regarded as an opportunity. The clear skies afforded by our kept-in-check industries and nonessential travel gave us a much-needed baseline from which to view the impacts of humankind on our airsheds and our viewsheds. Some scientists now are calling our temporarily diminished human traffic the *anthropause*.

In my household we woke one day to find a yearling bull moose ten feet away from a big picture window. We had never seen one so close. He nipped from a dogwood tree whose mid-March twigs had yet to bud. His nozzle of a snout draped over each branch end to draw it in and chop it off. How, we wondered, can those massive animals sustain themselves on such scant roughage? It was clear he was a bull by the nubs of antlers between the ears.

It was clear he was a yearling by his hint of a dewlap—the flap that wags beneath the neck like a biker's beard.

What do these two events have in common—our confinement from the novel coronavirus, and a moose settling into a neighborhood where we had lived for eighteen years? Maybe nothing. Every thinking person acknowledges correlation is not causation. A shortage of noisy cars and people yakking is not necessarily enough to have invited a moose to hang around for a week. And yet, the pandemic flattened demand for oil, and commuters stayed home. International travel shut down. US petroleum consumption fell to the lowest it's been in more than thirty years.

In nearby Palisades Park, five different moose took up residence that summer and spring. It was a record, said Craig Volosing, director of Friends of Palisades, who reported from his forty-five-year residence there. The mild winter might have been ideal for moose survival. The creatures might have come to populate our urban yards because their population outgrew more isolated habitats. At Glacier National Park, also quite nearby, graduate student Alissa Anderson's three-year study of Canada lynx received a boost. She was able to observe the animal, without the standard stress from humans, after portions of the park banned tourists during the pandemic.

Elsewhere on the planet, wildlife patterns mirrored those observations. "Nature Is Taking Back Venice," *The Guardian* newspaper in England titled an article. Seahorses were being spotted in the Grand Canal, whose murky water had become clear for the short term. In the absence of human traffic, animals began expanding customary boundaries. Not a dramatic rebound, but it was a revelation how our cars, boats, planes, and clatter banish them. Our comings and goings make us the noisy neighbors. When we shelter in place, nature begins to return. For parts of those two years, the shores grew tranquil, the skies clear, the streets quiet.

As internal combustion throttled down, as humans traveled less for work and pleasure, air pollution began precipitating from the skies. Noise pollution fell. Industrial smells settled. Water quality improved because factories shuttered and shipping ebbed. Visibility from outer space was the best it's been since the 2001 terrorist attacks blacked out commercial air travel for three days.

Normally smoggy Los Angeles, favored by coastal breezes, had some of the cleanest air of any major city. Bears, bobcats, and coyotes began to reclaim Yosemite Park in the absence of traffic. Citizens in Punjab, India, could see the Himalayas for the first time in decades. From Thailand to Florida, beachcombers reported increases in leatherback turtle nest sites. Wild boars were being filmed in Italian cities. "I don't know if these are the revenge of nature," Pope Francis observed, "but they are certainly nature's responses." What a fascinating thing for a pope to say. No Catholic leader before has ever intimated nature might need to take revenge.

Our human time in isolation offset customary tourist trips. With non-essential travel halted and social outings inconceivable, I found time to do some research and crunch some numbers.

Eleven percent of all transportation-related emissions in the United States originate in the massive aviation industry. Nearly a billion US passengers hop on planes each year. Those numbers are projected to double by midcentury. Personal carbon dioxide is measured by the metric ton. The best way to reduce our carbon footprint is to fly less, the *New York Times* reported. Travel may be quantified by flights taken, money spent, and carbon spewed.

Erin Florio, news director for *Condé Nast Traveler* in 2017, argued the problem is not that "too many people are traveling." No, she says, too many people are going to the same places. Travel promoters have made that argument for years, as if travel sites were boundless.

Demographics tell a different tale. The number of high-traffic sites increases every year—or they did, before the virus put the temporary kibosh on it all. My family's experience on the island of Koh Lipe in southern Thailand bears out the claim of overtourism at so many sites. The Indigenous people there, the Urak Lawoi, are suffering the harsh effects of travel's growth.

What does COVID-19 portend for the future of travel, particularly tourist travel? "My guess is we'll change very little," attorney friend Steve Faust said. "As soon as possible, we will go right back to rarely cooking our own food, driving all over the region, flying all over the globe, destination sporting events and conferences, and continued conspicuous consumption." How sad if our species needs a global pandemic to interrogate its behaviors. The numbers of air travelers in 2020 fell to a sixty-year low. Such reductions must be lucky and instructive.

The animal sightings give no hope for environmental historian Donald Worster that endangered populations will bounce back in his lifetime: "They represent the few who have survived, but they should not be taken as signs of a planetary recovery. That process may take thousands, even millions, of years. Industrial civilization, in contrast, will not take so long to recover." The many sightings of wild animals illustrate the consequences of our footloose ways.

Language also shows a growing awareness of travel as jaded eyes might view it. The Germans long have used the word *Reisefieber* for travel fever. Its semantic range is broad enough it may be understood both as holiday fever and travel nerves. A fever after all is a body responding to the onset of an illness. The Swedes might have it right—by coining *flygskam* for flight shame—that shaming one another into ethical travel conduct is the best response. Our English language has been slow to adapt to a growing awareness of the excesses of tourism.

If naming something confers power over it, the term *overtourism* marks a turning point. Since it entered English dictionaries in 2018, the phrase has taken solid hold. In the jargon of linguistics, it has filled an empty semantic niche. It shows dissatisfaction about our burgeoning populations in tandem with our travel habits. No other word has ever filled that niche so well. First-world residents whose homes have been hit hard by run-amok tourism have come to cling to that word as if it were a lifesaver. They've come to clasp it as if it were a buoyant donut thrown down to the drowning. Even travel businesses are using it, in a display of good faith.

The identity of some cities has been stripped by unchecked traffic. Travelers attracted to Amsterdam and Barcelona and Venice for their classic Old World charm saw that charm abraded by misuse, immoderation, and overtourism. Once again, we can note the irony of loving a place so much we help bring about its slow erosion. Before the pandemic, the infrastructures of those cities and others had become stretched as thin as the temper of many residents was stretched.

Tourist blades cut multiple ways. Locals feel besieged, and travelers resent the impoverishment of their experiences. Governments and industries keep profiting, though, behind the agitated scenes. Some locals have even taken to protesting in the streets. One sported a sign that read: "This is not tourism: It's a mass foreign inva$ion!!" Anthropologists met similar resistance when they entered isolated communities, but they never arrived in entitled droves. My characterization of tourists as rude and entitled is not mine alone. It is the outlook of the locals.

Scholars have been sounding warnings from deep within their silos. Fabiola Mancinelli, professor of urban tourism at the University of Barcelona, in an interview for the documentary *Crowded Out: The Story of Overtourism*, conjectured that her beloved city of Barcelona might ultimately "die of success." The problems there have grown so extreme she cannot sleep in the neighborhood where she lives. Residents of certain sectors of Amsterdam aim similar complaints about holidaymakers who party late into the night and take the parties to the streets. Many US cities, too, are seeing an increase in short-let rentals, especially since Airbnb stock went public.

Recreation professor Matthew Chase of Eastern Washington University uses a textbook titled *The Ethics of Tourism* published in 2013. A similar book, *Codes of Ethics in Tourism*, appeared in 2007. The titles of both books disguise the advisories on ethical breaches that fill their pages. The fact that two such books should appear in six years speaks to the perceived need to self-police the profession. Lax business protocols cause as many problems as boorish behavior does. COVID-19 quarantines, mandates to stay home, temporarily wiped blank the slate of unsustainable profiteering by a tourist-trade colossus in all its enveloping and invisible forms.

In 2019, one year after the word *overtourism* officially entered dictionaries, another book appeared. *Overtourism: Issues, Realities and Solutions* was edited by Rachel Dodds and Richard W. Butler, professors of hospitality and tourism in Canada and the UK respectively. Students assigned to study that as a textbook hope to make livelihoods within the industry. Students like Ambrosina, who served as our kindly hostess at the Conrad Bora Bora Nui Resort in 2019. Who can blame college graduates for chasing jobs that might allow them extensive time in paradise?

Their would-be profession is coining telltale buzzwords that offer them some cautions. Joining *overtourism* is the coinage *massification*: the availability of luxury products and services for mass markets. A counterweight to that word is the catchphrase *Instagramability*, used by tourists to describe the visual potential of a vacation location for distribution on social media.

The word *influencer*, too, ties to travel. It entered English in 2016. Travel influencers are those who entice on social media by showing attractive patrons here or there. Big brands pay influencers to get products in front of receptive audiences without the blatancy of traditional advertising, which consumers have come to regard with skepticism. *Business Insider* predicted influencer marketing would generate $10 billion in 2022. Influencers use Instagram, Facebook, Reddit, Twitter, YouTube, blogs, and many other platforms to gain followers and amass glances.

Social media has taken over much promotion, due to a growing tendency by prospective buyers to disregard standard marketing. The 2020 Netflix documentary *The Social Dilemma* makes that abundantly clear. To distinguish neutral coverage from stark marketing can prove impossible to the untrained eye. Such cunning subterfuge is by design. The cynic's maxim, that there is no such thing as candid objectivity, rings abundantly true in travel writing, particularly when resorts and tabloids subsidizing writers' expenses foreordain reporting's outcomes. If the untrained eye cannot distinguish neutrality from promotion, the eyes of other influencers can.

The excesses of the most heedless influencers have exposed them. One young woman faked a hiking picture to promote a Florida park by posting photos of herself in her own backyard and presenting it as part of the park. Another, a Swedish influencer, faked a trip to Paris by PhotoShopping herself on a bridge above the Seine, her high heels elevated above the bridge deck. Yet another influencer, Natalie Schlater, posing herself on Instagram in bikini underwear above a rice field in Asia, added a caption that read, "Thinking about how different my life is from the man picking in the rice field every morning." Other travelers have used the train tracks in Auschwitz as balance beams, the Berlin Holocaust Memorial for yoga poses, Jewish corpse photos as backgrounds for selfies, and Chernobyl for modeling new clothes. These might be exceptions, but an old maxim might also apply: that the exception proves the rule.

Rick Steves tells a compelling story of a German woman who ripped into him while touring on his way to Dachau. She showed him the entrance and exit wounds of a bullet that almost killed her during World War II. Another bullet killed her father. "I was stunned by her rage," he writes. "But I sensed desperation on her part to simply unload her story on one of the hordes of tourists who tramp daily through her hometown to ogle at an icon of the Holocaust."

* * *

Long before the advent of airline travel, transport technology was drawing criticism for its socioeconomic impacts. Frank Norris saw the rail industry as a monster that overwhelmed competition. In 1901, he published *The Octopus.* That novel's title references tentacles of the Southern Pacific Railroad in its sometimes-violent clashes with farmers. The title was inspired by G. Frederick Keller's 1882 editorial cartoon "The Curse of California," in which a devilfish railway engulfs miners, loggers, farmers, stagecoaches, ships, and banks. Keller's objections to the rail industry were never ecological. Both men objected to railroads for concentrating wealth.

Both men might be astonished at the reach of the airline industry today. In 2017, the Department of Transportation reported, "International passenger enplanements (107.7 million) reached an all-time annual high." By 2019, the DOT noted, "The annual number has reached a new high for five consecutive years." During the same period, not coincidentally, planetary temperatures were reaching their own all-time highs since record-keeping began. The word *enplanements,* another new coinage to add to the stack, indexes the impacts of the industry.

Thanks to quarantines, some bad behavior ratcheted back. As I was researching late in 2021, Europe again had banned American travelers due to our high COVID-19 rates. By the middle of 2022, though, as infection rates dropped, countries again welcomed all comers. But COVID-19 took a separate toll. When travel came roaring back in mid-2022, the airlines had too few employees to handle all the passengers, because so many workers had been laid off. Canceled flights and lost baggage were afflicting business and passenger routes alike. One of our sons went without his luggage for a week in Berlin, even though it was in the airport all the time.

The pandemic dealt industrial-scale tourism a massive blow. Passenger revenues plunged by more than $314 billion, according to the Air Transport Association. The share price of United Airlines fell from ninety-six dollars at the start of 2020 to twenty-two dollars in early May 2021. By June 2022, when passengers again were filling seats, its share price languished at thirty-six dollars. Alaska Air Group posted a first-quarter loss of $232 million. Airbnb laid off 1,900 of its 7,500 workers in early May 2020, delaying its IPO, which in December nonetheless exceeded expectations and brought in $3.7 billion. Those who chose not to travel nationally opted for short-let rentals close to home. Airlines began to consult and contract with psychologists to get reluctant passengers back in their seats.

Overall industry losses were not only a result of passenger aversion to jam on planes and fly. They were also an outgrowth of travel restrictions that 217 countries and territories levied. Even the wealthiest people could not gain entry. What such numbers do not calculate is the artificial inflation caused by excessive travel to holiday hotspots over decades. Had tourist travel been better regulated, that is, the pandemic's financial hemorrhage might have been less severe.

Justin Francis in England, CEO and founder of Responsible Travel, identifies five factors that have contributed to overtourism. First, he says, jet travel has become more affordable due to governments subsidizing it. "Aviation fuel is exempt from tax," he reports. "In the UK alone, it is estimated at a nine-billion-pound subsidy." By exempting jet fuel from taxes, governments allow more people to visit their nations and encourage more people to lubricate national wealth.

The cost of all the slopped carbon shifts to other nations and future generations. During the ongoing COVID-19 crisis, some of those same airlines applied for bailouts. Time will tell if their home governments consider them "too big to let fail" and forgive debts. Virgin was denied access to bailout cash. Some 90 percent of Virgin Australia's shares are held out of the country.

Mr. Francis puts travel writers in the crosshairs next. The complexity of travel writing has grown, especially since social media transformed the terrain. A half century ago, travel-industry inserts took up the largest parts of newspapers. Mainstream travel writing eventually proved too transparent, though, too overtly promotional. Clever readers recognized every bit of it as fluff. Negative travel reports rarely got into print. Old-school publishers, *National Geographic* and its ilk, are suspect, opening the way for media conglomerates to buy them out and make sweeping changes. Do travel promotions continue to feather magazine budgets? There is little doubt.

Awareness of the viral hazards of travel—the jamming into planes, boats, and resorts—will change the complexion of the travel-writing industry yet again in unforeseeable ways. Fears of death by infectious disease will not soon be forgotten. Fewer travelers will be inclined to risk tight crowds and customary modes of transport to earn vacation destinations. Tray tables on airplanes, waiters handling foodstuffs, throngs in public plazas—all such shared trappings of unreflective travel are apt to become suspect since viruses took the public imagination by storm.

Again, too, travel's hazards and awareness of the risks of contracting COVID-19 raise linguistic tensions. *Fomite*, for instance, many of us now know, is an inanimate object or substance, such as clothing, furniture, or soap, that can transmit viral agents or organisms from one individual to another. Language changes always follow wholesale cultural changes.

Justin Francis's third factor to account for overtourism is "honeypot sites." Honeypots are overdeveloped. They generate cash by concentrating visitors in tight spots. They put the destiny back in destination. Despite litter, vandalism, and strains on infrastructure, honeypot sites prove more attractive to certain sorts of tourists. People like me who critique industrial-scale tourism, of course, must be careful not to essentialize the people or the industry, not to portray or explain them away by stereotypical or innate character traits. Still, the analyses of pundits like Justin Francis represent a bold and hopeful development in the evolution of the travel trade.

A fourth factor he identifies, in the crushing circumstance now named overtourism, is the sharp and sudden rise in holiday apartments, aka short-let rentals. Airbnb, HomeAway, and VRBO have worsened crowding problems, research shows. Venice alone had eight thousand apartments listed for rent on Airbnb before the coronavirus crash. Our stay at an Airbnb in Barcelona, Spain's popular destination for international visitors, was cheerless and forgettable.

Across the planet, short-term residential rentals are coming under greater scrutiny than before. In California, the cities banning short-let rentals include Santa Monica, Pacific Grove, Monterey, and Danville. Residents of those cities position quality of life a notch higher in their gauge of priorities than the income to be derived by throwing open doors. Residential neighbors of short-let rentals are likewise demanding that their voices be heard above the commercial din. Many other US communities are having conversations about rentals and enforcing rules.

European towns and cities soon will follow suit. Communicable-disease concerns are triggering extra cautions among renters and landlords alike. Nor does nativism alone explain the barriers being erected to ban outsiders who would settle permanently in, especially perhaps those outsiders from those countries that have been virally hottest for the longest time.

Travelers reluctant to crowd in resorts and cruise ships after the COVID-19 scare might have contributed to the success of Airbnb, the short-let rental service. Since the company's IPO in December 2020, investors have been buying up tens of thousands of homes to convert into rentals. Those investors have made the squashing combat over home sales more competitive, and they appear to have contributed to the escalation of housing costs around the nation.

The trend toward short-let rentals stands to take millions of homes out of reach of middle-class families in the decades to come. Economic changes might force them to rent forever. If the ripple effects of the commercial tourist industry are indeterminable, as I have argued throughout this book, Airbnb as a growing sector of that industry is similarly inscrutable. By the middle of 2022, Airbnb was investing in television commercials—happy-go-lucky shot-gunned spots that feature songs by Dean Martin, Bob Dylan, Rita Lee, and Jay-Z.

As his fifth factor, Justin Francis joins dozens of other pundits by singling out cruise lines. That travel institution has come to be perceived as a breeding ground for COVID-19. Fairly or unfairly, cruise-ship companies bore a brunt of attention during the height of the pandemic. They "add little value to local economies," Francis notes. Moreover, the travel they cultivate is superficial. Francis classifies the experiences they nurture as "fly-by tourism."

In addition to the efforts of Justin Francis to make tourism more responsible, there is a movement that is afflicted by semantic noise. Going by many names, it is known variously as justice tourism, solidarity tourism, decolonial tourism, and critical tourism. Its advocates aim to critique the ways traditional tourism exoticizes and essentializes locals, reducing them to service providers and economic servants. The multitrillion-dollar industry, socially and environmentally consumptive, rarely improves communities. Critical tourism nurtures fairer exchanges, and it aims to create sustainable economies for those populations hardest hit by overtourism.

Kyle Kajihiro, involved in a group significantly named DeTours, tries to reconstruct the ways that tourists understand the Hawai'ian Islands. Speaking to Zeb Larson for *Smithsonian Magazine,* Kajihiro said: "I'd like to abolish the word 'tourism.' It does something really problematic by turning it into a consumptive, extractive experience. Journeying to other places and meeting other people can be a good thing, an enriching thing, a building of solidarity."

The experiences my family had in French Polynesia confirmed many of the critiques of traditional tourism. On the island of Mo'orea, we motored by 'Ōpūnohu Bay to watch whales. There, cruise ships anchor. They off-load day-trippers to a tender pier to tour the town of Papetoai. Blue whales used to be the behemoths of the sea, but cruise ships outsize them by many times. Those ships towered above our thirty-foot boat like skyscrapers above busses.

The tidings from the virus stand to hammer cruising as an institution. At the peak of the pandemic, Anthony Fauci, the leading immunologist in the US, remarked, "People on a large ship, all together, at the same time, all the time—you couldn't ask for a better incubator for infection." To sanitize a cruise ship serving three hundred thousand passengers per year must be a massive challenge. The notion of fomite will come right to mind for all but the most oblivious of passengers. Respiration vapors from thousands crowding for food and games is an even greater threat. A couple who are friends of ours ponied up $130K for a five-month all-inclusive cruise in 2022, a cruise that promised to have "only" nine hundred passengers. It was canceled. One of my relatives, a cruise-ship employee, has had to reinvent himself since COVID-19 hit.

Some cruise lines have chosen to install onboard water-filtering systems to counteract the single-use bottles. One overt purpose is to reduce the marine microplastics pollution generated when castoff bottles all break down. More than 90 percent of plastic fragments in the sea are smaller than a grain of rice. Some are small enough for sea breezes to carry them across continents. Larger bits enter bodies and lodge there, never to metabolize or pass through, as necropsies of dead birds show. Cruise line corporations are trying to limit the smog of marine microplastics by deliberating about which products to buy and distribute to customers onboard.

Cruise ships long ago gained bad ecological fame around the world. They discharge dirty water. They generate dissolved oxygen and turbidity. They disrupt seafloors and organisms. The hydrocarbons fueling them release sulfur oxides, nitrogen oxides, CO_2, and particulate matter.

One need not be an ecologist to be averse to boarding a cruise ship. Simple solicitude for human health will do. In February 2020, millions watched in morbid fascination as the *Diamond Princess,* a cruise ship holding the standard capacity of 2,666 passengers and 1,045 crew members, was quarantined during an outbreak of COVID-19. Novelist Gay Courter, a passenger who had yet to be chastened by the severity of the pandemic, called her stately cabin "a rather posh penitentiary." The ship's pastry chef was "the real hero" of that shutdown saga, she said. He kept her well-fed. The ship's two-week quarantine resulted in more COVID-19-infected passengers than if they had been evacuated promptly. Once the *Diamond Princess* passengers were off-loaded in Japan, they faced a second quarantine at air force bases in California, Georgia, or Texas. At least 712 of the 3,711 passengers and crew were infected. Nine died. Mokoto Rich, writing for the *New York Times,* dubbed that cruise ship "a floating epidemiological disaster."

A similar ordeal scared and sickened passengers aboard the *Grand Princess* on a trip to Hawai'i. Passengers boarded on February 21, 2020—after risks from the sickness had been known for a month. Its standard load of 3,500 passengers bent toward the upper end of the age scale, the most susceptible epidemiologically. Contact tracing later tracked passengers back to the nation's first novel coronavirus victim. Officials created a genealogy of the illness and learned that she had crossed paths earlier with others who had boarded the *Grand Princess.* To avoid contact for the medical crew, test kits were dropped by helicopter. Forty-five people were tested. Nineteen crew and two passengers tested positive, and at least one hundred more showed symptoms.

Family members of one elderly passenger filed suit. They said its day-to-day operations revealed the company never appeared to have contemplated or prepared for infectious diseases. Condiments were self-served.

Bridge games continued. Players handled the same decks of cards every day. After the panic began, infected crew members began to deliver meals to the rooms.

One eighty-six-year-old passenger, Rex Lawson, escaped unharmed. When his children said they never want him to board another boat, he said it will be hard to pass up the consolation cruise the company offered him and his wife for their distress. Mr. Lawson will have to go it alone or find another partner, however. His wife has refused to board another cruise ship again.

The dicey quality of life aboard cruise ships has generated the need for the International Cruise Victims Association. That volunteer advocacy association represents victims of crimes on cruise ships. Families, friends, and other interest groups make up its membership of several hundred. Some customers have disappeared and never again been seen, while others have been exploited with no available recourse, due to the jurisdictional uncertainties of the institution. In international waters, group members claim, victims are neglected, crimes underinvestigated, and criminals underprosecuted, free to commit offenses over and again due to scant follow-through.

Terry Hartle, senior vice president of the American Council on Education, likened the colossal holiday boats to college dormitories. The close quarters caused him to dub dorms "land-locked cruise ships." Neither colleges nor cruise lines stand to benefit from the analogy. In this recent sign that the pandemic will have lasting impacts both on language and on travel, the big boats have come to be shorthand for everything that can be thronged and virally hazardous.

Many vacationers cut their travel teeth on the TV show *Love Boat*. It began in 1979. The carefree disco beat of its theme song echoed "Copacabana" by Barry Manilow from 1978. The formula proved so popular it got a reality TV restart on US and Australian TV in 2022. The 1979 lyrics promised more than most vacations can deliver. "Love, exciting and new," the words began. "Come aboard. We're expecting you." The personal touch, the direct address, proved inviting in ways few other shows had tried. "Love, life's sweetest reward. Let it flow. It floats back to you." The show made the cruise ship a moveable feast, a mobile Bali Ha'i, an ecosystem of reciprocal exchange. "The love boat soon will be making another run," the lyrics assured.

For many elderly passengers, another run might be a long time coming. The corporations themselves admit that industry-wide changes can be neither calculated nor foreseen. Carnival Corporation's stock price fell in two months from near sixty dollars a share to less than thirteen dollars. (As of mid-2022, the share price of that granddaddy of all American cruise lines still had not cleared thirteen dollars.) Mass-media entertainments had primed audiences to sign on to cruise-ship excursions for a half century. A decade before *Love Boat*, in 1968, the musical fantasy movie *Chitty Chitty Bang Bang* starred comic actor Dick Van Dyke. That movie made ironic fun of cruise liners in ways the average viewer might not have detected.

Chitty Chitty Bang Bang's standout song, titled "Posh!," riffed on the word as an acronym for "Port Out, Starboard Home." That false etymology, that linguistic mythology, positioned savvy boaters between England and India as always booking the port side going out and the starboard side coming home. Alternating between the left and right sides ensured the choicest scenery both coming and going. The movie's mockery of travel lies in the scene where daft Grandpa Potts (Lionel Jeffries) struts in his imperial puttees and bellows the song "Posh!" Improbably aloft in an outhouse over the sea, he mistakes the toilet for a state room in an oceangoing vessel. Potts kicks open the door of the soaring privy and sings, "This is living, this is style, this is elegance by the mile!" Massified audiences must have guffawed at the spectacle and the slapstick more readily than they appreciated the piercing sarcasm of the lyrics. Potts, a delusional veteran of British India, hollers and gestures, "Oh, the posh posh traveling life, the traveling life for me! / First cabin and captain's table, regal company!" Not only does he confuse an airborne outhouse for a stateroom, but he boasts loudly of his attainments. "Whenever I'm bored, I travel abroad, but I do it stylishly." His boast prefigured customers of love boats such as the *Diamond Princess* a half century later, some of whom proved doomed.

The TV series *Love Boat* and the movie *Chitty Chitty Bang Bang* both brought to popular consciousness the possibility of heading out to sea for luxury short-term voyages and vacations. Massified audiences thronged to the siren call of all-inclusive buffets and entertainment. In the next four decades, the largest cruise ships grew one-third longer, to 360 meters, or 1,181 feet, expanded their widths to 60 meters, and doubled passenger totals to an unsustainable 5,400.

Had passengers on the *Diamond Princess* or the *Grand Princess* in 2020 read Elizabeth Becker's 2013 book *Overbooked,* they might have thought twice before signing on the dotted line. Every consumer, Becker pointed out with solid evidence, has reason to be chafed. They must bear the hidden costs for drinks and gratuities, starvation wages paid to the waitstaff, and predatory pricing for bling at foreign ports of call. The Carnival Corporation owns both boats.

Cruises also offend the environment by contributing to climate change. "The air pollution from just one of the docked giant ships," Becker writes, "is the equivalent of 12,000 idling cars every day." The average tourist cares little about pollution, of course. Part of the charm of being aboard those behemoths of the sea must be the oblivion or forgetfulness they bestow.

Patrons are encouraged to leave behind terrestrial cares and generate fantasies of love and abandon. And that of course is what vacations do— allow people to vacate day-to-day concerns, become oblivious, leave it all behind. Among the many forms of tourist travel that Elizabeth Becker dices, she reserves the sharpest contempt for cruise lines.

Those big boats throng ports at some of Earth's most beautiful spots. In a figure of speech adopted by many pundits while COVID-19 rates were high, the ships are mobile petri dishes. When travelers no longer dared to take a chance on Asia, the cruise lines shifted to Alaska and offered screaming deals. By early May 2020, those routes also had closed for a time. The delta variant of COVID-19 in the year 2021 curtailed their B.A.U. even further. The future is dim for humans in the hospitality industry if their credentials pivot exclusively on cruise ships.

Each boat generates an unseen motherlode of methane, a greenhouse gas that "traps eighty-four times as much heat as carbon dioxide over a 20-year time frame," the David Suzuki Foundation says. Invisible methane's main causes are fossil-fuel production, distribution, and use, at 33 percent. Livestock farming, at 27 percent, follows closely after the production of fossil-fuels.

In a wishful fantasy that ought to shame me to share, cruise ships all would sink into the seas—after passengers of course were first evacuated. The oxygen-deprived seafloor hulks would forever sequester the rich deposits of the carbon and the methane they contain. My shameful fantasy will never unfold, though. Each ship costs an average of $260 million to build.

Nathaniel Hawthorne inspired my apocalyptic fantasy. His tale "Earth's Holocaust" envisions a busk festival, a ceremony originating with the Creek Nation (Muscogee today). Useless, damaging, and outworn goods were heaped and burned in that Indigenous rite. In Hawthorne's 1846 appropriation, Anglo-Americans kindle up the fire. Those Anglos burn lots of formerly precious stuff in efforts to rid Earth of every emblem of injustice. They begin by torching the crowns worn by royalty and the coats of arms displayed by aristocracies. They conclude by kindling weaponry and other tools of capital punishment, such as gallows. The purgation brought about by the Muscogee busk festival let the people forget grudges, forgive debts, and regenerate community. The coronavirus, by crushing tourist travel temporarily, might indeed have positive long-term consequences that no one yet is capable of foreseeing fully.

In an image that could have surfaced from "The Rime of the Ancient Mariner" poem, cruise ships became ghost ships in 2020. Turned away from port after port, they drifted in search of spots to dock. Carnival's *Costa Luminosa*, rebuffed at Savona in Italy, floated in anticipation of Italy's ports reopening. The MSC *Fantasia*, its outing canceled, effectively held hostage its 1,338 passengers outside Lisbon in Portugal. The MV *Columbus*, owned by Cruise and Maritime Voyages in the UK, got stalled in the Andaman Sea off Thailand for weeks, until it undertook 7,842 nautical miles to return its passengers to England. Once they could disembark from those ghost ships, many of the captive passengers had no recourse but to travel on commercial flights. Doing so imperiled other fliers, flight attendants, and restaurant employees. Twenty cruise liners became *navis non grata* during the period when the virus preoccupied the world. In the 1798 Coleridge poem, the ghost ship drifts through alternating fog and drought, as penance for the mariner's having shot an albatross.

Backlash proved swift and predictable against international safeguards preventing ships from docking in 2020. Merchant mariner Mikhail Voytenko tracked alleged outrages in his *Fleet Mon* blog. Free-market champions like him blamed government overreach for hampering free assembly, free speech, and free trade. It was all a scheme, they said, to limit marine commerce. That same skepticism applied later to viral masking around the United States. Later still, it applied to state, national, and commercial requirements that patrons accept vaccinations. Masks and vaccinations became political acts, more so than travel itself has ever been or likely will be.

Every American cruise line but one registers in foreign nations, thus availing themselves of legal loopholes. They license in nations with laxer regulations—Liberia, Panama, Bermuda, Malta, Italy, the Netherlands. They court American customers while dodging American laws. Should a catastrophe take place, or a pandemic happen, remedies and rights prove difficult to apply. Moreover, cruise lines are "part of an industry that paid an average tax rate of under 1%, which is well below the required 21% tax rate in the United States." Still, many of the companies applied for financial relief in 2020, claiming a need for economic shelter for employees who might otherwise be laid off. Distribution of the funds was vague.

They call their foreign registries "flags of convenience," a phrase that's fraudulent on its face. By legal ambiguities, the companies in fact register in jurisdictions that do not oblige them to abide by US labor laws. That way, they also enjoy lower taxes. Elizabeth Becker, whose book *Overbooked* appeared in 2013, interviewed employees aboard the Royal Caribbean–owned ship on which she cruised. Some of those employees told her they earned only fifty dollars per month. They were accordingly forced to rely on customer gratuities, kindness from strangers, to survive.

For those in the upper echelons of the cruise industry, there is plenty of good money to be made supplying tourists with the amenities they crave. The largest cruise line, the monopolistic Carnival Corporation, has nine "brands": AIDA, Carnival, Costa, Cunard, Holland America, Princess, P&O Australia, P&O UK, and Seaborn. Headquartered in Miami, Florida, it is incorporated in Panama. Chairman Micky Arison had a personal worth of $5.3 billion USD in early 2020 and was the owner of the NBA team Miami Heat. He is also a friend of former president Trump, who conscripted him in his

Great Economic Revival industry group on April 14, 2020. By March 2022, his personal worth had increased to $6.5 billion, despite the numerous hits to the industry that resulted in several major cruise lines retreating into receivership. Like airlines, cruise-ship fortunes are made, in part, thanks to government subsidies.

Miami-based Walker & O'Neill lawyers specialize in maritime law. "I don't think the C.D.C. has protocols in place," the firm's James Walker told the *New York Times* in late March 2020 about the handling of the COVID-19 crisis. "Everyone is scrambling around trying to figure things out. It seems to me kind of a Mad Hatter type of environment . . . no one is taking the lead." Walker publishes *Cruise Law News,* a blog on "Everything Cruise Lines Don't Want You to Know." It dishes dirt on the love-boat industry supported by so many travelers. That dirt includes violations of air-pollution laws, illegal discharges within national parks, paint particles shed on dry docks and in the water, and court-required monitoring of repeat offenders.

In an industry that hosts more than twenty million people every year, an apologist might rationalize that accidents will happen. A different view would hold tourism as an industry itself responsible—a underregulated trade whose appendages prove elusive. Researching the impacts of its segments, though, is one small way of holding the industry accountable.

In that trying spring of 2020, two Carnival cruise ships motored for two weeks with COVID-19 patients aboard. After being turned away from South American ports, they were allowed to dock in Florida, after a long negotiation. Locals feared that care for foreigners would divert resources from their own region, where COVID cases had spiked. Once the *Zaandam* and the *Rotterdam* got permission to off-load folks at Port Everglades, four elderly passengers had already died. Dozens were sick. Carnival said forty-five mildly sick passengers would stay on board, but it had ten people to be shuttled to a hospital for care. It also acknowledged that some six thousand of its passengers were stuck at sea—stranded and at increasing risk of contagion.

The rumble of cruise ships and the roar of jet engines were still punctuating the air when Canadian editorial cartoonist André-Philippe Côté drew a seriocomic cartoon on March 18, 2020. In his foreground, a tatty bearded castaway on a desert island presses his back against the trunk of a palm tree. He is trying to hide. His face is grim. Behind him, a cruise ship looms. Coughs in French emanate from its several decks. "Keuf! Keuf!" they sound out. "Keuf! Keuf! Keuf! Keuf!" The cruise ship plows on. The castaway evades an unwelcome rescue by hiding. No cruise ships would leave a US port again till June 26, 2021, when the *Celebrity Edge* left Fort Lauderdale, Florida, holding some 40 percent capacity of passengers, most of them vaccinated. Many people shared the comic castaway's relief.

Our yard moose browsed apple branches, willows, rose bushes, and saskatoon shrubs. He would not scare. If a dog barked or a car started, then the neck swiveled, the great head swung, and the ears turned like antennae dishes to triangulate the sound. In that same period, travel traffic dropped to a sixty-year low. When the moose lay down in our yard to take a nap, the forelegs buckled at the knees, the haunches followed, and the cud rumbled up to chew. After a week in our midst, that bull moose just disappeared.

For several days in August 2020, though, a cow moose and two calves took the place of that bull and fed on our landscape as well. We hope they or others like them will return, though we have no certainty that day again will come. Soon afterward, the skies began to fill with contrails, the streets and freeways with cars and trucks, and the seas with raucous commerce.

among
the indigenous

13

Tracking Captain Cook

At Kahaluu Beach Park on the Kona coast, we navigated the parking lot, discovered a spot, and unhinged our limbs from the rented car. Young women in bikinis and families from middle America vied for bits of rock and sand. From those bits they entered the sea. We entered right beside them—snorkels, masks, and fins in hands—to take the lay of the land and water.

Rising near shore amid vigorous waves, the mounded shell of a large green turtle swayed. People crowded in to inspect the reptile. Its feet braced. Its beaked head tore live algae from ancient coral that had perished long ago. I recalled the Indigenous creation account from North America. Turtle Island, the people named their continent in the cosmos, the planet where we live.

Colonial sailors prized green turtles. Plucked from the ocean and flopped upside down on deck, the turtles "sobbed" but stayed alive a long time, according to firsthand travelers' reports. Fresh turtle stew lay always nearby. Turtle shells could be used to dish up turtle soup enriched with the fatty gelatin from within called calipash. In an early prescription, "The ashes of a Sea-Turtle mixt with oyl or Bears-grease causeth hair to grow," the seventeenth-century English traveler John Josselyn wrote. In parts of the Caribbean still today, farm-raised turtles supply upmarket restaurants that chop them to make soup. In French Polynesia, sailors busted in possession of turtles can have their boats confiscated, but they keep up the practice on the sly.

A century ago in Australia, the sport of turtle riding had its vogue. In that era, green turtles could reach five feet in length and weigh almost half a ton. Reptiles aiming to lay their eggs along the Great Barrier Reef were caught and overturned to become short-term tourist captives and steeds. Enacting a Pacific Ocean rodeo event, the animals were turned upright again, whereupon the sportive man or woman, dressed just so for a photo-op, hopped on. The frantic turtles headed instinctively for the haven of the sea, taking the riders with them. The most intrepid contestants, using rope harnesses, could steer their mounts and ride atop the waves. The turtle-riding feat was reprised in the London Hippodrome in 1931 for an audience of admirers. By the 1950s the pastime had declined, along with the size and number of turtles.

On our Kona beach, swimmers mobbed the feeding turtle. One pointed an underwater camera at the massive jaws and snapped. Her shot would show the animal glowering and trying to eat. Her partner, a tanned young man in swim trunks, posed with one hand atop the shell.

"Don't touch," our friend Bart cautioned him. Touching turtles is against the law. I winced at Bart's admonition all the same, keen to avoid a scene. The young man seemed to notice neither the beach signs nor the warning Bart had spoken. Posing, bending, touching, grinning—his was the air of a sahib on safari. Charles Darwin had wobbled atop Galapagos tortoises as part of an ignoble experiment, but I doubt that this young man had read him.

When he rested a foot on the turtle's back, that did it for an older bather, late fifties or so, who stepped into the surf and growled, "Get away from the turtle."

Ten feet separated them, those two squaring off, one in the waves, the other standing stiff and stony with his chest outthrust on shore. "What part of New Jersey are you *from?*" the elder fellow exhaled. Their words rose, their voices remained low, each man egging the other on. We onlookers wondered if this clash over an endangered species was going to devolve to blows.

A transplant from New York, the angry elder must have felt his whole head go red. How sick he was of pushy tourists, he muttered, backing down and returning to his lounge chair. Still pissed, he jabbed a finger and spat to anyone who'd listen, "That couple, good Catholics from Trenton probably, think God put that turtle there for them to photograph."

Two centuries after Captain Cook, we were searching for his legacies in Hawai'i. We were following his spoor. In the centuries since Cook claimed these islands for the Crown, waves had washed off every trace of his nation. The United States was running the whole show now.

On this big island, on February 14, 1779, islanders killed Cook. A few islanders also died, in the brawl that precipitated Cook's death, but their vowel-rich names rarely season the historical accounts. Too hard to spell, harder to pronounce, plus Cook's underlings and record keepers considered most Indigenous identities irrelevant. Some three thousand armed with stones, clubs, knives, and spears turned upon the English invaders to try to take their island back.

Cook must have been stunned to see his men's pistol balls bounce off the woven mats the islanders armored themselves with. Accurately hurled lava stones injured him and his men. Odd for a mariner, Cook could not swim. In the shallows near shore, he floundered in heavy regalia during the assault. Pierced with a spear, wounded in the side like Christ, he groaned. Or so the historical records show. That mortal groan might have goaded and emboldened the Indigenous people to topple him in the rocky water, to stab him and knock him on the head till he was dead.

* * *

Traveling had always meant camping for me. You traveled near or far, you pitched a tent, you prevailed on friends, you hiked for miles to earn prime rustic sites. Transitioning to a lavish condominium complex flung me from my comfort zone. It sported a café, restaurant, golf course, swimming pools, weight room, and activity signup desk. "I would rather sit on a pumpkin and have it all to myself," Thoreau had written, "than be crowded on a velvet cushion." Years ago in Wyoming, I coasted off a road after dark and lay a sleeping bag between some pines. No tarp, no tent, no fire, no hot food. Road-weary, I just crashed. Come dawn, the sandhill cranes were flocking, leaping, crying in a marsh so near they startled me awake. That bed was heaven-sent.

Following the altercation over the turtle on the shore, Karen and I wound ourselves down on a breezy lanai at condominiums named the Bay Club. We were the guests of Bart and Lindell Haggin, our generous friends who shared the timeshare. Kubla Khan decreed "a stately pleasure dome," in the 1816 poem by Samuel Taylor Coleridge, but our tastes were much more meager.

We would be gratified to sample fresh pineapple, we said to one another. In a stiffening noon wind, coconut palm trees began to nod and lash on the condominium's shoreside.

During our visit the second US-led Gulf war began. TVs blared in the airport when we touched down on the complex. Networks were broadcasting war reports fit for situation dramas, poetic in a clumsy and sensational way: "The Iraq Attack." "The War on Terror." "The Battle for Baghdad." In neighboring condos, in the café, even in the exercise room above the whirr of elliptical trainers, all eyes tracked the bomb blasts. We arrived early in the day and tried to doze on stone benches while waiting for the Haggins with the condo key to open.

As parents of two young boys, we found the patriotic fare unsettling. Vacationing so far from the kids felt wrong; our nation was prosecuting a war. Thoreau could refuse to pay his poll tax to protest actions by his government, but the only recourse we could see was to march in the streets, as we did at home, to protest the US invasion. Here we turned to the Pacific, wishing we could use the name of that great water body to preserve the peace and create conciliation.

Whales spouted everywhere. Karen got busy applying an antifog emulsion on our swim masks. She was charged up to swim with the parrotfish, the spinner dolphins, the green turtles.

News cycles distracted me. That same week in Scotland, the spear used to stab Captain Cook went up for sale. Made into a walking stick and passed down through an officer's family, it stood to fetch as much as £2,000 (USD 5,300), according to the Edinburgh-based auction house of Lyon and Turnbull. Such a prize irony would not have been lost on Mark Twain, who wrote harshly of Captain James Cook. In *Roughing It* and in letters sent home from the Sandwich Islands, as Cook named them after the Earl of

Sandwich, Twain laid out a Costco warehouse of historical facts and interpretations that we readers sample far less often than we do his novels.

Fiction is easier for many of us to metabolize than fact. Easier to spend a summer week with Huckleberry Finn and his companion, the escaped slave Jim, than to have to tongue the nasty savor of raw truth. Sooner subsidize multinational corporations bent on transforming volcanic deserts into paradise than score our feet on lava rocks while walking to the sea. Magma bubbles and pops, then cools to tiny caves or cups. Cratered and sharp, those concave hollows resemble tools for scooping melon balls. Unwary walkers can find the soles of their feet scooped.

Inside the Bay Club windows, sheer valance drapes softened the glare of the island sun. Curtains hanging heavy behind the drapes closed tight against the light and altogether shut it out. A song sung to thumping bongo drums crept to mind:

Condo, condominium.
Condo, condominium.
There's so, there's so many of 'em.
Can't get, can't get rid of 'em.

The song "Condo" hails from *The Earth First! Li'l Green Songbook*. Condominiums are the bread and butter, today, of the short-let vacation rental marketplaces VRBO and Airbnb.

* * *

When Cook sailed into Kealakekua Bay on January 16, 1779, it was makahiki time, a period of festivity dedicated to Lono, the fertility god. Normal kapu days, taboo days, were suspended. So were the frequent intertribal wars. Willing partners enjoyed sex freely. Everyone danced, ate, drank, and competed in friendly games.

Hawai'ian legend had it that the great god Lono, whose iconography depicted him as a wooden figure on a crossbeam, would return to Earth. In their eschatology, sheets of tapa cloth hung from the beam he clung to. Like Cortés, whom the Aztec people misread in Mexico, Cook appeared to be a promised deity incarnate. The tall masts and fabric sails of Cook's ship became Lono's sacred floating stage. Adding to the mythology, Kealakekua Bay had been named Lono's holy place. The people prostrated themselves in homage to Cook. They planted their faces in the sand. James Cook's crew needed supplies, and the resident Hawai'ians gave them all they had.

According to the earliest Anglo historians, the people of Hawai'i were too primitive to grasp the technologies of Europe. Ignorance blinded and safeguarded them. Such surmises tease and torment me, split as they are between the idyllic and the horrific, the cultural yin and the yang. As soon as possible, I planned to visit Kealakekua Bay and overhear what it has to say.

The Kona coast, where Captain Cook and his crew made landfall, reminds my eye of the Great Basin—Nevada, Utah, and Southern Idaho. The trees grow low, ground cover sparse, only eight inches of rain per year. But this small continent of an island has multiple climate zones. In highlands on the north side, vines and epiphyte-festooned tall trees drink in the 130 inches of yearly rainfall. That drenching from precipitation makes the forests exquisite in scent and sight. Swag-bellied clouds drain their capillaries of snows and rains. Little of wetness gets left behind to deposit on the Kona and Kohala coasts, where cacti and other spiny species thrive.

Mark Twain pronounced on Cook's demise "a deliberate verdict of justifiable homicide." Cook had returned all manner of "kindnesses with insult and ill-treatment" of the natives. He had parceled out a British justice—slain trespassers, burned villages, and amputated thievish hands.

After his execution, the islanders made certain that "His flesh was stripped from the bones and burned (except nine pounds of it which were sent on board the ships). The heart was hung up in a local hut, where it was found and eaten by three children, who mistook it for the heart of a dog." The lurid details of these colonial events fascinated Mark Twain. "Small blame," he concluded, "should attach to the natives for the killing of Cook. They treated him well."

In our condominium's mirror-closeted bedroom, behind eight-foot old-growth mahogany doors, Karen and I fluff our pillows to settle for a much-needed nap. The wave-slosh shushes in our ears at last, but our doors of perception fall and rise with the impress of the surf and tides. In my agitated sleep, aware of the children being cared for at home, I dream of the youngest and Home Depot. I have left three-year-old Chase to doze in the car, safety seat unbuckled, while I search for a home-improvement gadget. The irrational unconscious makes me a model Bad Dad.

Even more irrationally, in the landscape of my dream, the parking lot of the Home Depot has yet to be paved. Mashed grass and wheel ruts mark the passage of cars. Rainfall puddles instead of skimming into drains. Developers had hustled to prepare the spot for business. When I return to the neon dream-car, having scored the fitting for the toilet tank, Chase is awake and stumbling outdoors in the mud, fearful and calling for me, his cheeks puffy and bitten by bugs.

*   *   *

The patch of smooth water a whale leaves, after it breaches or sounds, is known as a fluke print. Hunters followed fluke prints, as if on dry land, to try to harpoon the beasts. Spy-hopping describes a whale thrusting its head above the water to look around. One humpback spy-hops and holds high for a long time to regard us in our boat. Breaching means a whale back has broken through. A spout is a jet of water and air, accompanied at close range by a snort or a groan. Sounding describes the flukes, or the tail fins, flying skyward to propel the animal below.

We see all these behaviors displayed off Waikoloa, aboard the ship *Sea Smoke,* on an afternoon outing to watch for whales. We are ecotouring, learning as we go, hoping not to be imperialist in our behaviors and tastes, wishing some book could guide us how. That wish is foremost for me when we tour exotic ecologies abroad. My scruples nag me when our wealth and privilege so starkly separate us from the locals. The water around this island has yet to be legally named calving grounds, and so tourist-laden boats can approach the humpbacks as close as one hundred yards, effectively hazing them. On Maui the distance is three hundred yards.

We trail one lone whale for an hour. The animal sounds, breaches, leads us, and follows. The crew share their informed opinion that he is a young bull, thirty-two feet long instead of the mature forty in length. Unattached, he has no female available to chase and impregnate, his plans to be an escort dashed. For a full minute he lies fifteen feet off our stern—flashing fins, blowing, groaning like an elephant or horse. He eyes us and behaves aggressively, in his peculiar way.

The crew guess that the animal has a cold, he blows so, but I have my own surmise. This bull is just being expressive—an oceanic bovine giving his audience his best impression of supremacy or territoriality. Approaching us and snorting, he is displaying in the only way he can. Barnacles crust his jaw's underside. When he sounds, his fins flip farther than the average whale.

Cook, on his last of three voyages, found evidence his men had pioneered an epidemic of venereal disease. Bare-breasted Polynesian women, sporting flowers in their hair, had swum from shore to meet the *Resolution*. No ship logs say whether those women, like the land itself, were declared to be the property of the Crown. Fascinated by the iron proliferating on Cook's ships, the Indigenous people traded sex for nails. Captain James Cook's voyage reminds me of Captain James Kirk, of the starship *Enterprise*, who likewise had his way with foreign females.

The women served as widgets or bargaining chips to be traded for scraps of this and that. Herman Melville, secretly smitten by maidens in the Marquesas Islands to the south, absconded from his ship and novelized his exploits in his first book. He arrived three generations after Captain Cook did. If Hawai'ians in Cook's time understood how vectors work, how European contact could make them sick, there is a chance their reverence for Cook was all a sham.

The science of island biogeography shows that secluded populations of humans or other animals lie naked to ecological change. Seclusion is both a decisive factor and the crux. Isolated species do not enjoy the protections afforded by crossbreeding and disparate genes. The rats that stole away in cargo from Europe ravaged Hawai'ian crops. To control the rats, mongooses from Asia were introduced, a goofy move that decimated ground-nesting fowl. No worries, though, hunters simply imported other birds. Grouse and partridges from Africa and India, chukars and pheasants from China, quail and turkeys from the US arrived to feather the islands anew.

Sporting types have always projected their frontier fantasies onto landscapes, as if on screens. They remake wild areas in their fondest philosophical ideals. During our sojourn on the island of Hawai'i, a mongoose prowls past us every day, even on the most populous of city streets. The cuddly Rikki-Tikki-Tavi of Rudyard Kipling lore has fangs—and the restless hunger its cousins the ferrets and weasels share. The mongoose is a legacy of empire, its predatory behavior a fit emblem for those who would take the whole world to tinker with as they see fit.

Unlike animals, though, volcanoes lie beyond human bylaw and control. They remind us that our dominion over nature has its limits and always will. Mauna Koa bleeds fresh lava when we visit. We hike to the continent's edge, pilgrims paying tribute to a peak. Lava blackens all the land, scorching and toppling road signs, sending up waves of heat, protruding into the sea.

Creation bubbles and smokes. We tramp a region never explored before, a territory newly made. The island is advancing. Those miles of glowing, bulging, and cracking lava constitute the true New World of legendry and lore, five centuries after Columbus, two centuries after Cook.

Red magma cools to lava before our eyes. The island is growing, glowing, throwing us back in time. Living magma pools beneath our feet. Its heart's blood hardens, becoming terra firma for seeds and birds, soil for sprouts and shoots. The Roman god Vulcan, dead to us except within the remnant cognate *volcano*, animates the enigmatic fires that puddle in hot peaks.

In public lands and waters, cultural friction is igniting debates with greater heat each year. All of us privileged travelers yearn for a piece of paradise, and we will pay more dearly for it as it shrinks. The needy may not scorch themselves on lava, though, because it takes cold cash to burn in paradise. Tourism is a pleasure friendly only to the most well-heeled inhabitants of the planet, to travelers who can well afford to melt their shoes and buy new pairs without a thought.

Awareness of shrinking planetary resources has led to a greening of the tourist industry, to a sweet patina of esteem for all things wild. Many tours are ecotours now. The $360 million Hilton Waikoloa Village commanded $150 a head, in 2021 when we visited last, from those who would loll with captive dolphins in a human-made lagoon. Such pleasant pastime is cleansed with a wink. Promo materials say the captive mammals "all wear smiles."

Gaze long, pilgrim, before every bit of it winks out for your descendants. The premises of paradise are fading fast. Places to get away from it all are finite. Alfred North Whitehead defined such calamities of our commons as "the solemnity of the remorseless working of things."

Upon friends and lovers, we lavish nicknames, terms of affection, epithets meant in some cases also to demean. The Hilton Waikoloa Village brands its beaches with its corporate logo. It scratches its hotel name on the sand. That brand, like as not, is breathtaking for those who view it from the seventh floor. The hotel might also have tried to copyright the quaint name *village*.

Explorers like James Cook named lands for patrons or pilots who never set a foot upon them. Names make claims. Because one owns a place—or can allege to have discovered, seized, or settled it—one may defend his right to appoint its significance for centuries to come.

* * *

At our condominium activity desk, we agree to listen to a pitch for a timeshare condo in exchange for a cruise to Kealakekua Bay. Our salesman, Barre, his name enunciated like Barry, pushes us hard. A tanned and retired military man, he was stationed at Fort Lewis near my former Seattle home. He flashes our geographical connection like some currency to be spent.

"I sell psychology," he tells us. The product he markets is not a week's vacation but a "lifestyle experience." His facility is exclusive. No "pimple-faced kids" will be found staffing the desks, he says. No "longhair with a bone in his nose" will be seen "dealing weed behind the convenience store." We agree to consider investing in his enterprise, and then we flee.

The product sold to the world here is the island itself. The ways it markets that product are manifold, tourism being the most extensive and poorly regulated industry on the planet.

At the Kailua-Kona Harbor we gather with two dozen others on the sixty-foot *Fair Wind*, a catamaran with a crew of eight. That fast ship will transport us to Kealakekua Bay. Advertised as an homage to Cook, near whose monument we anchor, the trip turns out to be a feeding and snorkeling frenzy. We prove to be moving parts of that craze. We line up right behind the others.

When we arrive in the bay where the explorer died, igneous cliffs plunge to underwater canyons. Invisible lava tubes corrugate the cliffs. In those tubes islanders buried their chiefs, we learn from a shipboard brochure. The *Fair Wind* drops anchor. Snorkels and masks hand around.

The monument itself to Captain Cook, a twenty-seven-foot obelisk of marble, looks like a missile blasting off. Its shape and size seem so right. Its color is white, its configuration the same sort shared by hardware for military aggression and for space exploration alike. Forbidden from going ashore, we have a view of the vaulting monument from seventy-five yards out.

One shipside brochure tells its story and reprints a photo of the bronze plaque dedicating the stone: "In memory of the great circumnavigator, Captain James Cook, R.N., who discovered these islands." *Discovered?* I read that assertion and I flinch. Such language generates rifts today between the colonizers and the colonized, between those who immigrate to the Hawai'ian Islands or tour them, and those whose ancestors have inhabited them for ages.

I toss aside the brochure, take up snorkel and mask, and plunge. Forests of pastel coral fall to sandy canyons undersea. Breathless and exhilarated, I spot legendary moray eels. One, white and black-spotted, flexes its formidable jaws from a grotto, until a swimmer jabs at it with his fin. Another eel, a four-foot yellowmargin moray—thick, brawny, gold-flecked brown—snakes along the bottom, still-hunting under cover before slipping across an expanse of sand to nose into the next floret of coral. Indigenous people call this species puhi-paka and eat it. In the cliffs above us, like cannonballs in barrels, the royals lie mummified within lava crypts.

Back on the boat after swimming, we lunchtime passengers brazen our way to the foods, many of us wearing undersize swimwear. One in front of me, with a little boy, packs her plate and explains how hard it is to have to load up for two. Several of the passengers, already seasick despite the stopgap capsules the crew hands out, cling to the railings or collapse on the stairs.

Arousing us from our after-lunch slump, a deck mate cries, gestures, and points.

A woman has clambered up by the monument to Captain Cook! Dressed in shorts and T-shirt, she stands against the obelisk, hands clasped behind her, as if manacled. We've been asked to stay in the water to save the reefs, ordered to avoid the sacred monument to Captain Cook. The deck mate, never noticing that the woman is dry, assumes she swam from the boat. But she's in fact an islander, a twenty-something local, solid, squat, her hair falling to her waist, her thighs and belly strong. She has hiked alone down from the road above the memorial site.

An Indigenous woman, she has watched the ship disgorge us tourists, as she has no doubt seen it do before. She has stood in silence at the base of the white stone. But now the mate is hollering at her, playing the heavy, ordering her off the monument and back to the ship where she should be. Her hands fly up like wings, manacles shed, as if to levitate her from the shore.

We have come to this sacred spot, a neon brigade in suits and swim masks, to be fed and swim and have a fine time. The *Fair Wind* has anchored at the spot the brochure names the Pathway to the Gods. But the rule-ridden shipboard lecture tells us nothing about the gods, loaded like cartridges in the cliffs above us, dormant or alive. Our barbecues are smoking, our fifteen-foot waterslide and high-dive platform splashing. Four stout poles, on the swift trip out, have trolled for billfish and tuna off the stern. What a sight we must be to residents like her.

Belatedly the mate realizes the woman is Indigenous. Explosive anger lights her face. She is wading into the surf now, stroking for our boat, pointing toward us every few yards. Off the starboard railing she stops and treads the water, unloading her words like so much weaponry. "You have no right to be here! You are ruining this spot! Why don't you go away and stay?"

We have committed kapu, defiled the living lands, the people, and the seas. She might still be smarting from the overthrow of the Hawaiian monarchy by US-backed forces in 1893. Five years later, the United States annexed Hawai'i. The kingdom of Hawai'i became a US territory, absent any input from the people and amid much opposition. Attempts to restore the kingdom have always failed. Too much mainland money is tied up here. In July 2021, the late Microsoft cofounder Paul Allen's sprawling, twenty-two-acre Hawai'ian property sold for $43 million.

This comely, muscular young woman begins to blur for me. She becomes one with the encrypted royals and the people whom Cook colonized. "Our unfortunate commander," one of Cook's crew wrote, "the last time he was seen distinctly, was standing at the water's edge, calling out to the boats to cease firing, and to pull in." Our Indigenous hostess, the last time we see her, is rising by the white marble monument, trembling with fury, black hair slinging spray.

The "spectacular marine environment" that our brochure touts, "like swimming in an aquarium," is squandered upon us. We have swarmed the coral in this "tranquil, secluded cove." We have listened to the captain's eloquence about "protecting and respecting" the environment. We have imagined we are heightening awareness, raising a collective ecological consciousness. We have yet to understand the profound relationships between local people and ecology.

Environmental education requires certain sacrifice zones, some pundits claim, places where ecological integrity must be relinquished for the sake of edification. The planet will begin to heal, they say, if people can absorb enough information and enjoy apt opportunities to bond. The same philosophy might hold sway within the tourist industry—that some locals need to be sacrificed for the betterment of cultural sensitivity and to build relationships on a larger scale.

If we infuriate the locals, when we practice slapdash environmental edification on their turf, we will have failed. Maybe Hawai'ian commerce instead ought to be propitiating the gods and risk affronting the tourists, like a certain healer at Lapakahi State Historical Park did for me.

* * *

Lapakahi lies on the Kohala coast, north of Kona and Kealakekua Bay. A partially restored precontact fishing village, its bits of old dwellings lie visible on the oceanside. We are fortunate to find it open, blessed to visit in the absence of commercial trappings so often found elsewhere.

Bart spurs up to the door carrying his hi-vis lime mesh sport bag. "No towels allowed," the woman keeper tells him. We stiffen before her office-cum-museum and clinic. Bart trots his gear back to the car, too sobered to ask why. Visiting hotel guests have littered, we can surmise.

"This is a holy place," she begins. "You enter the water here," pointing to a spot on a mural-sized aerial photograph. "Don't swim to the right or left. Go straight out only." We meet her steely gaze. We turn around and follow her kinked finger pointing to an alley out from shore.

That alley, steep and boulder-strewn, looks daunting. "To the left are sacred spaces where our ancestors lived and bathed. To the right, we've had too many people hurt when they got tossed up on the rocks." The cove looks like a graveyard, and she speaks like its guardian shade.

Her ancestors inhabited this place for more than six hundred years, she informs us. Foundations of their buildings crumble. Rows of low rocks, grass-roofed huts reconstructed in some spots. The site has now become a rustic park of some three hundred acres. She references the walls, plants, wind, and surf as the "lives accompanying you." She never gives her name.

Stern curator, she is riding herd upon us like any paniolo, enforcing rules, contending for reverence. "Don't make me follow you down there to keep you on the trails," she warns. Her job entails the tricky task of breaking tourists of being boors. We are her only guests in the entire park just now. Several hundred yards offshore, the humpback whales are spouting and sounding.

Before she will let me swim, she grabs my hand and focuses on it. She noticed a wound she wants to treat, to show me how her healing may take place. Above my cradled and upturned palm, her downturned hand caresses the air. I had sliced myself on a piece of coral when a wave flung me in shallow surf. "It's best to do it when the wound is new," she explains.

Now she has my full attention. Squat, gray, creased, and kind, she wears a ribbed tank-top above, a pair of baggy surfer shorts below, bone-print on the fabric. This docent is a welcome contrast to the starched and badged keepers we see in the forty-eight mainland states. Releasing me, she follows us partway down the sea-path, still lecturing, still contending for our reverence.

The ocean is roaring. The waves break in families—two big crashers followed by several seconds of hissing foam. Getting past the rocks is going to be hard. Coming back will be harder, the unseen surf driving us from behind. We stand with masks in hand and deliberate a while.

We want to swim here. We have come to swim. The coral clusters and the yellow tang fish hurled by currents look so good. But I have water qualms following Braden's drowning.

It is one thing to die of natural causes, "to cease upon the midnight with no pain," but it is quite another to tell fate to screw off and plunge in anyway. Signs all around the island beaches read, "When in doubt, don't go out." Still, I am the first to go out, floundering my way.

Karen follows, in part to guard me. Bart and Lindell follow moments later. I do not stray to the right or the left. I do not want to irritate the keeper. My mask is leaking. One temple throbs and pinches from swimmer's ear, the canal enflamed. The cut on my palm is smarting in the salt.

We see little, as it turns out. No matter, though. We are whole, we are free, and we are emparadised. We four shake dry like dogs, bake in the sun, pick bits of coral on the beach.

By certain scholarly interpretations, James Cook sacrificed himself for empire. "When the Hawai'ians took away Cook's body and stripped the flesh from the bones, he was nearer deification than he had been in life," one scholar wrote. All of us like to valorize our forebears, translate them into heroes not scoundrels, charitable not greedy. Traditional historians, some of them creaky apologists for manifest destiny, have taken up Cook's legend and spun it into gold.

Whether he was being deified or snubbed after his death is a matter of interpretation. The part of him most worthy of preserving was one buttock, though, a diary from a sailor shows. "The Taboo Man had a bundle under his arm & he caryed it down into the Cabbin where he opened it and presented to us a Spectacle that struck us with Horror; this . . . large piece of human flesh, the whole of the upper part of a Thigh with the bone taken out, smelled strong. He told us repeatedly it was the Thigh of Capt. Cook & that he was carrying it over as a present." The locals mooned the Englishmen after hostilities broke out, flashing their asses to taunt them.

Back on the mainland now, I inspect my left hand and find the spot where I was injured, where a shard of coral cut me and seeped my blood into the sea. I choose to call it a sacrifice today, a bit of bodily substance I left behind. A tribute to the gods, that they might find peace.

After our kids were old enough to travel, Karen and I packed and took them with us on a series of trips to Mexico and Central America. Water always strongly draws my spouse. She has training as a lifeguard and experience as a swim-racer. Both boys, early on, also learned to swim.

14

A Mayan Apocalypse

Like a frigate bird afloat on thermals, Karen is frolicking in the Belize surf and calling out to me to join her. The salt that seeps from our sweat glands, the salt that crusts upon us after swimming in the ocean, never devils her. She hauls us abroad on travel junkets often, and I do my best to set aside the watery qualms that roll my way like so many waves.

From the sand I rise and join her in the surf. We dive, blow spray, and clasp one another. Like a promise the Caribbean lubricates our skin. Some starlit evening on our holiday here, we plan to wade in deeper. We will agitate the salty liquid at waist-height and make the day-blind phosphorescence glow.

We clamber back to shore, pat dry, and dab on zinc sunscreen that protects the reefs. An iguana like a statue has crept atop a cast-off wheel and tire nearby. Melancholy ochre rust stains streak the wheel where salt has had its way. The tire's heat-trapping and radiant black warms the lizard's sluggish blood. It never flinches while our boys above it toss a ball in a game of catch.

On that overgrown beach, in that humid clime, many lizards camouflage in foliage. Unlike the succulent vegetation, iguanas can withstand some crushing. Snub-nosed and scale-plated, the lizards are rugged survivors, much like the Indigenous people of this region. They can wedge tight in Earth-cracks and baffle every effort to extract them.

That adaptive gift came plain yesterday when a pair of boys and their dog chased one into a rockpile. The boys dislodged the basalt. The dog beside them yapped and dug. The iguana crept ever deeper within the rocky recess. It sucked in air and blimped itself.

I approached the boys and asked them, "Why do you chase him?"

"We like to eat wish-willy!" one sang out.

Their smirks told me they were messing with me, goading the gullible gringo. *Wish-willy* is an endearment for a subspecies of this hardheaded lizard. Still, people in Belize do eat iguanas. They dub them *gallino de palo,* which translates bamboo chicken, or chicken of the trees.

Good thing Karen did not witness that pursuit. If she sees an animal injured, neglected, or distressed, a sharp pain stabs her in her solar plexus. She proves powerless to forget or turn away. Every living thing is precious equally.

A larger iguana, spiky like a dragon, appeared two days ago. We tiptoed near, hoping not to scare it. From behind a pine, a tall man rose. He had the creature tethered as if managing a dog. What were the two of them doing on that white-sand beach? The handler with his banded straw hat and aviator glasses, the lizard lashed to a harness so it could not wriggle free?

Just then a pair of white legs in Bermuda shorts approached and bent to snap the iguana's image. The handler moved between the two, his hand outstretched, his prickly living prisoner a source of income. The pair of shorts reached inside a vertical pocket and paid up.

Karen is lying face-down on a towel now. The jungle throbs with birds. More iguanas than ever have swum into our vision during this sojourn in Belize. Sloe-eyed, spine-ridged, they are suckers for sun, hogs for heat. On an overlook above the Macal River, a pair were seen sunbathing on the spindle limbs of deciduous trees a hundred feet above the jungle floor.

It was the year 2012, and we were on vacation in advance of the Mayan Apocalypse. The implications of that day of reckoning fascinated me. Some people believed the planet Earth was apt to undergo a welcome spiritual renewal, while others predicted the world's end by arcane catastrophe. The date signified everything under the sun, from the end of one era to the start of another, from cataclysm to rapture, from destruction to salvation.

Later to be dubbed the 2012 Phenomenon, it was the culmination of the Mesoamerican Long Count Calendar's 5,126 years.

Historians and ethnographers who read Maya writings had swiveled public heads toward some Armageddon, some enigmatic marvel. Whether or not upheavals were to take place in a few days later—as pundits claimed they might on December 21, 2012—I set myself the goal of sussing out significance during our stay. I would discover explanations that underlay the hype.

* * *

Barton Creek Cave opens to a lengthy river within. A "single-passage re-surging stream cave," our guidebook tells us, the site is one that prehistoric people used for religious purposes. Early explorers found the passageway extending eight kilometers underground, only the first few safely accessible. The nation's Archeological Service regulates the cave today.

Stone shelves served the first inhabitants as altars. Above the fluctuating waterline, the people gathered seepage fallen from cenotes on those shelves. That water, we hear, was used to embalm sacrificial victims. Those victims were mostly females, their relict pelvic bones showed.

We huddle in our canoes and whisper. Water drips. Calcite, limestone, magnesite, and flint flowstone contour the cave mouth. Stalagmites and stalactites, some of them still growing, some long dormant, rise and fall like grinding teeth. Bats roosting in the shadows impart a steady ambiance. Guano streaks the walls. On the surface far above us, puddles form from eroded limestone and water migrating underground to the cave stream, puddles known as cenotes.

From the cave mouth a cold breeze blows. It is as if the ancients are admonishing us, warning us away. We decide we do not need to paddle far within. We opt for a shorter tour, an underground excursion the brochures publicize as instructive and fun. Our guide, Noel, implies that the Maya continue as a potent presence, their energies contracted in that watery spot.

Noel's mestizo mix is Indigenous and French. Previously a cab driver, he speaks skillful English. He profiles the ancients as barbaric, ritualized, protohuman. The beam of his laser pointer, a proxy for his voice, guides our gaze. Old ceramics glow in his red probing light.

North Americans in this region overtop the mestizos. The mestizos patronize the African creoles. The creoles intermarry with the Maya. The Maya people dig postholes, erect cabins, lay tiles, and pluck pubic hairs from toilets. An apocalypse by any other name is coming into view. A judgment day of cultural change is tilting primordial habits off their axis.

Anthropologists and archaeologists refute one another on key points. *Allegedly, reportedly,* and *supposedly* pepper the journal I keep. What is certain is that the cave's discovery brought on wholesale looting. Twenty-eight sets of human bones lured collectors and pothunters.

The rain god Chac demanded sacrifices. Human blood appeased him. The dripping of blood, I conclude, both mimicked and inspired the rain the people needed to survive. The Maya people enjoyed a good run, but the apex of their civilization was destined to decline. Homage to a pantheon of brutal gods brought about the murder of their slaves and women. The fittest and most nubile among them were singled out to die. It was a form of unnatural selection. Too few baby-bearers remained to thrive and plenish their ranks.

Other causes of their decimation are subject to competing theories. A scarcity of food and water diminished their populations. Mercury and blue-green algae, experts now believe, toxified the aquifer and drove them from the city of Tikal, deepening the sundry other miseries they suffered. A rise in volatile Caribbean cyclones weakened their adaptability more.

Humans were created in caves from corn dough, the holy text the Popul Vuh says. There, hypersexual underground gods exhaled a gendered sentience. Religious leaders heaped personal and social anxieties about ecological crises on the heads of those subterranean superbeings. In material terms, the gods helped the people to decide when to plant crops and how to instigate rain. In ideal terms, religious explanations verified the universe remained in order.

We duck, scrape, and pivot our canoes beneath stalactites in the cave. The ancients, to navigate their passage in high water, sawed or snapped off those mineral daggers, we are told.

Pottery shards date from 200 to 900 CE. Part of me wonders whether ceramics on shelves were placed there rather than found. Relocated to augment wonders for innocents abroad like us. Travel is partially an art of second-guessing sources, sifting through the throngs of artful dodgers.

* * *

Tourist travelers have become the shiny coin of the realm in Belize. Businesspersons erect fresh ventures where the Maya people used to worship. Entrepreneurs troll for sightseers in places the ancients chose to gather. Such concurrences add apocalyptic tension to our ventures.

Canadian expatriates Mike and his son Brian rent us our canoes. Alongside their gothic cave show, they run a zipline. A little kiosk sells pseudo-Maya curios and barbecue. We sucker up and buy a blowgun the boys want. Primitive drawings circle its wooden barrel; its darts are colored at the ends, as if dipped in poison. In a blue tattoo beside one tricep, Brian has name-checked the rock group Iron Maiden. A corrugated metal cuff is clamped upon his ear.

The smack of the ersatz extends to stories we hear told. Limestone notches betray paths where priests conducted sacrificial virgins. Hot water poured down a drain can force out troublesome spirits in a home. Iguanas change up colors with the angle of the sun.

On a night tour we take, our naturalist guide Mario conducts us along sweltering jungle paths to try to find night-thriving kinkajous. In the distance, grinding booms like factories ring.

"What's that, Mario?" Karen gestures toward the booms.

"Those are cane toads. Their *familia* traveled to our country and they stayed."

The next morning, I make my way back to the wetland to see the toads. They are huge, too elusive to capture and to hold. My research tells me they are native to the nation. Mario might have transferred his beliefs about first-world colonists to the local toads.

Cane toads, *Rhinella marina,* resident to South and Central America, are expanding their habitats, coming to govern every riparian niche. Those most massive of all toads on the planet have the appetites and abilities to swallow others of many genera. They dart tongues to capture prey. They ratchet wide mouths wider. They deploy forelegs to cram in writhing insects, birds, mammals, and other amphibians. Their croaks like hand-rasps punctuate the night.

Like their kin the Colorado River toad, *Incilius alvarius,* cane toads harbor cocktails of neurotoxins beneath their warty skin. Those cocktails hold DMT, a psychoactive stuff that has been fabricated for recreation and therapy. Locals and some visiting trippers dry and smoke it.

Unlike LSD or psilocybin, though, DMT comes on fast. Its toxic high earned a reputation as the businessman's trip—up and down, in and out, rapid to destinations and back home. Ingested by recreationists accompanied by guides, the toad venom needs to be crystallized before it can be consumed. Others confess to have slurped soups of cane toad carcasses to soak open religious insights. At the most primitive level, live toads may be seized and tongued.

If it sounds too fantastic to be true, that is the Caribbean for you. The blue-beyond-belief seascapes shed tensions. Ruins left behind by the Maya people prove too trippy to refuse. Foreigners voyage inwardly and out. Cane toads have what it takes to gratify certain outsized postcolonial appetites that wing in on the jet stream every day.

Fascinations with altered states originated among the Maya long ago. Stephan and Carl Borhegyi, archaeologist father and son, make the case that "hallucinogenic mushroom rituals were a central aspect of Maya religion." Accidental ingestion of *Amanita muscaria,* they believe, inspired a cult. Their evidence includes some two hundred carved human figurines the Maya crafted with caps that look for all the world like toadstools. Iconoclastic Catholic missionaries, aiming to subdue the pagan faith, smashed many of those so-named mushroom stones. Journalist Michael Pollan agrees that psilocybin "was brutally suppressed by the Roman Catholic Church after the Spanish Conquest and driven underground." Pagan religions, sprouting from the land, were forbidden by the missionaries who colonized the people.

In Mexico, Costa Rica, the Cayman Islands, and Belize, we have given over weeks to our vacations. To our vacays, as popular parlance clips it. Like Philip Larkin's speaker in his poem "Church-Going," we tourists blink aside some tropical sensations and consider others a delight. Larkin named our species "ruin-bibbers." People thirsty to imbibe the vestiges of an antique past.

* * *

In a water taxi, a tiny Maya woman sits. On the edge of her bench, proud head held high, one hand clinging to the steel rail, she scans the watery horizon for her endpoint. Her hair is done up in a bun. Her short-sleeved blouse has fringes at the collar and the cuffs. Silver filigrees hem her light-blue bodice. Across one shoulder she has slung a bag of purple Guatemalan cloth. A melon-hued floral skirt dangles to midcalf. Well-worn flip-flops sheathe her feet.

Her young grandson, from all appearances, nestles underneath her arm. On her opposite side, the boy's mother sits, clothed the same way as her mother, who has chosen their seats well, considering what might happen if this craft should crash or swamp. The rail where her hand rests is the only exit for the craft. This water taxi would be illegal by North American standards.

Taxi-boats are a standard kind of travel on this coastline of Belize. Locals rub shoulders with us Norteamericanos. Clad in strappy sandals, we are incalculably wealthy by their norms.

The woman seated near me never looks my way. I regard the watery horizon. December 16, five days from the alleged apocalypse, we find ourselves moving to the north of Ambergris Cay, enunciated *key*, a barrier island to the west of Belize that borders on Mexico. In-country we will spend more than twenty hours on boats. Once we dock, the woman and her family go one way. My family and I head the other direction to our short-let bungalows.

My beloved partner always structures our vacation days by excursions. Its Latin etymology means *run out*. From beach cabins and huts, we run out to take in ruins, jungles, and marine reserves. An older use of the same word entails military expeditions, martial sallies, hostile armed campaigns. In front of our bungalow, Earth's second-largest barrier reef extends.

Snorkeling off Ambergris—Karen in the lead, the sun fierce—we ogle lionfish, yellow tangs, parrotfish, a lobster. After dusk descends, pier lights lure tarpons and stingrays: shadows ghosting in the water, their red eyes agleam. Dogs from nearby cabins skulk for scraps, ribs on show, heads hung low. A waiter trying to shoo one cur away gets his calf nipped and bloodied.

Outside this resort town, guards wielding AK-47s patrol the jungle byways to keep bandits at bay and grease the rails of the tourist trade. Many Indigenous people set aside their pride to bend and reach for foreign dollars. As in Hawai'i, tourist pressures in Belize have some of the locals hypnotized. Foreign burdens have put them in a daze. How can they maintain a modicum of dignity, I wonder, while benefiting at the same time from the influx of US dollars?

The legendary Mayan Apocalypse, the end of a 5.5-millennia cycle, might never have been foretelling the future of our planet. Only Indigenous destinies might have been foreseen. We first-world travelers develop compassion. We grow, I hope, through exposure to other lives.

We sign up for an excursion led by marine naturalist Abel, his name enunciated *Ah-bell*. Handsome, fit, erudite in ecology, this Maya man guides us across the water. His mustache gives him a serious air, but he is capable of play. He feigns an attack on Chase's hand with a captured crab. To get at all the biological marvels, Chase shoves to be the first in line. Two years from now, after his head injury, he will recall this sojourn, a memory that might help him heal.

Abel Coe used to bust his knuckles as a mechanic and pilot a water taxi. Hired as a leader of ecotours now, he seems to have found his calling, his life an instance of the tourist industry's improving an Indigenous person's quality of life. Such benefits as he enjoys are not sustainable, though, as shown by the crushing downturn many Indigenous people suffered in the pandemic.

Abel beaches the boat at the foremost Belizean breeding slough for American crocodiles, *Crocodylus acutus*. They multiply in a brackish inner pond screened by trees. Drag marks from their tails come into view once we step to the shore. Every televisual trope about being marooned on desert islands comes into focus for us on our secluded strand. We imagine we have been abandoned.

Red mangrove trees, taking root upon and buffering the beach ridges, stabilize this islet. Pneumatophores, or aerating roots, rise above the surface to help the trees to breathe. Leaves, turds, carcasses, flotsam, and shells upraise and fertilize the littoral forest. Sand washing in from sea storms shores up this ephemeral islet year by year. Mats of mangroves, becoming little islands in themselves, often become waterborne and wander. They take root where they can.

In mangrove branches above our slough, boat-billed herons nest. Crocodiles scarf fallen nestlings and fledglings. Herons feed on fresh-hatched crocodiles in turn. It's all ecology in motion, as exemplified by the Egyptian ouroboros, the mythical snake seen tumbling hooplike and clasping its tail in its jaws. That snake's spherical enclosure, changing always while it keeps its shape, makes it a fitting emblem for enduring heavy weather and civilization's sieges.

Adult herons squawk and flap off nests at our approach. Ten feet up a tree, a nestling turns a wary eye upon us from its slumping spot, facedown on twigs, the slender neck not yet strong enough to support that boat of a bill. Crocodiles, underwater charismata four to eight feet long, slink from shore. An old croc nest beneath our feet reveals crinkly epidermal shell debris.

We hike in single file following Abel. Red knots in a flock, migratory shorebirds related to sandpipers, fidget near us in the shallows. Scuttling crabs tantalize our boys to chase them. A banded wolf spider three inches from my knee materializes just in time for me to dodge it. Abel thrashes the overhanging branches to put off snakes that conceal to look like limbs. Mosquitoes and biting deer flies go for our "fresh blood," Abel teases, his blood having glutted them.

Our second stop with Abel finds us snorkeling in a Technicolor reef. We follow him down deep to concave slots and coral cut-banks. Modeling good ecological practice, he places a single finger on underwater rocks and coral ledges to hold himself stock-steady there. That single finger safeguards microbiotic crusts. We peer into the shadows alongside him. Our pupils dilate.

Abel spots underwater animals. He points out an eel, a nurse shark, a spiny lobster. He probes dark crevices to trigger hidden creatures to reveal. Finning up behind a yellow ray that lies buried in the sand, he gives its tail an impish tug. The animal flees twenty feet before calling a halt at a separate silty spot. It scoots fore and aft, like a brood hen settling on a nest, to conceal itself and still-hunt once again.

We fin in Abel's wake for a mile. Eagle rays, electric rays, rough-tailed rays, yellow rays, and manta rays pass overhead. Those cartilaginous fish flapping by like lazy lapwings on their tranquil way nowhere cause us reflexively to duck. Abel thrills the boys by placing a constellation of starfish in their hands. Squiggly bristle stars, puffy cushion stars, spooky serpent stars. After each encounter, each abduction undertaken to enlarge their zoological delight, he places the creepy-crawly back in its exact same spot.

Our final dive takes us snorkeling amid coral gardens mostly smothered by silt from some hurricane—Alex, Arthur, Karl, one of the many that have ravaged through. The seafloor looks like the 1980 volcanic eruption's aftermath from Mount St. Helens that clouded massive portions of our bioregion back home. Seafloors and deserts correspond to one another. Belizean underwater geography differs little from topographies that typify the North American Southwest.

Not just the sandbars, the silt deposits, the blast zones, canyons, rocks, and ravines, it is also the coral growing and grown, live and dead, like cacti. Unseen currents, rather than hot winds, rustle the waving plants and weeds, the underwater shrubs and trees. The barrel cactus finds its terrestrial counterpart in the barrel coral. Terrestrial palm fronds resemble marine fan coral. Underwater weeds correspond to towering saguaros.

* * *

Always an edgy traveler, I work to regulate my breath when I scuba-dive or snorkel. Deep breaths center me and keep at bay the intrusive sea. To be thriving and alive in the same hostile medium that forever spirited Braden away differs little from a miracle. It is as if I have sprouted wings and entered some celestial elsewhere. "I am a little world made cunningly / Of elements and an angelic sprite," poet John Donne wrote in 1633. After a day on the sea, my horizons warp and weave, the consequence of inner-ear turmoil from wind and waves.

In "After Apple Picking," Robert Frost lyricized the state of nocturnal stupefaction after a day spent ladder-harvesting tree fruit. "Magnified apples appear and disappear, / Stem end and blossom end, / And every fleck of russet showing clear." Repetitive motion sickness makes him so dizzy he finds it hard to sleep. That same state occurs whenever bodies surrender to waves.

Thoreau, undertaking a nose count of fish in Walden Pond, grew woozy too. Staring long into the watery abyss, he could narrowly distinguish the sky from the reflective medium beneath it. "Sky water," he named it. "It is a mirror which no stone can crack, whose quicksilver will never wear off, whose gilding Nature constantly repairs." Had Thoreau had a diving bell, what trips he'd have taken, insights he'd have relished, transformative experiences he'd have gained.

On the Sea of Cortez in 2018, Karen and I met a Mexican man who fed his family and earned pocket change by plunging to quarry chocolate clams. Clad in a raggedy wetsuit, he came up clams in hand, teeth chattering. He had yet to adapt to Mexico's changing economy.

Better adaptations are to be seen in other nations. Sustainable harvest initiatives in Honduras, balanced forest management in Brazil. The scarlet macaw hunters whom the Costa Rica government pays today to preserve the birds they used to shoot and serve as food. We saw those birds screeching with no fear in low trees. Indigenous people around the planet are proving gifted in their shifts from subsistence ways of taking to protecting and sustaining.

After our snorkeling excursion, we limp back to our bungalow. We throw together a supper of rice and beans and shrimp ceviche. The boys fade fast. We almost follow them to bed, but a second wind freshens Karen and me. We lock the door behind us and slide into the sea. Bioluminescent plankton swirl and mirror the stars gawking at us from above.

The staring stars remind me how some locals must regard us. "An ugly thing, that is what you are when you become a tourist," Jamaica Kincaid wrote in *A Small Place*, "an ugly, empty thing, a piece of rubbish pausing here and there to gaze at this and taste that." She dubbed her book about Antigua "a prolonged visit to the bile duct." Her literary seepage gained my esteem, setting off a wet dull tingling inside me. She made me wonder if we were tourist trash already.

Phosphorescent critters in the water below us winked like stars above. The smell of brine took me to a dreamy place and time. As a youth in the Salish Sea of Washington, I dove from anchored docks into the cold salt water with my friends. The bioluminescence agitated by our diving shone. Paths shorn by our bodies traveling through the water looked like shooting stars. On the Belize beach, Karen and I discover teeming luminescent jellyfish that rub against and shock us dully. Our soft splashes increase the brilliance of their glowing.

Drifting to sleep that evening, my mind's eye rocked as if I were on a hammock. The bed became a raft. Waves reared and disappeared. The Mayan Apocalypse, like the Y2K bug, came and went, but its energies tinged my memory forever. Noel, Mario, Abel, and others adapt to an economy in Belize that is undergoing rapid change. May they flourish and their kind increase.

The best way to obstruct apocalypse might be to prioritize the beating of one's own heart. My heart throbbed time to the shore slosh and to wishes for the people whom we met. Having begun as a skeptic, I felt like an interloper. Today the nation conjures up a durable reverie in me.

* * *

Unlike the tropical shorelines of Belize, the coastal portions of my native Northwest are temperate rainforests. Rains and snowmelt from inland mountains feed the Columbia River and its tributaries, where commercial travel and hydroelectric power generate intercultural scrapes.

The following emotional geography meanders through history. It loops in and out of agencies, industries, utilities, and the corridors of state capitals. My story spells out why so many of us share concerns about the planet's rivers, the species they harbor, and the quality of water. Those concerns press hardest on Indigenous people, whose livelihoods tie so tightly to streams.

15

Loved Badly on Your Bank

Man's like the earth, his hair like grasse is grown,
His veins the rivers are, his heart the stone.
—ANON.

Unfolding his six-foot-five frame from the car, my father drew a bandana from his pants pocket and blew his nose. Then out he lounged toward the nearby basalt cliffs. Casting his eyes up and down the steepling columns, he was looking for something hidden in the shade.

"Nita!" he called. "Come here!" My mother, flexing her lower back by the open car door, settled both hands on her hips. Her body language let us know she did not want to make the walk. Sisters Diane and Jill, pivoting from the Columbia River that flowed below us, shaded eyes with their hands and gazed toward our dad. Behind a bush, I finished my business and zipped.

By the time we caught up with him, Dad was wielding his bandana like a flashlight. He pointed it to rock drawings that gathered shape in the shade. "Indians drew those pictures," his voice echoed off the rock. One drawing resembled a face. Shafts like sunbeams spread from the head. Spokes of light, tendrils of hair, power blazing from some brain. "They painted it with their fingers," he dribbled to a whisper. I turned and gazed, wondering where those Indians went.

Back in the car, I rubbed knuckles above my ears to feel the buzzcut Dad had insisted I get. "Lower his ears," he had told the barber. The seatback's stiff velour shared the texture of my haircut. The seat's fabric made an easel I could scuff to try to replicate those rock drawings.

Though I had no way of knowing it, a dam was building downstream from those cliffs. Water was scheduled to rise above the pictographs our father pointed out. The Columbia River on that stretch would never flow free again. The charms of sage grouse, coyotes, spiders, whitewater, and Indigenous petroglyphs would be flooded by the sluggish rising reservoir. The reservoir would come to be dubbed Lake Wanapum, a name appropriated from the local tribe.

The people of that tribe who hunted and fished there for millennia would lose the rapids for catching steelhead and salmon. The petroglyphs would be lost, along with spots they buried their dead. Secret places, sacred sites, handed down for generations—every bit of it swamped by my clan's drive for lower energy rates. Cold comfort it would be to the Wanapums when Grant County awarded them kickbacks and a riverside site to build a heritage center. In much the same way as the tourist economy has made captives of people in Hawai'i and Belize, so the energy economy of the Northwest, its mighty hydropower, would marginalize my region's tribespeople.

"MAN'S LIKE THE EARTH"

Imagine you are hovering above the Columbia River, a continental watershed that drains all of Idaho, most of Washington, large parts of British Columbia, Montana, and Oregon. You watch its tributaries like arteries and capillaries pulsing far below. Rivers and creeks like mammal arteries shuttle lifeblood from the heartland out to the continent's shores. Rain clouds pick that blood back up and trundle it back inland from the Pacific Ocean to the watershed's core.

Squint westward toward the setting sun and you will see the river shimmer as it drudges to the sea. Fourteen major dams along its route impede it. Dozens of dams incise the Columbia watershed's upcountry rivers and streams. Those dams look like bad bling on a cashmere jacket.

This is my bioregion, the place I have lived for most of my life. When I liken water to blood, when I compare geography to human anatomy, I am making more than a flip analogy. "Not only is blood mostly water, but the watery portion of blood, the plasma, has a concentration of salt and other ions that is remarkably similar to sea water," Natalie Angier wrote, in "The Wonders of Blood." We know full well how harmful it is to hinder circulation, to bind up veins, to inhibit the delivery of bodily fluids. The same holds true for our planetary waterways.

Think of calcified aortas working overtime to siphon. Think of physicians performing bypass surgeries by embedding stents that ease the function of congested hearts. Call all of it the world's body. Call water the planet's blood. The ratio of water on the surface of our home globe measures the same 70 percent or so as the water in us Homo sapiens. The salts in earthly water are found to be suspended in just about the same ratio as they are in our circulatory systems.

The Gaia Hypothesis, too absurd for every US legislator on record, holds that the planet of our habitation shares the processes of a single organism. That it lives, combats pathogens, has sentience or intentionality, and that our industrial excess sickens it. James Lovelock originated the Gaia Hypothesis, which characterizes Earth as a self-sustaining entity, much like you and me. Holistic interpretations of nature by earth system science vindicate it.

When I was a toddler, I saw the Green River south of Seattle overflow its banks and saturate the Kent Valley. That snake of an organ wielded forces beyond our purview and control. Much like the flooding Nile fed its delta before the advent of the Aswan Dam, the Green River replenished the dairy fields and truck farms in Kent and Tukwila. Volcanic ash from upcountry headwaters fed downstream fields. Those fields, nourished by the river, nourished us in turn.

In the Green River's upper reaches, my sisters and I slipped down slick rock chutes on inner tubes. We bobbed downstream like platelets in blood. Tannin from red cedars and fir trees bathed us. The deeper we plunged into the rivers and lakes, the more fragrant the tannin became.

Tannin is that "yellowish or brownish bitter-tasting organic substance consisting of products of gallic acid" in plant tissues. Tannins abound in red wines, teas, berries, barley, nuts, chocolate, and squash. Tannic water functioned like aromatherapy for us. It was pleasing, never bitter. Scientist Boris Tokin in the 1920s and '30s discovered that volatile tannic oils, exuded by conifer trees, benefit our species by reducing blood pressure and boosting immune function.

In those years that we were playing on the Green, we heard about a river-floater savaged by otters and taken to hospital. The otters felt a threat when the teen bobbed through. Since then, I have seen river otters in other waters behave with territorial angst. They had been the apex predators of our freshwater bodies until the end of the last Ice Age. That's when humankind began to depose them. By mistreating waters the otters evolved in, we reduce aquatic mammals to subalterns. Still today, we Homo sapiens menace them. The prospect of flashing incisors on the Green River made our summertime recreation the more delicious for the risk.

The Green River downstream becomes the Duwamish River, named after Chief Seattle's tribe. Before it slumps into Elliott Bay, the Duwamish has grown slow and sick. A sluiceway for industry, a conduit for chemicals, spanned by girders, trashed by factories. To serve the cities and the state, the Duwamish has been straightened, dammed, diked, and hammered into shape.

Its flood zone still held a wild vitality I could taste, though. Nosing there like a hound one day, I came upon a cluster of mushrooms. "Bland-mannered," in Sylvia Plath's fine phrase, they took "hold on the loam" and "acquired the air." Detaching caps and taking spore prints at home, I identified them as *Psilocybe semilanceata*, the magic mushrooms people know as liberty caps.

The pamphlets and the manuals I consulted, the reports of experts and the anecdotes of friends, none of them advised how many to ingest for recreation or health. Most people eat them dried not fresh, making yet another variable. Still, I took a chance and "shook the snow globe," in the figure of speech used by psychedelic researchers today. I choked down twelve fresh ones.

Those fungi fostered original ruminations. They clarified my views of the man-made world—the manufacturing plants, the airports, and the helipads that surrounded me. The Boeing Company, the foremost manufacturer of military rockets and commercial planes today, compounded my ruminations. So did the strobing radio transmission towers, runways, and flight paths. Jets virtually zoomed through my dining room and kitchen.

My mirror revealed a dude in the underground comix, a guy from a Robert Crumb strip. My eyes bugged out, my spectacles askew, my hair like a Halloween cat's tail. Years later I would discover the ideal lines by poet Mary Oliver: "Tell me, what is it you plan to do / with your one wild and precious life?" At that point I still had no idea, no solid plans. All I knew was that the Duwamish River had deposited some fantastic fungi like a plea to keep the wildness alive, even while the world was falling beneath the yoke of industries and humankind.

Some friends and I in high school had to get away—to escape the trappings of the travel trade, the military hardware, and the Duwamish River throttled into strict submission. Ours was a mixed-sex cohort whose parents would have cried foul had they known. Sue almost blew our plan. Peeping out from my antique panel van, she shouted, "Paul, get some butter!" The van was carpeted, its windows shaded in drapes ablaze with stars. Cresting the Cascades after dark one Friday, after the end of school in June, the six of us motored toward the Columbia River.

We took turns roof-surfing, flat on the van's top, faces arrowing forward, fingers hooked inside the window wells to ride out bumps. "Born to Run" was roaring from a tape deck. When we reached the Columbia River's windy shore, we made a shelter for our beds by stamping flat some cattails. Those reed maces rustled and sung above us like wind harps through the night.

CIVIL JUSTICE

While we were having our fun, Nisquallys near Tacoma were striving to gain their civil rights. Tribal members were being beaten, gassed, and jailed, their fish nets confiscated or stolen, just for harvesting fish in local rivers as their ancestors had done. Lengthy legal battles ensued.

At stake was the lawfulness of 1850s treaties that ensured them salmon and steelhead in perpetuity. In 1917, the US had appropriated 3,370 acres of the Nisqually reservation for Fort Lewis. Military muscle masqueraded as eminent domain. Tribespeople in the 1970s were falling under siege by

Anglo fishermen trespassing on their tribal grounds. They were overtopped in salt water by white-owned boats and better gear, fired at by rifles to try to chase them away.

A hero-leader rose from the fray like a god to set things right. Billy Frank Jr. made it his goal to preserve the river traditions his ancestors had bequeathed him. His scarred and weathered face, his calm, strong manner, attracted national notice. He became a commander in what were named the Fish Wars in Pacific Northwest rivers. Adopting tactics from antiwar protesters, Billy Frank and others of the allied tribes coordinated protests they called fish-ins.

They borrowed strategies from pacifist sit-ins that took place during the Vietnam War. They broke the law by defying state orders. They cast nets on the Nisqually and Puyallup Rivers, demanded treaty rights, and refused to abide by the sanction of seasons, limits, licenses, or laws.

Billy Frank was arrested more than fifty times over three decades. Celebrities rallied with him. Dick Gregory spoke. Jane Fonda showed up. Marlon Brando was arrested. The ACLU and the NAACP made common cause. Even the Department of Justice came around to Frank's way of thinking. What seemed so radical to pundits at the time seems so commonsense today.

He was as consequential an activist in the Pacific Northwest as our region has ever seen. He led the charge from family property called Frank's Landing—the six acres of Nisqually River frontage his father had found the funds to buy after the government dispossessed him in 1917.

The campaign for Northwest rivers set up a precedent for other tribes around the nation. After hearing three years of testimony, Judge George H. Boldt in Seattle ruled in 1974 that the Indigenous tribes had valid claim to half the salmon. And that Indigenous people should manage the fisheries in tandem with the states. The finding in that case, the Boldt Decision, is the only one in judicial history to gain an eponymous celebrity status for the judge who handed down the law.

It also laid the groundwork for cooperation between state and Indigenous governments. Ensuing rulings would likewise favor tribes. One of those rulings was the 1988 Indian Gaming Regulatory Act, which allowed tribes to open and run casinos to help fund their governments.

Backlash to the Boldt Decision was swift. Commercial and sport fishermen gathered in Tacoma and the state capital of Olympia. In overalls and rain gear they hailed us motorists as we drove by. They waved signs saying, "Indians Are Racist" and "Shuve It Boldt." All the bluster on behalf of Donald Trump in 2020 brought that era rushing back like kitchen jets for me.

Anti-Indian bigotry, continuing today, has gone to the blogs. One bigot wrote of Indian fishers in 2016, "Disgusting. Should be hung by there necks. And left to rot!!" During that heated period of the 1970s in Western Washington, I fished the Pacific Ocean. My father, friends, and I chugged diesels out to sea, sometimes puking overboard between salmon strikes.

During the 1970s, too, an influx of Vietnamese refugees roiled the waters of the Salish Sea. Some of them tried to fish to make their way. More shots were fired, more protests. A boat was scuttled. Some soldiers who had slogged the jungles of Vietnam fanned the backlash.

In the entitled eyes of more than a few locals, Asians and Indians alike were conspiring to deprive whites of jobs, to encroach on God-given rights. Mutterings about an "Asian invasion" were overheard up and down the coast from San Francisco to Seattle. A shirttail female relative reported she flung a Vietnamese woman to the floor in a secondhand store.

The Ninth Circuit Court of Appeals upheld the Boldt Decision, and Billy Frank became a luminary. His charm in part was due to his gift for aphorism, long before the locution *soundbite* came to be. "When an electric light is turned on in Seattle," he said about the hidden costs of hydroelectric power, "a salmon comes flying out." His capable equation went around the world.

He met with presidents and led national committees. He did not stop with rights for his tribe and other tribes. He also exacted promises from timber companies to roll back logging operations alongside salmon streams. He lobbied the United Nations to ban drift nets. He fished, at long last, in his tribe's "usual and accustomed places" between Tacoma and Mount Rainier.

LOVED BADLY

At that same period around Seattle, the literary lion Richard Hugo was writing dirges for rivers. His 1965 poem "Duwamish Head" shows embryonic ecological insight. "With salmon gone and industry moved in / birds don't bite the water." Skimming birds no longer hit the Duwamish River's surface due to pollutants that ravaged the baitfish that fed the birds. "Once this river," Hugo keened, "brought a cascade of color to the sea."

The color-cascade from spawning salmon drew to drab close after key links in the food chain snapped. Everything about the Duwamish River in Hugo's philosophy grew gray. In mine, too. The sludge that tainted the Duwamish River seared the vegetation on its banks.

Richard Hugo's Seattle differed from other frontier towns after World War II. Its pace of change was driven in large part by the multinational corporation and jet manufacturer Boeing. Still ruling as the world's largest aerospace manufacturer, Boeing is rivaled only by Airbus in Toulouse, France. Hugo worked for Boeing as a technical writer. During that same period, Hugo was studying creative writing under Theodore Roethke at the University of Washington.

Moving inland later, he retooled as a professor and a poet. He enjoyed a second career at the University of Montana. He left behind those agents of ecological change—the jet and rocket industries, the military contracts in Seattle, the heavy-metal waste those manufacturers made. One of my distasteful jobs was disposing of that waste at Western Manufacturing in the Kent Valley. From that gross job I wear scars. Sulfuric acid drenched me and burnt off my pants.

Hugo was an ecologist before the first Earth Day, an outdoorsman who chose poetry as a tool to effect social change. He grieved towns gone to seed, ramshackle homes, social isolation, and family dysfunction. Rivers that were wheezing like his Duwamish rasped the big man just as badly: "Jacks don't run. Mills go on polluting / and the river hot with sewage steams." Jacks, those male juvenile Coho salmon, spend a year in salt water before they fin back inland.

Fifteen years after he published his chapbook *Duwamish Head*, Hugo still was grieving his favorite stream. Its oversaturated waters drenched his imagination. In a 1980 poem he wrote for fellow poet James Wright—"The Towns We Know and Leave Behind, the Rivers We Carry with Us"—he lamented the presence of "mercury in the cod." His best poems adopt a tragic tone.

Anglo-Saxon scholars know that somber mood as *ubi sunt*. It is a phrase from the Latin that translates as "Where did they go?" The ancients deployed that formulaic language maneuver to ruminate on the brevity of life, the weight of mortality, the cosmic loom of loss that wove their doom. In the Bible the book of Lamentations mourns the destruction of Jerusalem. Northwest rivers still weave rapture in abundance for those of us who recreate upon them.

The Cedar River, part of the Duwamish and Green watershed, once ran thick with fish. As a kid I saw its color-cascade in full splendor. The Cedar-Sammamish watershed drains to the southern end of Lake Washington now, where a kokanee sockeye salmon fishery persists in dribs and drabs. Those fish grow scrawny by comparison with their oceangoing counterparts, the anadromous sockeye. Food in the Pacific Ocean proves more plentiful than in Northwest rivers.

In one tongue *kokanee* means red fish, or landlocked sockeye. Those fish turn red when they spawn. Now the word *kokanee* is all but eclipsed in the US consciousness by a brewery in British Columbia that has drafted the word to brand a beer. The Okanagan diction that seasoned our regional speech took a hit with that commercial appropriation. Names from nature often get usurped in corporate boardrooms for commercial use. Nature holds no copyright, or any right.

One of the most forceful lines Hugo wrote about the river sounds as confessional as any by poet Robert Lowell. "River, I have loved, loved badly on your bank." I picture Hugo in an erotic mood and making amorous plans—cattail patch stamped flat, blanket spread for a compliant lover—before a spasm of hereditary self-consciousness overcame and withered him.

My imagination envisions him turning crimson in a disastrous act of outdoor spawning. His biography *The Real West Marginal Way* gives instances of his gawkiness with women. Apostrophe—that figure of speech used to address an absent or inanimate entity, that figure now considered an antique poetic manner—has fallen far away from popular tastes. Poets no longer feel as if they can address a river. Or an absent ancestor. Or the sun, like John Milton did.

Three years after the publication of Hugo's second full-length book, *Death of the Kapowsin Tavern*, the Wild and Scenic Rivers Act came into being. That 1968 act nominates US rivers to be preserved for their outstanding beauty—for recreation, geology, natural history, culture, and much more. Such designations are meant to protect and keep rivers from being dredged or locked up for hydropower projects. From being stoppered, plugged, and riveted shut.

"River, I have loved, loved badly on your bank." Hugo probably was confessing he had failed a lover, but he might instead have been confessing to the river he had loved it badly. That he neglected to protect it. Today the Duwamish River delta in Seattle's southside accommodates a Duwamish Longhouse and Cultural Center adjacent to a $342 million Superfund cleanup site.

IMPLICIT RISKS

Back East where I went to graduate school, most river mouths had been dredged to form deep ports. Channelized, excavated, made subservient to the commercial will. Classmates and I scouted waters wild enough to provide respite from the grad-school grind. The Youghiogheny River in West Virginia filled the bill. We rafted and paddled that watercourse like a clan of otters. Its current diminished the academic stress. It brought us all together. It leveled every ethnicity and creed. We classmates grew grateful for one another and gain trust.

Paddling whitewater, an extreme sport, is comparable to nothing else. Implicit risk is a calculable bit of its equation. Even practiced paddlers sometimes drown, even those who wear, as federal law demands, a personal flotation device, or PFD. The paddler might tumble from the craft and get clonked on the head. Get flipped over and trapped beneath the hull. Swamp and get Maytagged—swirled underwater in a so-called keeper hole. Unlucky paddlers might broach the boat against a rock or fallen tree, as happened once to me. Broadsided in a frail canoe that almost buckled, I found myself soused like a noodle in a strainer, water pouring through the fallen tree.

Living and working in Pocatello, Idaho, after graduate school put me in striking distance of other Northwest currents, including the Henrys Fork tributary of the Snake River near Yellowstone. That stretch of Idaho stays memory-etched as one of the most stunning places I've sojourned on this dirt-and-water body we call Earth. The Big Wood River that runs through Hailey and Ketchum in high-mountain Idaho comes in a close second. Idaho is a living contradiction for visitors today, its lands and waters combining with scarlet far-right politics.

Before I gave up spin-casting, I hurled a lure in the Big Wood. It was pulsing with alpine chill and insect life, its foliage neither burnt to a crisp from overgrazing nor sheared to grow crops. Heavy vegetation overhung the water so far that I could not hurl the fishing line overhead. Branches would have snarled it if I tried. In its shade, I practiced bow-and-arrow casting. I crouched, pinched the lure with ginger fingers, and bent the fishing rod to double. Pointing it downstream, I released the lure and cleared the vegetation. It worked, right there in the river city of Ketchum, where Ernest Hemingway spent his final years. After paying homage to his granite slab of an outdoor memorial, I thought about Hemingway and his writings for a good long time.

Rivers delivered sanctuary and flight for Hemingway. He set *A Farewell to Arms* in Italy. Wounded Frederick Henry flees execution there in World War I via a river-plunge. Later, the Isonzo and Tagliamento Rivers buoy him to a neutral nation. Hemingway lived in several countries, but he returned to the South-Central Idaho mountains and its rivers many times.

He recognized, like few American writers aside from Twain, the redemptive power of big streams. The progress they embody, their promise for the human prospect. Hemingway's Nick Adams, home from World War I, suffered family alienation and PTSD. He made his way to the banks of "The Big Two-Hearted River" to rediscover a soul-balm no humans could provide.

Near Ketchum, I drifted on the Salmon River for a week. Its yawning canyons shadowed the stream and kept it cool. Its Class 4 rapids tossed boats like bark chips. On an outfitted trip to uproot invasive knapweed, my paddling partner and I knocked heads and saw daytime stars.

Idaho senator Frank Church set aside that river corridor by sponsoring the National Wild and Scenic Rivers Act, inked into law by President Lyndon Johnson. Upon Church's death in 1984, the 2.5 million acres were given his name. The Frank Church–River of No Return Wilderness, along with the contiguous Selway-Bitterroot complex, is the largest official Wilderness in the Lower 48. It would be plugged up now, if not for Church's fight and foresight.

CIVIL INJUSTICE

Indigenous fisher David Sohappy was first arrested by federal agents in 1968. In a 1982 scheme now known as Salmon Scam, he was netted. A Wanapum tribesman who served in World War II, his ordeal began when he lost his sawmill job and moved his family to Cooks Landing on the Columbia River. Cooks Landing was one of dozens of sites the government gave Indigenous people after it built Bonneville Dam in 1938. There, the Little White Salmon River pours in.

The federal government has always shoved aside Indigenous people, and this time was the same. The National Marine Fisheries Service persecuted Sohappy. Agents called the Little White Salmon River site a boat launch, not a lawful residence. They called Sohappy and his clan squatters. The fish they sold—the state called them permissible for ceremonial purposes only.

David disagreed and fought the law until he died in 1991. He fought the law by arguing that his spiritual principles made fish, fishing, and trading fish a right. His Seven Drums religion and his ancestor, the prophet Smohalla, foresaw a return of people to the ancestral homeland. That prophecy would come true. Capturing salmon exercised their traditional religious beliefs.

Anglo allies rallied when David Sohappy went to prison. They dubbed him a prisoner of conscience. To bolster his defense, Jackson Browne and Bonnie Raitt organized a benefit show.

The American Indian Religious Freedom Act (AIRFA), overdue as a federal law, was not passed until 1978. AIRFA preserves and protects the cultural practices and privileges of Aleut, Inuit, American Indians, and Hawai'ians. Those practices include worship through ceremonial and traditional rites, access to sacred sites, ownership and use of sacred objects, and repatriation of artifacts and bones unearthed in digs or held by museums. That law, applied in court, might have saved Sohappy a lot of grief. Access to rivers and fish might have qualified under AIRFA.

A member of the Wanapum People of Washington State, Sohappy and his ancestors had enjoyed Cooks Landing, in present-day Skamania County, long before the John Day Dam was built in 1971. But federal agents claimed Sohappy was trespassing and illegally selling fish. They stung him in an undercover operation. Agents entrapped the people of his tribe by slyly asking to buy some fish. Seventy-five other tribal members were drawn into dragnets with David Sohappy and his son David Jr. The two of them got convicted and sent to a series of federal prisons.

Chilling in the joint for thirty months, shuttling at age sixty-two from state to state, Sohappy had a stroke. Worse, he suffered a broken spirit. In 1988, Senator Daniel Inouye of Hawai'i traveled to the Geiger Corrections Center in Spokane to work with Washington governor Dan Evans and gain Sohappy's early release. Discharged on a snowy day, Sohappy in the documentary about him can barely walk. Cradling an arm as if it were a sleeping child, he tries to address his kinfolk, tries to speak to them in the old tongue, but he breaks down in coughing fits and tears.

Prison had crushed him. He fought the law, and the law won. Two years later, cuddling that arm and disabled by the stroke, he fought removal from Cooks Landing and prevailed. Some of his offspring live there still. His granddaughter Loretta, a Gates Scholar and a friend of mine, completed her graduate degree in urban and regional planning at Eastern Washington University.

Sohappy Sr. did not live to wield influence like Billy Frank did, but his disobedience set a powerful precedent. In the 1969 decision *Sohappy v. Smith*, in the trial of his relative Richard Sohappy, US District Judge Robert Belloni awarded Indigenous people a "fair share" of the harvestable surplus of the Columbia watershed's salmon. Five years later, in the *U.S. v. Washington* decision in the Billy Frank case, Judge Boldt defined Belloni's fair share doctrine to mean half the harvest.

CATCH AND RELEASE

By the time I gave up spin-casting in 1995, fishing rules had grown byzantine. Habitats were being trashed. Fishing license fees supported the rearing and planting of hatchery trout. Put-and-take, it was called. Put in the fish for dudes to take away. That ain't fishing, I slurred.

State trucks vacuuming trout from concrete troughs, spewing them for people to catch, did not smell like outdoor glory for me. Catch-and-release became a similar sham once I read statistics about high mortality rates. Catch-and-release is a cure-all for the tourist, a catchphrase to make itinerant fishermen feel good. Some 20 to 30 percent of hooked fish don't survive the palate-piercing, the barbs on hooks, the hauling to the boat or shore, the netting and the handling.

Writer David Quammen used to be fishing guide, but he gave it up: "Small flies with the barbs flattened are an excellent means for allowing the fisherman's own sensibilities to be released unharmed—but the fish themselves aren't always so lucky. They get eye-hooked, they bleed, they suffer trauma and dislocated maxillae and infection. Unavoidably, some die." To foul-hook a fish means to snag it, whether deliberately or accidentally, anywhere except the lip.

I once used flies and barbless hooks to go easy on the fish and help them to survive. A prole of a fisherman from the get-go, I was never one of those Zen poetic types. My mode of dress on rivers and lakes was hand-me-down khaki and five-dollar shades. A popular bumper sticker says a bad day fishing is better than a good day at the office. I chose to hone the slogan to say there's no such thing as a bad day fishing. Just to be a silent participant and view the line looping, the waterbirds swirling, the river crooning its ceaseless tunes proved enough. The fact that fly-fishers rely on undammed rivers ought to persuade all of them to outlawry.

Outlawry tempted me near Oldtown, Idaho. Driving through the town, I found myself thirsty and stopped at a bulge of asphalt—the Albeni Falls Dam lot on the Pend Oreille River. The Army Corps of Engineers had gotten up its visitor center gift shop like a destination resort. It made me seethe to see. I yearned to do some *nachtwerk*, in Edward Abbey's phrase: slip back with spray paint and get all decorative. Every bit of civility was required to chill out my hot ire.

Bending over the drinking fountain inside, I realized that gilding a lily always requires the gilder to kill the lily. Standing up, I had a fresh perspective. Through my narrowed eyes, the starched and ironed functionaries behind the desk became cogs in wheels revolved by organic machines. At once I grew tender with an empathy for their lot. Had I not halted a misbegotten undergraduate degree in biology and natural resources, I might have sat behind that same desk beside them starched and ironed. And I would have found a way to excuse the uniform I wore.

"How do we forgive our fathers?" Thomas Builds-the-Fire in the movie *Smoke Signals* asks. His question resonates, as the film wings viewers high above the Spokane River. Sherman Alexie wrote the screenplay. Like Richard Hugo, he laments the slow violence forced on local folks. In poems and stories, Alexie bridles an abiding anger about a shattered past. In his poem on the Spokane Falls titled "That Place Where Ghosts of Salmon Jump," the word *love* erupts eight times. How can Indians ever love again, he wonders, when the salmon now are ghosts?

Places revered for centuries by Northwest Indigenous people have been trashed by dams in the Columbia River watershed. Grand Coulee Dam—for years the largest concrete structure on the planet—required upstream tribes to pry their dead from graves before the water flooded them in 1940. The water rose and did not stop behind the dam. It flooded Kettle Falls beneath ninety feet as part of the reservoir now named Lake Roosevelt. The joint loss of cultural legacy and fish runs gave rise to the Ceremony of Tears for ten thousand Indigenous people in the region.

Filming Sherman Alexie's *Smoke Signals* in 1998, director Chris Eyre also experienced an awakening. He learned about the vagaries of river flows due to mismanagement by the local utility. Upon discovering the falls of the Spokane River, which run through Spokane, Eyre was stunned with wonder. Perfect for the scene, he decided, where Victor Joseph scatters his father's ashes from high atop a bridge. His film crew, costing him seventy-five thousand dollars a day to retain, arrived to find the falls switched off at the dam. Only dry stones remained. Getting hold of Avista Utilities' flow schedule, Eyre returned at the preprogrammed time and shot the scene.

After Karen and I moved to Spokane, I toted our son Reed in a backpack to the same bridge that Eyre filmed. Above those stunning falls, showered by April spray, I leaned against the railing and looked down. From his backpack Reed craned, his eyes settling on the rush and flood, his jaw dropping. The binky that plugged his mouth went spinning to the drink.

Two decades before we made Spokane home, boosters were gearing up to host Expo '74, the International Exposition on the Environment. Spokane was hoping to be the smallest city in history to host a world's fair. But the burg needed buy-in from corporations and nations to keep from drowning in red ink. Ford and General Motors were dubious prospects for funding.

In the summer of 1973, Ford and GM agreed to be wined and dined and scope the site. A businessman named Walt Toly, fabled for his sales skills, set up lunch at a posh restaurant below the lower falls that usually went summer-dry to generate electricity. Toly persuaded Washington Water Power—renamed Avista in 1999—to switch on the falls so a showy flow might brighten the lunch. Awestruck, the company representatives agreed to shell out for exhibits at the fair.

The subterfuge of modulating flows for cosmetic and economic purposes has figured in American exceptionalism for donkey's years. John McPhee titled his book *The Control of Nature* where he wrote about the Atchafalaya River and the engineers that twist its spigots and the Mississippi River's. A painting by Thomas Cole from 1826, *Falls of the Kaaterskill*, might never have been completed without a hireling in hiding behind a cliff. In southeast New York State, an old gentleman "performed" those falls for tourists and artists alike. He cranked a handle for a fee.

Thomas Cole, the founder of the Hudson River school of visual arts, focused panoramic canvases on rivers. Viewers also admire *Niagara Falls* by his protégé Frederick Edwin Church (1857), *Among the Sierra Nevada Mountains, California* by Albert Bierstadt (1868), and *Grand Canyon of the Yellowstone* by Thomas Moran (1872). Our nation needs to keep its rivers healthy, if only because they stand as a living record and repository of great American art.

In the century following those canvases, dams began to alter our tastes in the visual arts. Z. Vanessa Helder, trained as a Precisionist, gained distinction for her watercolors that depict the construction of Grand Coulee Dam. Several of her original canvases are on display in Spokane. The Bureau of Reclamation commissioned hundreds more artworks to valorize its federal dam projects in the 1960s. In doing so the agency aimed to manipulate public sentiment and steer eyes away from tamed rivers. Because the agency had come under such scrutiny, painters valorized the engineering feats that thwarted those streams. Paintings by Nicholas Solovioff, Fletcher Martin, and Anton Refregier prettify the construction of massive Grand Coulee Dam.

Paintings from two centuries earlier were entirely supplanted—paintings such as Paul Kane's *Below the Cascades, Columbia River with Indians Fishing* (1846) and *Hunting Salmon at Kettle Falls on the Columbia* (1848). Undammed rivers and sublime wildness, whose appeal had dominated American visual arts for two centuries, were kowtowing now to technological feats.

Today in the Columbia Basin, some three hundred hydropower dams more than one-tenth megawatt in size are churning. Some two hundred smaller dams have been built for irrigation and flood control. Tell me, what is it you plan to do with your one wild and precious life?

CONTROL OF NATURE

By 2012, the same year Chase and I paddled the Clark Fork River delta, my regard for dams had withered to contempt. Agency mandates had stanched those capillaries for us all. The Clark Fork used to massage its way into Lake Pend Oreille. Now it erodes the shore, its erratic emissions regulated by dams both upstream and at the outflow of that great lake. Floodgates, forebays, siphons, aqueducts, and pumps unravel the shoreline of the Clark Fork River delta.

Bad management damages wildlife habitat each year. Water officials adopt the dodgy talk of bureaucracy to greenwash it all. They acknowledge the need to remediate "the erosion of wetland habitat types in a delta ecosystem due to altered hydrologic conditions." Those last three words are a stellar instance of euphemism from the top, a crafty kind of language magic that camouflages the control of nature responsible for those same conditions.

The Clark Fork of the Columbia flows into Lake Pend Oreille and out again forty-three miles later as the Pend Oreille River. There it winds to the Columbia River. Kayaking the Columbia's Hanford Reach in 2015, Karen and I could feel the mighty Columbia's muscles flex.

Dams have yet to atrophy the Hanford Reach. At fifty-one miles long, it is the largest untrammeled stretch of the Columbia River, as well as its most productive spawning water. The muscular flow told us we'd be lucky to survive if we swamped. Our best bet would be to clutch the kayak like a

PFD and kick it to shore far downstream. Then we would have to lug the boat up a steep and sandy bank. Facing such odds, we hugged the riverbank and loved it.

The greatest blight in the Columbia watershed is the Hanford Nuclear Reservation. Its production of plutonium helped manufacture the Fat Man bomb dropped on Nagasaki in 1945. Visitors can take buses to "the site," as locals call it. Rebranded now as the Manhattan Project National Historical Park, proudly open to the public, that euphemistic park commemorates "The Dawn of the Atomic Age," among other events, and "the creation of the atomic bomb, which helped end World War II." The would-be tourist attraction plays down the dispossession and displacement of David Sohappy's people, the Wanapum band of the Yakama Tribe of Indians.

Subsistence fishers were dislocated when the government claimed eminent domain once more, that time over 560 square miles on and around the river. Indigenous people still fished, but they had to scatter both downriver and up-. Fish-heavy diets exposed them to the radioactive effluent that cooled the nuclear fuel rods. Ignored as downwinders, the people became downstreamers—a portmanteau to describe the hazards that flow south and west with the Columbia River's current, compounding the radioactive hazards that drift north and east with the prevailing winds.

Indigenous people were hit harder than the whites because they relied more on the salmon, sturgeon, and mountain whitefish for food. They smoked all three species and preserved them for winter use. According to a study, boiling the ribs and spines of the fish to make stews can set free more deadly and invisible radioactivity than just eating the meat does.

CULTURAL SURVIVAL

In the degradation of fish runs that fed the people, scientists have difficulty separating cause from effect. Dams, farms, pesticides, road runoff, and nuclear waste all afflict Northwest tribes. In the Pacific Ocean likewise, fish runs have flagged so badly that orca populations in the Salish Sea have registered a thirty-year low. The so-called killer whales rely on Chinook salmon.

Nor are fish alone at risk. Dams also add to climate change. A writer for *Undark Magazine* reported, "Aging reservoirs have become inefficient . . .

and research suggests that hydropower reservoirs may be a much larger contributor of methane—a greenhouse gas roughly 30 times more potent than carbon dioxide—than previously realized." Organic material builds up in reservoirs behind dams. It consumes oxygen, releases methane, and abrades the ozone layer.

Cultural survival of regional Indigenous people depends on the flow of rivers and of fish. Federal judges, year after year, have demanded the Bureau of Reclamation and the Army Corps of Engineers double down to restore at-risk fish, even if that means breaching dams. So far, those federal agencies have stonewalled the available science to uphold bargain-basement energy rates.

But global rivers are immortal. They might be more resilient than the people and the various species that rely on them. Free-flowing water is always being freshened by natural circulation. Rivers never really die, it gives me comfort to realize, even if the fish and the people depending on them do. Dams are only interruptions. Water will always find its way.

The Elwha River, far west on Washington's Olympic Peninsula, was set free in 2014. Two privately owned dams that shackled it for a century were dismantled—a result of creative vandalism, battles in Congress, and massive fundraising. It is the largest dam removal to have taken place anywhere on the planet. The Lower Elwha Klallam Tribe had lobbied to tear down those monolithic dams since they were built. Faster than fisheries experts expected, Chinook salmon recolonized areas upstream of the former dam sites. We in the region, Indigenous citizens and others, have grown hopeful that those dam removals might just be the start of something big.

In 2017, the news from the Northwest continued improving. Idaho Fish and Game limited fishing to catch-and-release in the Snake, Clearwater, and Salmon Rivers. Runs of anadromous fish were unsustainably small. Any harvest of sea-run migrants, wild or hatchery-raised, would put them too much at risk. Midseason, though, buckling to pressure from sporting groups and key legislators, that Idaho agency reversed its hivemind. It allowed fish again to be toted home.

That is when the unexpected occurred. Fly-fishing groups organized and voted to oppose all Idaho harvests. Fishermen and -women who wade in wild waters know a few things the officeholders seem unwilling to acknowledge. That water is the lifeblood of the land. That oceangoing fish are the counterparts of healthy red blood cells swarming in the planet's body.

River crises are acute in Eastern Washington where I live, but there is cause for hope in recent years. That hope rests with the Columbia River Inter-Tribal Fish Commission, a consortium of the Nez Perce, Umatilla, Warm Springs, and Yakama Tribes. Those tribes are taking the lead on salmon restoration around the Columbia Basin, the same basin where I leapt from cliffs, hunted birds, stamped flat a patch of cattails, and saw the Wanapum Dam go in.

BEING BIOREGIONAL

County, state, and federal agencies manipulated by agricultural interests and other commerce will never spearhead restoration efforts alone. The tribes verify "it will take everyone who lives in the basin to restore the salmon." That pitch sounds a lot like bioregionalism: the will of locals to gain control of their ecological and economic destinies. People learn from and remain attached to geographies like other animals do. Jesus lived and died at sites that lie eight kilometers apart.

Bioregional campaigns can succeed, but only with collective action. In early 2018 the Supreme Court agreed to hear a case by twenty-one tribes on culverts blocking fish migration in Washington State. By June 11, 2018, in a 4–4 decision with one judge conflicting out, the Court ruled on behalf of the tribes. The ruling means, within the treaty area, that the State must replace or repair 817 culverts at a cost of billions. This salmon crisis is acute. Everyone, including taxpayers, will have to pitch in to restore fish. Thank Indigenous people for taking the lead.

The best cause for hope that salmon might once more color Northwest rivers rests with the tribes. For the first time in eighty years, salmon now swim upstream of Grand Coulee Dam. To begin a new life cycle for the fish, the Colville Confederated Tribes released them there on August 16, 2019, passing soft rubber custom buckets hand to hand to release the fish from tanker trucks into the river. Prayers, songs, and speeches followed. The hopeful goal is that the fish will spawn and their fry prove small enough to pass destructive turbines to the sea. In the Pacific Ocean they will feed, grow, and return to butt the dam. Then they will be captured and transported once more to the upper reaches of the Columbia River, above the dam, to repeat the ancient cycle. That hypothesis rests upon an abundance of hope and technological intervention.

In 2022 the Coeur d'Alene Tribe tagged and reintroduced fingerling Chinook salmon to Latah Creek, a major tributary of the Spokane River, which itself is a major tributary of the Columbia River. Latah Creek, a bygone habitat for the fish, is fouled by agricultural chemicals and eroded soil. The tags will track the fish throughout their journey, all the way to the Pacific Ocean ideally, a journey fueled by aspirations that they might become anadromous again.

In the summer of 2020, at a Leavenworth bed and breakfast in the Washington Cascades, Karen and I rented rooms for a working vacation. AC made our rooms too cold. We asked the hostess how to dial down the thermostat, preserve our comfort, and conserve some BTUs. She just laughed. The hostess said to throw the slider and the windows wide, no need to go easy on the AC. Leavenworth is so subsidized by Chelan County PUD, she pays only 3.22 cents/kilowatt hour. Rocky Reach and Rock Island Dams on the nearby Columbia River afford her those bargain rates. New York City residents, by contrast, were paying 19.6 cents in February 2022.

The willful negligence of our hostess vexed me. Call hers an insouciance, an entitlement, a studied ignorance, or something worse. Good dog that I am, indoctrinated by silent grinding, I clamped my tongue between my teeth and lodged it there. Tourism is such an economic force the tiny town of Leavenworth has made itself over as a Bavarian village. Tourists overrun it every month, much to the chagrin of locals who moved there to escape the Seattle throngs and masses.

Those of us who feel strongly about river issues have had to learn to choose our quarrels. Someday, like Henry Thoreau, I might wonder what demon possessed me that I behaved so well. And if I repent of anything, it will be my good behavior. Travel and its challenges have taught me to pick my quibbles and develop good rapport with locals, however difficult that might be.

Bad dams in my bioregion might not be bypassed in this lifetime, but their utility is finite. Tons of sediment build up within those reservoirs.

Regular dredging keeps cargo barges from running aground. Barges haul sawdust and paper pulp milled from trees shorn off federal lands. Those same barges tote fish past federal dams. No matter how many hatcheries are built, salmon will be superheated and shredded by turbines, until river rapids and spawning grounds come back into geological play. Breaching the worst of the dams would bring about a glorious dawn.

Alternative energies in time will allow Northwest rivers to run free again, a welcome reversal. My family and I have done our part by installing solar panels, by investing in an electric vehicle, by throwing our support behind the right nonprofit groups. Removing the four dams on the lower Snake River, before it joins the Columbia, would expose passage to five hundred miles of habitat. Fish could fin to the base of the Sawtooth Mountains in Lemhi County, Idaho—all the way to Redfish Lake, so-named for the few lone sockeye salmon that still survive migration and thrash their way there. People will celebrate that reclamation when it takes place. They will acclaim the date when Indigenous cultures and treaties come to be honored at last.

Some people's heart arteries get clogged from eating bad food. From lack of exercise or genetic predisposition. Medical providers carve side channels for oxygenated blood to help those hearts plug away. Dam breaching is the landscape-scale equivalent of heart-bypass surgeries, procedures that allow the blood to flow freely again, the rivers to enjoy refurbished circulation.

The world's body resembles our own more than we think. It might be more like ours than we *can* think. No planet except Mars shows signs of running water, much less evidence of rivers and climes that function in tandem to keep the good stuff flowing, the liquids lifting and drifting back down, the systole and diastole by any other name performing the complex circulatory work.

16

Nomads of the Sea

When I used to watch TV, *Mr. Magoo* was my favorite cartoon. Wealthy and educated Magoo is an elderly man whose eyesight is failing. He bumbles blindly and hopes for the best. He gets into scrapes and near-misses, needs rescuing, and falls on his feet. His catchphrase is "Oh, Magoo, you've done it again!" He means well, but he's a goof. The UPA animation studio made the show, and actor Jim Backus voiced him. The name *Magoo* plays on Scotch stereotypes, profiling him as too frugal, too Scottish, to pay for eyecare. On his behalf I gasped as a kid, especially when he dared to travel. In one episode he is seen driving a car up the Eiffel Tower.

At all events, I think of him when I go abroad. Like Magoo, I am often at risk of falling. My catchphrase is "There are so many ways to go wrong." Swimming in open water, I blunder like a kayak that has lost its rudder. For some twenty feet I stroke facedown before peering up to assess my destination. Oops, off-target again by several degrees. I correct my course and try to get back on the straight-and-narrow. Swimming with Karen—much stronger in the water than I am, a former Idaho breaststroke champion—I keep her fins or feet in view. That pattern continues out of the water when we travel in tandem. She sets the fine itineraries, and I follow along. The goofy Magoo to her silent guidance, the bumbling blind man to her keener foresight.

* * *

We are bound for an island governed by Thailand in the Andaman Sea. Patience and time have carried us this distance, far south of Bangkok on the Malay Peninsula. Muslim headgear mingles with Buddhist statues. Many of the people blast by on scooters. The women's garments flap and flow at highway speed, like actress Sally Field's in *The Flying Nun*. Helmeted toddlers, balanced on gas tanks, hold tight to handlebars. Their parent's outstretched arms surround them.

Karen opens the window of the chartered car for relief from the humidity. The rush from traffic is heavy. The roadside billboards are few. At the shack where we stop the chartered car for lunch, our servers honor us with the *wai*—the bent head and prayerful hand gesture available today as a telephone emoji. The intricacies of this gesture, this silent expedient for gratitude and social leveling, take some time to master. We travelers may return a *wai* whenever one is shone upon us, but we ought not instigate it with anyone but elders. Thailand is principally Theravada Buddhist, and this respectful greeting, this *wai*, originated within that strain of faith. The gesture might have arisen originally to show no ill will was in the offing, no weapon being concealed.

The smidge of island where we are heading, named Koh Lipe, has earned the nickname "the Maldives of Thailand." It is the only inhabited spot allowed within the Tarutao National Marine Park. Tourism drives the economy of Koh Lipe in the Satun province. Tourism likewise is the largest moneymaker for the Maldives in the contiguous Arabian Sea. We have flown from Bangkok to the Hat Mai airport to find our island. I try the window on my side of the chartered car, but the wind from our velocity offers no relief from the heat. Shore breezes will be better.

Aboard the twenty-four-person water taxi that beelines us from the mainland to Koh Lipe, we are the only Anglos. Waves are heavy, the sky gray. Wind gushes above the gunwales. Spray soaks our faces and hair. Some passengers, after squeals of delight in the first wave splash, grow solemn and withdrawn. Faces turn pasty, barf bags pass around, and heads drop to partners' laps. Other passengers sit solitary without stirring, bent as double as a living body can be bent.

The water taxi leaps like a rodeo horse—catching air, banging back down, a stiff-legged bronco trying to throw its rider. The tortured frame of the boat groans. Our skipper sees the need to ratchet back on the throttle. He might batter and bruise his passengers otherwise, slam them to the seats and the walls. Our velocity slows. Clenched hands come off the seatbacks and whitened knuckles unwind. This ride will cost us privileged travelers an extra hour due to nasty weather.

The skipper is a black-skinned Lawoi. His face bears deep acne pits. He never utters a word. Even with his mates, he does not try to talk. We can only guess he knows little or no Thai language. His skill is to read the water, parley with it, capitulate to its mandates when he must.

His throttle hand feeds three loud Honda outboards, each engine harnessing 250 horses of power. At length a bearing starts to whine and grind. It shatters in a metallic racket and the skipper sloshes us to a stop. Tossed by waves, the boat pitches, wallows, dips. The first mate balances and disassembles the outboard. He claws out the shards and replaces the bearing.

Our idled craft gets underway again, and at length the island of Koh Lipe comes into view. Everyone is grateful to be making landfall. We will explore the jungle and salt water. We will come to know the people in the ways that we know how—chatting, dining, touring. In 2004 when the killer tsunami came by, Koh Lipe was spared. Intervening islands blocked the wave. In other environs to the west, the death toll reached a quarter million, the head count only a guess.

We clamber from the water taxi to a longtail boat to reach the shore. On the dock we stretch, gape, and regain our land legs. Koh Lipe, we can see, lacks much infrastructure. Tiny and remote, sheltered by the marine park in whose boundaries it lies, the island accommodates no cars. My jaded gaze says developers will have their way, just as water always finds its level. Fiscal pressures will guarantee that piles are driven, docks built, concrete poured. We wheel our baggage bumpety-bump across rain-slick diamond-plate decking meant to offer purchase.

The sky has cleared. High up on the shore, motorbike-taxi drivers wait for us passengers to make our way. Their folded arms rest on the handlebars of their carts. Each driver's legible shirt names his resort. There is ours now: Serendipity. The driver of our motorbike loads our bags. On a seat behind him we three bump shoulders—our son Reed, Karen, and me. Sticky from sweat and salt spray, we are keen to check in at Serendipity to shower or rinse in a plunge pool. Our ride to our resort takes us on a rutted road past dwellings of the Indigenous Lawoi people.

In several locales around the world where travel is the richest industry, we have seen how poorly the local folks and ecology often fare. Koh Lipe's Indigenes—the Urak Lawoi, known as *chao ley* or *chow lair* in the Thai language, dubbed sea gypsies by English speakers—are no exception to the tourist rule. Commercial growth on Koh Lipe has become precipitous. Absentee investors have scooped up much of the habitable shoreline. These Lawoi, the tiniest ethnic group in the region, inhabiting shanties at the island's highpoint, are being shoved aside. They are disconnected from the same geography their culture historically ties them to, this land and water that has nourished them for millennia, this Adang Archipelago on the Andaman Sea.

The bungalows of our Serendipity Beach Resort sprawl along a cliff. Vines underlie the slope. Steep hardwood stairs zigzag uphill and down, and the pitch of the cliff demands stout handrails. Boulders stud the precipice. My right hand slides the rails, my left suspending my wheeled suitcase. The open-air waterside restaurant below the bungalows has been scooped from among smooth stones. A wayward place to have built, but so it goes. Johnny-come-latelys to the land rush have been buying up every worthwhile building site on this Thai island.

Religious icons animate the restaurant's shadows. Carven Buddhas in shady niches peep like bracelet charms. Large Buddhas, small ones, etched from stone or native hardwood. Tiny baby Buddhas, like so many stilled GIFs, creep on hands and knees. Stormy weather and neglect have partly marred the features of some of these figurines.

Fifty yards below the diners, so pleased before their meals, the Andaman Sea yawns. An unnamed island a quarter mile to the west, backlit at sunset, resembles a postcard. An illuminated money shot at the end of every day. Insensitive travelers often say, "I did Thailand," or whatever other nation, as if the nation they toured through were a wham-bam accomplice in a tryst.

Nothing is not to love in Thailand, apart from jammed Bangkok, Chang Mai, and Phuket. The beaches are powdery white. The food is prodigious. The baggage handlers, housekeepers, drivers, and cooks so sweet in disposition and visage. Just as Costa Rica has its verbal brand Pura Vida, under-scoring an ethic of sustainability and health, Thailand has its own verbal logo: Land of Smiles. Sincere, lovable, unforced smiles summon our sympathetic beaming in return.

The smile is the idle the people return to between gears. They know which side their bread is buttered on. Their economic interests lie in being kind. We come to share a sense of shame if we do not repay their every beaming. We taste disgrace if we have no proactive smiles ready for every chance encounter. They have yet to experience the burnout of overtourism. Or if they taste its burn, they constrain themselves by the device of *jai yen*. It translates as cool heart.

These islands call the masses from afar. Much like Hawai'i and Cancun serve North Americans, these Andaman Sea islands serve the Asian nations. Places to escape for a long weekend. To spend money, get pampered, gain mental space away from tedious jobs. Tour promoters trigger itches and labor zealously to scratch them. People of disposable income grow grateful for fresh spending outlets, for foreign products to buy, novel services to try. Mine is the legendary Thai massage. Pain and pleasure, elbows and knees, press upon my pliant flesh. The stern madam of the studio, high upon her catbird seat, keeps an eye on me and the masseuse.

The internet, the chief source of literacy for international travelers, spreads distortions about how to define the locals on this island. Some sites categorize bar owners and staff as locals—a false labeling, however innocently made. Providers arrive from other nations or from the mainland to chase jobs. In the loose and easy locutions of the internet, though, all Thai people are locals. One resort claims in online promotions it uses the Lawoi people to capture all the seafood that it serves. Such feel-good assertions distort the truth. The Lawoi, the legacy locals, are as invisible to casual travelers as mainland entrepreneurs inside their countinghouses. We travelers in our behaviors might be invisible to ourselves. If retirement-account managers admit foreign real estate investments, then you and I might be underwriting resort sprawl.

Within two decades, an island path on Koh Lipe has become a thorough-fare. Commerce has grown from two groceries and a single resort to twenty resorts. The internet has become a game changer in the ways it propagates tourism. So-called influence marketers throng the social media byways. They earn in terms of the online followers they can amass, the page-clicks or the screen swipes they can tally. The rise of travel influence has been so precipitous it is being categorized as an industry itself. If promotions were audible, the screech of PR might deafen. There is lots of money to be made, especially from newly affluent Chinese so nearby.

The practical boat to get through sea channels, the shore craft of choice, is the longtail. It gets its name from an improbably long propeller shaft at the stern that resembles an ovipositor on a wasp. Like a setting pole on a keelboat, the shaft is spun or elevated to clear flotsam or coral. The boat itself has a high bow. Paint, fabric, or flowers ornament its proud bowsprit. The boats serve much the same purpose as the herds of semi-wild horses did for the American Plains tribes. Constructed of precious teak, each boat can weigh a full two tons. Longtails rest upright at low tide on flat-bottomed hulls. Lanyards tether them to shore. Skippers slop from the shore to clamber aboard. The skipper stands to steer his craft, to turn the tiller and goose the throttle.

So many longtails buzz around the bays that a swimmer might resemble the blind and bumbling Mr. Magoo sleepwalking across an urban thoroughfare. Swimmers must rely on an abundance of luck. They must stay alert to keep from getting hit. Low tide is the best time to swim. Never after dark around this island. The Lawoi benefit as the only licensed skippers of longtails, the most experienced in this archipelago. They are predisposed to know the ropes.

If one buys into geographical determinism—the notion that environment shapes human nature, just as it shapes the evolution of other species—then genetic disposition has equipped the Lawoi to navigate these seas. Seascapes and landscapes craft character, or so hypotheses go. The Lawoi have a keen ability to hold breath underwater for minutes at a stretch, accounting for how they can spear-fish so well. More remarkable, they can see, can keep eyes open wide in salt during underwater work or play. A pupillary reflex gained by training, or nested deep inside the genome by now, has bestowed on them a full-immersion vision, a keen marine ability to see.

Nothing, though, has prepared the Lawoi to traverse the rush of tourist traffic. Nor has any genome prepared them, despite the idealistic notions we might harbor, to manage resources sustainably or to live in ecological balance. Most scientists discredit any "balance of nature" and consider it romantic. Random periods of natural equilibrium punctuate erratic and often violent upheavals. Indeed, that is a basis for Darwinian natural selection. Adversity and upheavals effect evolution. Such an upheaval is underway for these microminorities in the Andaman Sea. Whether they will evolve to meet industrial contests, or get assimilated, has yet to be revealed.

Heading to supper on a footpath leading from the beach, we pass close by a dog on a porch. We worry he might bark, rush us, bite. We have all three been bitten by dogs. Reed got it on the face when he knocked at a neighbor's door. This dog does not raise its head, though, only twitches its tail a single time. Karen baby-talks him off the porch. He rises and approaches smiling. Yes, this dog has learned to smile like people do. He draws back black lips and grins.

For a distance he shadows us on the packed dirt path, wetly nosing our warm legs. "The greatness of a nation can be judged by the way its animals are treated," Mahatma Gandhi said. If Gandhi was right in that assertion, the residents of Thailand on this microcosm of an island are demonstrably great. Not only kindly, never a harsh face or noise or word or gesture, but their happy animals reflect a kindred temperament as well. One might enlarge on Gandhi by suggesting that a nation's kindness may be measured by the conduct of its domestic beasts.

At the restaurant Nee Papaya, a server draws us in to supper. She draws us in without the force we've seen in other countries. She wears a hijab and jeans. Bling studs her back pockets. The menu is so well-thumbed, the pages flake between our fingers. We three often share dishes. Reed orders crabs in garlic butter. I get green curry pumpkin, tofu, and rice. Karen has sliced green eggplant with basil in oil sauce, sticky rice and mango, fried and sliced tofu above a grated cabbage bed. Dining on the equator in mid-June, I sop through my shirt and begin to feel sloppy. I deplete the table's tiny pink napkins by mopping my face before our meals arrive.

We are drinking half-liter beers, Singha brand, to try to cool off. I don't like beer, but I thought I would give this one a try. Sun and rain nourish tropical plants along a dirt and lath-laced path that meanders both indoors and out and leads me to a squatty potty, a four-inch triangle on the floor.

At the edge of the kitchen, I pass a cook dicing a clump of green onions. His left hand serves him as his cutting board. He swings a heavy cleaver with his right.

When I drift back to the table, fuzzy and flushed from the beer I've drunk, I wonder aloud about the breeze I feel. Has the weather changed? Monsoons begun? Reed doubles over and laughs at my oblivious manner. He points out three fans blowing at my back. Oh, Magoo, you've done it again! Soon I will fall into bed at our bungalow. The Serendipity lodgings have no AC, but a big-bladed fan overhead stirs indoor breezes and affords us comforting white noise.

In the morning we have restful breakfasts then hire a longtail guide for a snorkel. Before we may board the boat, a lecture from a water guardian is needed. Scowling, uniformed, he is an ecological cop in a black beret. He instructs us how to care for the water and the coral. We pay him every due respect. Our Lawoi skipper on the longtail boat, training his son to take over the trade, begins by showing his young man how to manage the ladder and the anchor. A Japanese couple in their sixties, clad in matching Speedo sunproof water suits, earnestly tune in. A Korean couple and their two toddlers round out our little crowd. Once we buzz out to our first snorkeling site, the son lowers the anchor, and the skipper guides us into the water.

Curious creatures creep beneath. A squid, an animated mop head drawn by its beak along the bottom of the sea, tentacles drifting like the sensitive membranes of a ghost, proves rare enough that the skipper splashes back for his camera. Squid and octopuses, chameleons of the sea, change colors so fast they resemble a dust cloud one second, a blushing and embarrassed face the next. Rarest of all beneath these waves, and scariest for us northerners, we see a black-and-purple sea snake. We slip overboard four separate spots to snorkel, never far from shore.

Back at our bungalow we decide to swim to the nameless islet a quarter mile out to sea. The descending sun, like a cherry on a sundae, tops that islet's concave peak and foregrounds every sunset. We want to snorkel-snoop for critters among coral beds. A tide is running sharp, though, the longtails roaring back and forth. We neither hit slack tide nor evade the going boats.

The resort has lent me a too-small snorkel, its gauge meant for smaller mouths. Sucking in air enough proves tough. I ought to have brought my own from home. I sidestroke out, then rest on a granite outcrop to catch my breath. We fin around the island but see little sea life. When I crawl-stroke back, snorkel tucked in my shorts, I keep one eye open for longtails. On shore two swimmers rear near in the shallows, engrossed by themselves and their telescoping selfie stick.

Tourists were culprits in the decimation of Maya Bay on nearby Phi Phi Leh. *The Beach* starring Leonardo DiCaprio publicized the site. Nasty blowback could have been foreseen. After the film's release in 2000, Maya Beach endured a thirtyfold increase in traffic. By 2016, five thousand tourists, most of them Chinese, were visiting the bay every day. Coral reefs perished outright. Thai officials closed the beach for a period in a token effort to rest the environment, regenerate the water quality, and try to lure back sundry fishes that had fled. Ironically, two years before *The Beach* hit theaters, the movie star created his DiCaprio Foundation to focus on environmental causes. He helps now to fund several other environmental groups and acted in *Don't Look Up*, a tragicomedy about climate change that went over most viewers' heads.

We visitors to Koh Lipe grow hyperaware of our threat to water quality. Rules forbid us to flush any toilet tissue. We deposit the soiled paper in a wicker bin, as we did in Troncones, Mexico, during a yoga retreat there in 2022. We use a handheld bidet at Serenity Beach Resort for cleansing. All week we sleep in the same sheets. Quasi-military troops stalk the beaches and preach a green gospel—scolding, penalizing, apprehending flagrant offenders. But the sheer mass of humanity populating these beaches defies the most benevolent of ecological intentions.

Groups of women on the island display a pasty face paint. These are Burmese immigrants who ceremonially make the paint from thanaka trees. They grind and mix bark, wood, roots, and water in slate basins. The paste imparts an eerie appearance to their beings. The bleaching cream, handed down for two millennia, functions as makeup, sunscreen, and cultural marker. The environment, again, shapes them; it upholds their beauty and well-being. Thanaka kills acne and fungus, the Burmese claim, helping to heal and sustain their skin throughout this steamy region.

Compare the makeup first-world women wear. Perceiving cameras ever at the ready, many self-conscious Westerners dress for watchers who are inclined to post snaps to social media. Everyone wants to see and be seen, especially in tropical vacation hotspots.

The Wat Hantalay Temple beckons us in our rambles, a monastery on a sidehill, a poor sort by Thai standards, as poor as the landlocked Lawoi have become. At an entry gate we bump into a collection box, unstaffed and open to passersby. That honor-bright device has much to recommend it over the long-handled baskets reached down aisles by settler-colonist Puritans.

We drop 150 Thai baht into the collection box and enter. No one is about. We approach a plywood platform. Where effigies of a tortured Christ might be, a gold Buddha beams. On one side falls a Buddhist banner. Opposite it, a spider and its web anchor a Thai flag. A cross-legged monk facing away from the gold Buddha greets us silently with his eyes. Reed and I remove our shoes, ascend the stage or platform, and sit. A cat proves skittish when Reed extends a hand.

Karen approaches but does not ascend the shrine and does not enter. She has read that women's bare knees make for a kind of violation here. Unlike most Christian faiths, Buddhism offers ordination to women. Buddhist nuns, or bhikkhuni, while they are living in their monastic communities like the monks, choose to remain celibate and never marry. The Buddha allegedly said it is not possible otherwise to make good as a holy person. Our monk, in loose orange string pants and a sash, raises a hand and a glance when he leaves the stage.

We keep walking up the hill and over. Our map tells us we will find a restaurant named Cliff Beach at a site called Sunrise Beach. The place where we sleep is Sunset Beach. Mundane names obviously spun toward vacationer tastes. Everyone wants to be on a beach or close to one.

Even the Lawoi do. Their quaint local label, "sea gypsies," takes an ironic shape when one considers how they have been sequestered inland. Curbed by a centripetal force, they have been marginalized to the least pricey environs on the island. Neoliberal capitalism decides the lifeways of these project-affected people. At one time a nomadic tribe of sailors in Thailand, these former nomads no longer can wander. Their depreciation is an instance of a business externality: a cost incurred by a producer which the producer, in this case the tourist industry, never has to absorb or pay for. We reach steep Sunrise Beach and rattle down a sheer flight of stairs, in the process passing an unnamed bistro-bar to discover Cliff Beach at the waterside.

The barkeep is playing Hindi music intermingled with wailing prayers. We are his only patrons. He stiffens when he sees us with our swim gear. Without a word he enters the water and shoves logs off the beach to bare a patch of sand. He propels the logs to a neighboring beach. We are learning it's all about beaches here. Visits are valueless in the absence of water and sand.

We order beverages and go to the beach. Gingerly we enter the water to rinse the sweat and cool off. What we see there is the only thing to scare us in our time in Thailand. A snake looks to be coming for Karen, causing her to back-paddle fast. It is a banded sea krait, whether being territorial or rising for air. Herpetologists claim its venom has ten times the potency of a rattlesnake's. Kipling wrote from India that the venom of terrestrial kraits is as powerful as that of a king cobra. In his novel *The 8th Confession*, James Patterson has a serial murderer deploy kraits as murder weapons. Resort disinformation calls the snake's mouth too small to bite.

First my near-miss with a coral snake in Costa Rica ten years ago, now this toxic ribbon of a reptile that feeds on moray eels. Like morays and kraits, sea urchins pose a calculable risk to swimmers. We dare not drop our feet to the ocean floor without looking first wherever we swim.

Travel as we do it is not for the effete. We try to beat feet off the beaten path. We run out to take in the local people and the species. The ubiquitous mosquitoes can carry dengue fever, an illness resulting in rashes, enduring headaches, fever in some, death in a few. The Hantalay Temple, our guidebook informs us, harbors "industrial-sized mosquitoes," bugs that drink the blood of monks and chance visitors like us. Mosquito larvae wriggle in a swamp the road runs through. My light shirt, worn to keep cool in the drip of this nonstop humidity, proves thin enough for the mosquitoes to sting right through. Swatting proves futile. Spray-on repellents fail.

At Serendipity Resort, pythons and iguanas gobbled up three kittens of a litter before employees could rescue the rest. The workers moved the babies inside the crawl space beneath the restaurant's floorboards. Now the mother cat eats with customers, her kittens secure beneath.

In nearby Indonesia, we hear, a twenty-three-foot reticulated python has eaten a middle-aged woman this week. She was gardening after dark a half mile from her home. Searchers found her flashlight and umbrella. Too sluggish to move, the python was soon discovered. Backward-slanting fangs hook its prey, which it squeezes to death and swallows head-first. Villagers killed the snake and found her packed like a sausage within. Would her clothing have digested? Strange question to ponder, but I do. The usual prey of Thai pythons is wild boars and monkeys. Smaller Burmese pythons have taken over the Everglades, some of them released by owners who grow weary of caring for them, others by travelers who smuggle them to sell.

We hoof it to the town center for our evening meals. We either mush the beach or take an inland route through jungle where workers live. Tonight, we dine at Papaya Mom—a space for sixty diners in the style of a barracks, an extensive tattered menu. One family on trencher tables near us is eating fast and pounding Chang beer, their gorged throats like the vocal sacs of frogs.

Across the lane, a cook has set up the equivalent of two food trucks, nothing more than grills on wheels. Their roofs stave off rain. Bullfrogs groan in the standing damp. Between a tree and one of his carts, a strung hammock helps him grab a nap when commerce goes slack. During the busiest tourist times, he spends the night. I wonder how he and his kind have stayed afloat since the pandemic throttled unsustainable tourist travel for more than two years.

Something draws us toward the Wat Hantalay Temple a second time. To get there we pass rain ponds, shuttered stores, trash piles, and swamps full of croaking frogs—peepers and bullfrogs alike. Tree-trimming machines at the storm-littered monastery screech to clear debris. Laborers chatter and climb. The storm last night was savage, its wreckage littering the streets.

We sit on the lip of a Buddha-ed platform and try to quiet our storm-tossed minds. Its curled plywood decking stands in stark contrast to the lacquered gates and marble floors in sanctuaries elsewhere in the nation. Two resident dogs welcome us. Most are a Chinese breed—brown fur, narrow hips, curled tails. Five more dogs trail a monk walking nearby. The offering boxes, our guidebook says, help to afford pet food. The same is true elsewhere. The Sangeh Monkey Forest in Bali went from six thousand tourist visits per month, which afford food for the sacred monkeys, to zero when the island banned all travelers due to the pandemic.

The monk, now sweeping leaf litter and water from the platform, meets my eyes. Shoes off, hat off, I try to meditate facing outward in lotus pose. The stark hierarchy afflicting island people focuses my contemplation. "Skeetoes," I hear him whisper. I open my eyes and smile. I've been shooing bugs unconsciously amid the babble of my mind. The monk sweeps around us.

At our favorite open-air restaurant, Ja Yao, we arrive early for some lunch. Most of the staff appear to be sexless. One waiter near us strips basil leaves from stalks. Then they rise, lift a water vessel, and bear it to the roadside. Our solemn waiter, facing the shrine before the restaurant, performs an upright bow. Then they fingertip-sprinkle the pathway that runs out front. The sprinkled liquid is known as lustral water. Somewhere a great monk has blessed it. The sprinkling may also be intended to appease a resident deity. Roads and paths are animated and worthy of a sacred drink. For old Romans, the resident god of hearth and home was Lares.

Are all Thai people reverent? Are reverent people more honest? Riding a motorbike-taxi on a steep and rutted road, we drop a wallet. We miss it only after we enter our bungalow and settle in. Frantic searching ensues. Within ten minutes, the driver comes back, returns the wallet and its contents of a thousand US dollars in Thai baht. Grateful near to tears, we reward him.

"What a world, what a world," the wicked witch mutters as she slumps to a puddle at the conclusion of *The Wizard of Oz*. Her dying cries must have signified she was incapable of accounting for an environment like Oz where such upright morality prevails. The Thai people around us seem so utterly caring that it would take a lifetime to begin to return their favors.

When I travel, it is not to escape the hordes. Or to build character. Or to claim bragging rights from having seen the world. My purpose is to fulfill the desires of my beloved. She craves travel. She favors blue water abroad. Her compass points toward the equator. She says, "I never feel more alive than when traveling in a foreign land." Travel is part of our tacit marital compact. As an attorney, she earns the surplus funds. When she wishes I travel with her abroad. I say yes.

She is a member of Gen X, often perceived to be directionless, that generation born after the baby boomers from the early 1960s to late 1970s. Her given name, Karen, has become a stand-in for white entitlement. "What a

Karen!" people exclaim on social media. Online videos by the dozens illustrate the name. A Wikipedia entry on that fraught topic spools five thousand words to sketch the scapegoating, the unfair and unfortunate cultural back-and-forth. My Karen's generation, like many aspiring others also in stereotype, often holds the view that they have not arrived in merit until they can afford the freedom to travel freely through geographical space.

Travel proves alluring because I have someone always agitating to go. Not only agitating, but keen to make the itineraries, book the flights and shuttles, evaluate the lodgings, and find the best sites for our treasured ecotourism. "My bags are packed" has become her ready catchphrase. Intrepid, I call her. Accommodating. I do my best to set aside a concern that we are practicing an unreflective neocolonialism, colonizing in fits and starts. I do my best to be present always.

* * *

In the island's center, rutted twisty roads weave through Lawoi lodgings. Taxis fast on errands storm past the dwellings built from thatch and corrugated tin. Stilts raise the dwellings against floods, tsunamis, and monsoon mud. The Lawoi gaze from pallets or from hammocks, from beds that invite rare cooling air beneath them. Dully they regard the taxis and the tourist blur. The nearby equator radiates heat. Their dogs dig burrows against high temperatures and steam.

Long ago a ruler deeded the Lawoi people this land. That deed, however, included no jobs or educations, no ready means of subsistence. A marine park surrounds them now. Outsiders in their midst have retrofitted precious motorbikes with seated box beds or sidecars, converting them commercially to become pickups, supply-haulers, taxis, and status markers.

Information about the Lawoi people proves scant and erratic. The original inhabitants of the island, they are the smallest ethnic group in southern Thailand. They might have originated in Burma, Borneo, Indonesia, or Malaysia. They overlap ethnically with the Moken. An inborn savvy helps them survive the frequent storms and interpret tides. Geographical determinism again appears to have favored them. Preternaturally, they foresaw the 2004 tsunami that devastated the Indian Ocean and the Andaman Sea. Dodging in time to higher ground, they lost none of their members.

They did lose prime waterfront parcels. Only a monopoly on longtail services that move tourists between the beach and offshore pontoons allows them to stay afloat today. Disruption brought about by tourist traffic intensifies distresses. In 2020, sovereignty activists "asked the government to pass the Ethnic Groups Protection Act" on Koh Lipe. The *Bangkok Post* reports that "the Department of National Parks, Wildlife and Plant Conservation is trying to reclaim part of the land occupied by local people and new investors." Amid such reclamation, the Department hopes to secure protections for Lawoi homes and restore some ways of life.

Guidebook publisher Lonely Planet has come around to criticize tourism's impact on the Lawoi people. Such criticism is a trifle ironic, given the historic tensions the publisher itself fermented. Founded in 1973 by UK couple Maureen and Tony Wheeler, Lonely Planet was compromised from the get-go. It was unable philosophically, that is, to sell books that spur tourist traffic and to preserve the pristine and wild allure of getaways like Koh Lipe.

Lonely Planet's recent about-face is a PR gambit. The company had come under fire for attracting unwanted backpackers to the so-called Banana Pancake Trail, that series of popular but geographically indefinite routes that Western tourists favor. For a different set of reasons, the Trade Union Congress of Britain, with the weight of its six million members, enacted a political boycott of Lonely Planet and caused the withdrawal of its guide to Burma in 2009.

The Wheelers sold a majority interest of their company in 2011 to BBC Worldwide for £42.1 million. That deal propelled them from "hippie backpackers to multimillionaires." As of 2016, the publishers employed six hundred staff and writers and had offices in seven major cities. During the pandemic, Lonely Planet closed offices and laid off hundreds. An instinct for public relations is leading them now to levy tough love for locations they used to plug.

The Lonely Planet webpage for Koh Lipe begins by lamenting its lost glamor: "Once a serene paradise, Ko Lipe is now a poster child for untamed development on Thailand's islands." (The poster-child analogy conjures photojournalist John Everingham's images of Lawoi children and the simple life they enjoyed in 1982.) The Lonely Planet page continues: "The centre of Ko Lipe has been transformed into an ever-expanding maze of hotels, restaurants, cafes, travel agencies and shops. The biggest losers have been the 700-strong community of *chow lair* . . . who sold it in the 1970s."

Sold it? Such claims add to the erratic data—the errata—about the Lawoi. No evidence of the role of travel promoters in the tribe's lost glamor is on offer. Nor does the Lonely Planet page admit specific blame for the numbing fate of the island that it used to tout. If the Lawoi sold any of their environs, they did so in the forcible way that Indigenous Americans sold theirs.

Cultural and legal challenges besiege these Indigenous Thai people. Videos show how their massive fish traps, the size and shape of igloos, bamboo-framed and sheathed in nylon netting, charm fish by dangling lures inside. The people haul, set, and lift traps from longtail boats. Tender-hearted tourists sometimes dive down to the traps and slice the nylon netting to liberate tricked fish. The Lawoi then need to weave stout wire strands to mend them. They fillet their catch and spread the slabs on boats or on the shore to parch, flies atop them often crawling.

In the new ecological ethos that governs Thailand, the system fines Indigenous people caught fishing in the parks or in protected areas without a permit. So-called blast-fishing gained them historical bad fame. Igniting dynamite underwater, they stunned the fish and made them easy to gather. Such offhand explosions blasted healthy coral reefs to rubble. Elsewhere in the Andaman Sea, forced relocations have limited their travel, fragmented their communities and culture. The people make their way today by ferrying tourists and by netting or spearing fish for tourist banquets. Too bad they cannot build casinos, like the US tribes have successfully done.

Demoted to sedentary lives, ensnared in webs of misinformation, the Lawoi used to be nomads of the sea. But tourism so far regulates the Thai economy that communication about the people has become propaganda, misinformation, unreliable lore. Tourism equaled propaganda from the start. The World Tourism Organization, before it joined the United Nations a century ago, went by the name of the International Union of Tourist Propaganda Associations.

Even Project Urak Lawoi, so promising on its face, has been press-ganged into English by the We Love Travel Guides Koh Lipe. Though the

Lawoi did not always have "a valid deed or title," the Project website notes, "it was not possible to implement the policy of moving people out of parkland." Outright evictions would have been too damaging to the image of Thailand Smile. Officials "strongly discouraged Urak Lawoi from their nomadic foraging." The pattern is familiar in North America, whose nomadic foraging Indigenous people were herded to reserves.

A refreshing neutral source of news about these disappearing minorities was the site assembled by John Everingham. That site is gone now. A photojournalist during the Vietnam War, he hails from Australia. He had lived unbeholden to tourist tangles in Thailand for more than forty years. He began his photo-rich weblog in 2016 to chronicle lost Lawoi lifeways. One recalls that *nostalgia* is rooted in Greek *nostos*, for a return home, and *algos*, for a painful state.

Due to his celebrity, Everingham was exempt from typical tourist internment, until 2021. A feature film revealed his love for the Lao woman Keo Sirisomphone and her rescue from the communist regime of Laos. He swam her to freedom beneath the Mekong River using scuba gear. Their son Ananda Everingham is recognized as an actor and a model today.

Some of John Everingham's photos for the weblog were taken of the people on Koh Lipe at Haad Chow Ley, the place-name he favors over Sunrise Beach. Other photos were taken on Rawai Beach in Phuket, the largest island in Thailand. Lawoi children frolic in the photos, middle-aged men heap clams in boats, and elders act out stories for the children after dark. Infiltrations from outside their region now have exacted a familiar toll on the Indigenous people.

Everingham has taken down his photos. His rationale must trace back to his new tourist enterprise. His sacrifice of art for commerce proves the almighty inescapabilty of the industry.

Sovereignty activists are trying to reclaim the role of art for cultural preservation. One Lawoi painter, hoping to reestablish some of the lost autonomy, has depicted people dancing in "a jinx-dispelling ritual." The jinx they reference is industrial tourism. In a twice-yearly ritual during the full moon, the people build a model boat to carry their misfortunes out to sea. By enacting that ritual, they aim to regain a measure of the independence they now lack.

Even though Thailand is the world's second-largest rice exporter, tourism earns it far more money. Demonstrators in 2008 discovered the best way to achieve short-term political ends was to occupy and shut down the airport, holding hostage the economic lifeblood of the nation.

*   *   *

No matter how left-behind they might seem today, the Lawoi are not relics on the march toward civilization. They will prove lasting and dynamic. Ebbs and flows will recur. Peripheral people like theirs get drawn into, or hover on, the edges of the urban landscape so that they may savor its abundance. Other far-flung Lawoi might have set out by design to flee from their own kind.

A generation or more later, if exploitation and indebtedness have confined them, they or their descendants can trickle back from the margins. They can relearn how to thrive. They can rejoin those who remember. We are lucky to have them still to preserve the ancient skills—the fishing, sailing, reading tides, so much more. They alone uphold the old attachments to natural forces. The identities of those whom we consider "the other" often prove more complex than we know. People can get lost in our modern world. Get lost, persevere, and display great resilience.

To travel is to sit upon an open cart as it advances, rarely casting glances backward as we go. Patches of light and shadow flash out and cry from either side, taking shape only afterward as people, lizards, vines, and trees. Space and time conflate. William Faulkner wrote about how easy it is to confuse time "with its mathematical progression, as the old do, to whom all the past is not a diminishing road but, instead, a huge meadow which no winter ever quite touches, divided from them now by the narrow bottleneck of the most recent decade of years."

Our wonder days are often unrecognizable when we are in their midst. We will recall the silicone shampoo bottle chewed by our nocturnal rat as part of a high time. Not "the gnawing pestilential rat" seen by Anne Sexton, ours will inhabit only its glossy burgundy fur. The pint of sweat leaked from my pores in an hour's hike-time will cleanse my memory forever. The shock of the sea krait surfacing between us will return as heroic endeavor, happenstance reincarnated as deliberation. Our stable structures often seethe within. Travel itself is the relinquishing of consciousness to time, a refusal to grow blemished. It is a hope we might remain forever new.

People make great claims for sojourns, even when surrendering awareness to itinerary. We soldier through some vacays to keep pace with calendar dates. If it's Tuesday, it must be Rome, the language of the old joke goes. Sightseeing can be an empty undertaking to suspend time, freeze it, fill old-school photo albums or social media pages with glossy shots. If, as writer Rick Steves says, only 4 percent of the world chooses to afford international leisure travel, then the number of those who take lengthy trips at a laidback pace, unlike we can afford, is minuscule indeed.

My lifelong habit of focusing on travel's downsides must be managed if I am to treasure time with my family. Focusing on pollution, sea rise, or tourism-marginalized Indigenous folks will make me a bad companion. Living splendor will grow threadbare. I will risk resembling A. A. Milne's character Eeyore from *Winnie the Pooh*, whose catchphrase is "I knew it was too good to be true." Mr. Magoo, that cartoon doofus, continues to be cheerful as he blunders through the world, no matter how his failing eyesight might impede him. His catchphrase—"Oh, Magoo, you've done it again!"— shows him as one who can claim responsibility for his conduct.

The Buddhists have much to teach me on every score. An aspect of mindfulness, learned from the Reverend Zensho Roberson, whom I sometimes sit with, is to find the flow and enter it. Be in conscious inner harmony with whatever activity is undertaken. If the coveted flow does not always arrive ready-made, I can discover ways to create it, ex nihilo, in the here and now.

Several strategies can help invite the flow state. The first is to give technology a rest. Every resort has Wi-Fi, but I resist the lure, switch off phone, make it available for emergencies only. Find the internal pleasure buttons and press them—family, books, nature's futile beauty. The head-bowed tourist peering at a tiny screen is an archetype of purgatory in paradise.

Rather than brooding on the long-term consequences of tourist shocks around the ailing globe, I shall live in and for the present. Revel in the squidgy insects crept from underworld to be stepped on, the resident rat nibbling on the cracker wrappers after lights-out. Bless them all for the ways they ground me and mine. Thank the creepy-crawlies in the water and the land.

Counter inborn penchants to fret about Earth's future. Let low notions roll off the back. Relinquish hope that much of substance can be done for Indigenous cultures from my distance. Nor may any one of us, alone, impede the sixth extinction of other species that is bearing down so hard upon us. Economic and ecological barrages might meet with unforeseeable justice in the end. *De rien* ("You are welcome" in the French language) translates literally as "It is nothing."

In a fond fantasy, I will gain an ecstatic suspension of time and merge with eternity. If only for sixty seconds, I will rest myself in lotus pose, leave my husk of a body, and rise until my noggin knocks on whatever cloud or ceiling asserts itself and returns me. That would be a fine way to travel, an eternal merging that would gratify me both going up and coming down.

Thunderstorms slash in the latter part of our stay. Sheet and fork lightning combine to electrify the air. The weather changes and bares the shoulders of the monsoons. Rain cools the atmosphere. We no longer need our ceiling fan. Every bungalow has a private plunge pool inside a fenced enclosure. The privacy makes clothes optional. From our secret pool we can see the sea.

Karen, her long hair sleep-frazzled from the bed, recommends herself to the water. Both of us plunge in to rinse ourselves and wake. The water manages to be the ideal temperature for ablutions, an antique Latin construction that signifies "a ceremonial act of washing the sacred containers." She is the sacred container, the vessel essential. No peeping from the husk of safety grown thick after the loss of Braden would otherwise be possible for me. Braden's brother Reed takes a slo-mo video of raindrops bouncing on his plunge pool. And I am glad to see him honor this wet weather rather than lament it, glad to see him keenly share our Thailand time.

Our resort employs a lot of people. In the office, which is an open-air affair above the restaurant on the hill, several employees have doffed their flip-flops on the walkway outside. Behind computer screens they beam as I approach. My errand is to hand over our order forms for breakfast. On each form we are asked to specify what we want to eat and the time to have it delivered. Deliveries are done barefoot on slick stairs, the great trays balanced shoulder-height.

The waiter rings the outer bell and awaits our call to enter. Inside, he kneels at our low table. Balancing the tray on table edge, he lifts bowls and beverages plastic-wrapped to shut out bugs. The breakfast salads for us vegetarians include tiny quail eggs. What keeps him and the others going so long and strong? Gratuities from patrons? An inborn desire to please? Hope for advancement? Or a tacit recognition that their fortunes are more blessed than many others?

Up and downhill from restaurant to bungalows, waiters tread the twisty stairs above the jungle floor. Beneath them, great creatures slink unseen. A horned striped lizard with red head. Massive black-and-yellow millipedes. The rat whose eyes reflect from rafter shadows. Geckos that chirp and twitter so shrilly they stymie sleep. Four-inch grasshoppers at the bottom of the food chain, deep-fried in markets beside crickets and other bugs, twenty grams of protein per.

In our privileged lives, we journey above the hidden circumstances of our destinations. Monsoons bathe us. Mosquitoes sing. Landings below each set of stairs give walkers opportunity to pause in Serendipity, to catch breath and gain perspective. Step a few more stair treads down; level the head to the falling water puddled on the landing. Watch raindrops bounce and roll like ball bearings across each living puddle before they merge, return, and become part of the whole.

17

Island Time

If you try, you will find me, where the sky meets the sea.
Here am I, your special island. Come to me, come to me.
—"BALI HA'I," FROM *SOUTH PACIFIC*

What is it about islands that attracts the well-heeled traveler? It may be their remoteness. On far-flung island locales, few of society's pressures encroach. Long checkout lines in grocery stores, jams on freeways, red eyes and broken teeth lofting signs at traffic lights—such mainland stressors do not trouble island tourists often. Islands might entice by sheer abundance of water. Vast expanses of moving blue prove restful to the eye. Sea waves, lapping and receding, echo the systole and diastole of hearts at rest. In blue latitudes the sun, that cosmic clockwork, substitutes for digital and electric timepieces that instruct us when to jump. Islands might prove seductive also due to what it costs to get there. Not costs as gauged by extra dollars alone—costs, rather, incurred in transit and in time. If e-commerce costs consumers less and delivers faster, everyone might cherish island sojourns more than other places for the travel time it takes to gain them.

Whatever it is about island life, my family and I are following the French to Tahiti while we can. We are mindful of the climate changes erasing some of the low-lying lands of Oceania. That region, named Oceanica in 1832, includes our own sprawling piece, Polynesia. Its regions lure sun-starved northerners. We will tour four isles on our visit. In George Orwell's novel

1984, the word Oceania describes one of three superstates to which the Party confines the people.

First-world wanderers decline to be confined. Confinement is akin to incarceration. We tourists flit from place to place like birds of passage. Not like snowbirds—those human fowl that inhabit the same drear northerly and southerly sites as seasons change. No, we are more like passerines, spreading seeds that cling to our feet and sprout. Making change, wherever we go.

Malena Ernman, mother of Greta Thunberg, cowrote a book that records her daughter's evolution as a leading climate activist. "Everyone wants to be successful," the authors observe, "and nothing conveys success and prosperity better than luxury, abundance and travel, travel, travel."

ON TAHITI

Our first port of call is Pape'ete, the capital of French Polynesia, on the northwest coast of Tahiti. The name Pape'ete takes the Tahitian enunciation of four syllables, elevating the first "e" powerfully, like the English interjection *eh*. Artist Paul Gauguin looms large among noteworthy former inhabitants of the town. His paintings of carefree Tahitian maidens, some of them topless and bearing fruit baskets, entice tourist travelers still today. Tahiti entices writers, too. Its islands rank among the priciest and most exclusive of global destinations. Foods must be flown or boated in from afar to gratify discriminating palates. Nor may potable water be assumed. Bottled water is the surest and the safest choice, offered for a price at every meal, the bottles too often discarded and adding plastics pollution to the water and the air.

Tahiti is the largest of the 118 islands in the French Polynesian archipelago. When Gauguin was tenant, selling paintings here and there, mostly struggling, he was suffering from syphilis, a woe he allegedly contracted from a Paris prostitute. Perpetuating a long colonial pattern, he shared his incurable illness with island women and underage lover-girls. To try to heal himself, he injected the arsenic compound salvarsan. Tahiti is the busiest isle, a hub for travel to the outer islands, a stopping-spot for cruise ships.

For a century overtourism has afflicted Pape'ete. James Norman Hall, who lived on Tahiti most of his adult life, got grouchy about the throngs in 1929. Hall is best known for coauthoring the celebrated Bounty trilogy with Charles Nordhoff, which includes *Mutiny on the Bounty* in 1932. In that book, Fletcher Christian's conquest of the maiden Mauatua whetted the appetites of readers who hungered for a sensuous celebration within an island cornucopia. In an unpublished letter to Frank Pratt on Whidbey Island in Washington State, Hall wrote:

> We have had more than the usual allotment of tourists the past six months, and for the most part tourists of the objectionable sort, a noisy, hard-drinking lot. One of them at least was requested by the French authorities to leave the island. I'm afraid that I shall have to go on to the island I told you about, Mangareva, before many years. I do love this island, but it is being so rapidly spoiled that there will be no living here five years hence if changes go on at this rate.

The Hall family, self-rusticated eleven miles from town, commuted to Pape'ete for supplies.

When I say we are following the French, I mean we are crowding into planes, boats, and restaurants alongside them. We Anglos are once again minorities in our travels. Karen and I have a smattering of French, enough to get along, enough to bluff it when we need to. In their long and carbon-intensive hegira, the French people travel from Paris to Los Angeles to Tahiti. The first leg of their trip takes thirteen hours, the second leg another eight. There's talk now of a direct flight in the works. At the present time in airline history, the longest nonstop flight by duration appears to be eighteen hours and fifty minutes, from New York's JFK to Singapore.

Before we shuttle back to the airport to board another jet and embed ourselves in our second island, we overnight at Hotel Intercontinental in Pape'ete. The property shows off a replete breakfast buffet, an infinity pool, a swim-up bar, and a salt lagoon that hosts captive sea urchins. The wealth on display here would make my Danish ancestors uneasy. Those ancestors, as common as old shoes, disclaimed conspicuous displays. Paintings in the style of Monsieur Gauguin splash the walls of our hotel rooms. We come to call those kitschy reprints Fauxguin art.

The blood of my ancestors, diluted but still flowing in my veins, prompts me to add up all the hundreds of unhoused people our hotel stay might shelter in my hometown, the carrots and potatoes that could be air-dropped to feed wallabies in fire-ravaged regions of Australia, the campaigns we could subsidize to unseat hidebound legislators in the American South. Scenes from black-and-white films by Ingmar Bergman compound my brown study. His winter-addled landscapes. His Lutherans who have never been instructed how to suffer fun.

If marriage like politics is the art of compromise, how difficult could it be to accompany a hardworking spouse to live out her dreams in the southern Pacific's sunny reaches and escort her for three weeks? On opposite shoulders in vintage movies and cartoons, a dark and a white angel perch. One angel hisses out a series of doubts, while the other angel lisps encouragements into the witless listener's ear. Unable to hark to angels, I busy myself by trying to decide which attitude to heed, how much hair to let down, and the right ways to thrive in a warming world.

BATTENING ON PINK SAND

The islet where we land in Tikehau is named Tuherahera. It has the only resident airstrip and two small markets, both shadowy and flyblown. We shuttle to the boat dock in a minivan. Greeters drape gardenia leis around our necks, a single bloom behind one ear. After much ado, we board a water taxi and roar past tiny islets. Islets so low a stout wave might flush them clean away, wash them out to sea. Wrongly called islands in the promos, these glorified sand spits are in fact geological atolls. One beach displays pink sand. We make a note to paddle kayaks there.

The boat ride to Tikehau is short. The check-in office lies right at the dock. Overwater bungalows—OWB in promos, the most expensive lodgings—tower architecturally as if on stilts, a structural hedge against rogue waves and rising seas. In our bungalow set back from the water on a sandy expanse, the AC is blowing to offset a wilting humidity. The porter leaves our bags outside the door. In this Pearl Beach Resort, we will be detainees for every meal for a week.

The tiny islet takes twenty minutes to walk around. From the tops of cone-bearing trees, white terns burr, their melodious name *Gygis alba*. Everything as far as we can see is white. The sun that beats without ceasing, the gardenias that scent the air, the beaches of granules chipped or tide-scoured from coral, the coral grains excreted by parrotfish. Dig beneath the sand, and spines of once-live coral show black. Atolls rise from undersea. Coral grows on the lips of volcanic fissures. Some of the coral dies and traps sand. Grasses, bushes, and spindly trees sprout and take hold. In the last stage, we hungry Homo sapiens close in, supplanting geological succession with civilizational succession, replicating global-scale conditions that have created the Anthropocene.

A channel inside the islet has been dredged. A dredging barge and a shipping dock are harbored within the channel, stashed really, out of public view. Golf carts creep paved paths like so many laden worker ants on task. They haul supplies to restaurants and bungalows inside. They haul trash outside to wooden pallets in the channel. On the islet's public side, boardwalks rumble out to the OWBs. A whiff of sewage wafts up often, robust enough in spots to sting the eyes. Each resort treats its own sewage and returns it to sea as "grey water." Bonefish and parrotfish, drawn by handouts in the day, by dock lights at night, twine alongside black-tipped reef sharks.

Jacques Cousteau, leading a research group to Tikehau in 1987, found it to have the most fish in the world, *le plus poissonneux du monde*. Equatorial currents run fast between its islets. So fast that swimming can seem like ripping down a river. Tidal currents thermoregulating the water cool and refresh it. Swimming near Tikehau is like flying, our finned feet like wings. The fearless fish would willingly feed from our hands, if we were careless enough to habituate them.

Artists visualize a peaceable kingdom to be like this. Around our bodies, three-inch reef shark pups take refuge from the current. They crowd around us and never nip. Underwater we spy octopuses, spiny lobsters, skates and rays, coral mounds awash with angels and clowns—fish so named for imaginary wings and paint. Channels in nonstop motion between islets propel us. The churning current borrows us, bears us, carries us as if toward some unknowable goal. The saline warmth of the water makes us nimble. We feel weightless, little need to stroke or kick.

In the afternoon we load kayaks with snacks and paddles. We are headed for the pink beach. Its pink derives from the finely ground debris of corals and crustaceans. One has to squint to see it as pink, like the influencer marketers do, those who generate promotional content. Comic artist Gary Trudeau characterizes their work as "toxic narcissism." As if to prove his point, a couple in nuptial white is dancing in the shadows of this late afternoon. Below them, a videographer animates from crouching to standing to crouching again to capture fresh angles. Seabirds hover and plunge a quarter mile off the islet, their clamor out of earshot far away.

We haul the boats ashore on a pinkish spit and take a walk. Grains abrade our heels and toes. From a house beneath pines, a resident rooster heads our way, territorial and alert, an avian guardian of this bleached domain. The animal pecks at flotsam that washes up on shore.

The day is about to end. The sun turns red. Water that had been a cobalt blue goes silver. The sand grows red. To gain a sight of the setting sun's possible green flash, we hop back in our kayaks and paddle fast to carry us past a distant islet that blocks the tumbling sun.

We have traveled far to see these places firsthand. Some of them might soon be gone forever. Sea rise is taking its toll. The coral, due to acidification, is blanching in spots. Some travel commentators might name our interests doom tourism or last-chance tourism. Those phrases apply as well to natural wonders as they do to afflicted human cultures around the globe.

The Marshallese people northwest of Tikehau suffer from sea rise, cyclones, calamitous drought, bleached reefs, and crashing fisheries. Some in that archipelago live mere feet above sea. Low islets and coral banks in Tikehau "will very likely disappear in the next 50 to 100 years, thanks to their inability to keep pace with a warming ocean," a writer for the *New York Times* asserts. Marine biologists forecast sea surges here to rise two to four feet by century's end.

If the future bears them out, if all the dire projections come true, how much blame does tourist travel merit? The answer ties to the questions that agitate public opinion about climate science itself. Every one of us needs to decide how far our civilization's carbon discharges are contributing to climate warming. In short, how much our industrial species is altering the globe.

We did not have to travel to French Polynesia to brood on climate refugees. In southern Louisiana, outside New Orleans near where we have family, an entire community of Indigenous people is being resettled to safer ground with the help of a $48 million federal grant. Some Isle de Jean Charles residents belong to the Biloxi-Chitimacha-Choctaw Tribe, others to the Houma Nation. They are the first climate refugees in the United States. Futile lawsuits were filed to hold oil and gas companies responsible for the destructive erosion. An area of land the size of a football field in their homeland is washing away every hour. New blows keep coming. In 2020, it was Hurricane Laura, the worst storm to hit the state in a century. In 2021, it was Hurricane Ida.

A loss of ancestral land always precipitates a loss of heritage. Right there the greatest kinds of conflicts live. Secretary-General António Guterres of the United Nations, at Columbia University on December 2, 2020, said, "Making peace with nature is the defining task of the twenty-first century." To make peace with nature also means to treat with justice those who live the closest to it, those most in need of refuge, as formerly stable climates undergo great change.

* * *

Our Son Reed again has traveled with Karen and me. Younger son Chase, still suffering from his car wreck and brain injury, stays home. On this budget vacation, the three of us share a bungalow. The love Karen and I feel for one another goes on hold. When Reed is sunning or swimming, we share a worry he might return. And so, we buy time alone at night outside.

We take towels and say, in truth, that we are going skinny-dipping. We barefoot the paved paths to the shipping channel at the far part of the island. The tropical night is warm. The sea laps the sands, pine trees screen the moon and stars, and the landscape no longer has any color. Everything has turned gray. We spread our towels on the sand, shed our clothes, and yield to the taste of eternal life that lovers can confer on one another. We slip into the sea as if it were a grand immersion tank. Dredge spoils in the channel break the waves. The salty water buoys us.

In the moonlight we break flesh with one another. No one may hear us

ISLAND TIME   229

singing out or see the scattered leavings of our clothes upon the sand. Some tourists like to venture to tropical climates to reach outside themselves, to carry indoor habits out of doors and savor island time.

Next day, we rent bikes and water-taxi them to Tuherahera, where our little plane touched down. We buy a few groceries, place them in a rickety bike basket, and pedal ourselves around the entire islet. The bikes are rusty, the chains dry, the remote path circling the airstrip rocky, the risk of blowout great. We pass a bungalow whose walls are made of coral: an instance of how resourceful these Indigenous people are. The coral's bony corrugations look like cheese graters.

Abundant palm trees shade the yard. Coconuts continue as a useful food and unit of exchange, but wild rats relish them as well. Rats will scale the trunks, gnaw the husks, lap the milk, and eat the meat. Aluminum strips, in populous spots, band the trunks to baffle rat traffic. Their nails can get no purchase on those slick strips. Only five atolls in the entire Polynesian chain remain free of rats since their arrival with Europeans. The whole chain is open to invasion. Prior to human contact, these atolls generated evolutionary changes. They were workshops like the Galapagos for biodiversity. Rats today, those proxies of human civilization, decimate species of ground-nesting native birds as well—albatrosses, petrels, shearwaters, and unguarded others.

Burrowing and nocturnal rats seldom trouble tourists. We have no baseline view to draw upon. Nor are we sojourning abroad to census wildlife. We travel far to lounge, swim, sun, and make love. The few groceries we tote back from Tuherahera last us no more than a single meal, and so we join fellow visitors by the clock and make our way to the Pearl Beach restaurant.

The menu is lavish, the all-you-can-eat breakfast buffet a good way to start the day. The foods are those that French folks favor: baguettes, croissants, *confiture, fruits fraise, figues et dates sechees, pain au chocolat, des oeufs*. The supper menu one evening features *le poisson du jour lorsque*, fresh-caught fish of the day. From our several sojourns in France, we know how the French prefer to serve their fish—heads, fins, and tails intact. We diners skin and bone our own before we eat. Eyes glazed, skin crinkled, our orders of fresh fish arrive. One nearby French diner must have missed his nation's culinary memo. He throws a tactful fit when his whole fish arrives. He sends the waiter scurrying away to redeliver it discreetly as a mound of flesh.

WRITING POLYNESIA

Many books have "nurtured collective European fantasies that Tahiti was a hotbed of unbridled erotic pleasure," wrote Sylvie Largeaud-Ortega, of the University of French Polynesia. Some of our firsthand experiences confirm that stereotype. Robert Louis Stevenson, Somerset Maugham, and Jack London gained inspiration here. In 1846, Herman Melville penned the novel *Typee: A Peep at Polynesian Life*. In that book the sailor Tom, "Tommo" in the Indigenous enunciation, jumps ship and lives four months among the locals, besotted by the lovely Fayaway. Melville himself absconded from the whaler *Acushnet* in 1842 and lived among the islanders. Opinions split about how much firsthand experience informs his first novel, how autobiographical it is.

My hope is that the talented Melville found his own fond Fayaway in the month of island life he spent. We will never know, though. Historical lives are often sanitized. Writers in earlier centuries, for instance, scrubbed how ship captains allowed Polynesian women to be abducted and kept as sex slaves. The exploitation of those women, from Captain Cook's 1769 tour to today, makes fantasy fodder for key groups of readers and tourists alike. The allure of ready sex tourism sharpens certain first-world desires to touch down in tropical ports of call like Tahiti.

Melville chanced a scandal when he wrote about a shipboard visit made by Marquesan maidens. His sailors yielded "to every species of riot and debauchery. Not the feeblest barrier was interposed between the unholy passions of the crew and their unlimited gratification." Melville's editor saw fit to jettison those sentences as too steamy for his Victorian readers.

A century after Melville, the play and movie *South Pacific* gave the gaze to a single male. In James Michener's ethnocentric tale "Fo' Dolla," from *Tales of the South Pacific*, Lieutenant Joe Cable gapes at local women. He sees them "walking about with no clothes on above their hips." He gets aroused. "Their breasts disturbed him mightily, and when one girl clutched anew at a melon, throwing her gingham sarong awry, he both blushed and found himself unable . . . or unwilling . . . to look away." Cable's "nubile adolescents appear in unbelievable profusion."

The comeliest maids are white-smocked and isolated in a nunnery. Nuns prevent GIs from assailing them. GI Joe Cable, a century after Melville, gains his own Fayaway. Her name is Liat. Her isolated island, Bali Ha'i, is approachable only by officers in the Michener fiction.

Much like today's elite tourist resorts, Bali Ha'i is set aside for those of most prestige, who can shell out to gratify their dreams. In Central America, Thailand, and Polynesia, well-off tourist Tommos hire male and female Fayaways to satiate their erotic whims. Amid the myriad species of tourist travel, sex tourism casts long shadows. Its veiled market strengthens claims for tourism as the planet's largest trade. Neither in Victorian times nor in our own can one track sex tourism freely. Margaret Mead might have inspired Michener. Her 1928 book *Coming of Age in Samoa* was subtitled *A Psychological Study of Primitive Youth for Western Civilization*. Mead believed that sexually active adolescent girls in Samoa helped to loosen ruinous social constraints. Those girls filled their culture with pleasure and drained it of suffering and pain.

James Michener as a naval historian traveled the South Pacific during World War II. One may credit his male imagination for a Bali Ha'i in our mythology—an island liberated from sexual restraint. Michener has Liat's money-grubbing mother, Bloody Mary, offer her daughter to Lt. Joseph Cable. Michener consigns the blood-blame to Mary rather than to the American man. It is a scene straight out of harlequin pulp where the smitten Cable strips Liat of her white smock and her virginity. After he has had his way, he uses her smock to wipe up the blood.

Back in Tikehau, commerce has supplanted sex. Black pearls, for sale everywhere we turn, are the signature prizes of these islands. Karen eyes a strand at a gift shop. Its asking price is $38K. Just in time, we need to leave for our next island venture. We pack our bags, water-taxi back to Tuherahera, and stretch out on the stone floor in the open-air hangar for two hours. Then we board a nineteen-seat Beechcraft. Once we are aloft, the island of Rangiroa ranges below us. Karen adds that blue-water item to her bucket list. Lifeblood and the flooding lust for travel, if planetary pandemics are kept in check, will allow her to schedule a return one day.

ROUGHING IT ON BORA BORA

We arrive at the Bora Bora airport after dark. The wince of sewage again fills the air, but rescue is nearby. A trio of crisp uniforms is greeting us and handing us cool drinks. Then they conduct us three, the only passengers, aboard the grand catamaran for the Conrad Bora Bora Nui resort. We motor off to Moto Toopua, the site in Bora Bora where our five-star lodging lies.

The moon stalks the water. The Southern Cross comes into view, a constellation visible at last, one of Karen's travel ambitions. Songwriter Stephen Stills wrote, "When you see the Southern Cross for the first time / You understand why you came this way / Because the truth you might be running from is so small / But it's as big as the promise, the promise of a coming day." What his song lacks in lyrical allure, it compensates for in earworm harmonies. Like the Roman senator Seneca two millennia before him, Stephen Stills positions travel as escapism.

Our French hostess on the boat, Ambrosina, aka Amber, earned her degree in hospitality. She boasts how Kim Kardashian and her family boarded this boat before us. A writer for *Paper* magazine found the overexposed celebrity shines like "a beautiful anime character come to life."

Suddenly, illumined by the moonlight, the signature twin peaks of Bora Bora vault into view. Mounts Pahia and Otemanu mark the extinct volcano that formed this island seven million years ago. Those jagged peaks qualify this old atoll as an island. Peaks that will never erode out to sea in one of the region's cyclones, never be overwhelmed by wave rise and storm surge.

Their height and remoteness and picture-postcard beauty ensure its continuation, unlike either the Turneffe Atoll in Belize, where we visited during a windstorm, or the tiny isle of Tikehau we just left. From the air, this atoll is a vast lagoon that displays huge mountains at its apex. It lies, we realize, precisely midway between Chile to the east and Australia to the west.

Amber loads us and our bags in a golf cart, the terrestrial favorite for traversing islands. On route to our bungalow via intricate cart paths, she points out the many amenities: unlocked bikes for all to use, several restaurants, a workout facility, and an infinity pool. The boardwalks range a mile around this vast property, boardwalks of local hardwood a long time growing.

Amber unlocks our bungalow. A sweep of her arm becharms the mirrored walls, the see-through minibar packed with booze and food, the master king bed garlanded by tropical blooms.

All of it lords over a deck that features a private freshwater plunge pool and a hammock suspended above the ever-roving Pacific. That hammock resembles a trampoline—a tramp meant for lounging, stargazing, and inviting sea breezes to play beneath it. Underwater lights show how green the sea can be. Taking her leave, Amber bends a knee, scrapes a toe, and wishes us good sleep. We will eavesdrop all night upon the wave-slosh, punctuated by occasional bird cries.

After sunrise, various watercraft from the resort headquarters nearby begin to come and go. Jets descend to the airport several miles away. Travelers of restless conscience used to have the option of adding carbon offsets when they scheduled trips abroad, an option offered by travel companies like Expedia and Travelocity. It was like tithing. One checked a box, added voluntary dollars, and felt as if flying were blame-free. Such contributions were meant to offset the CO_2 emissions that result from airline travel—the damage those emissions enact upon the planet.

The extra money funded sustainability projects, but I always wondered which and where. Carbon-offsetting became an act of faith, a tax, a duty. One needed to credit the integrity of business and industry to settle those funds upon deserving projects. The tithing obligation has shifted to the airlines today. A United Nations agreement that grew from the Montreal Protocol of 2018 is called the Carbon Offsetting and Reduction Scheme for International Aviation.

Our Bora Bora resort limits opportunities for excursions. The sprawling self-containment of the campus undercuts the foremost reasons why we travel—to gain independent access to wild environs. We try snorkeling underneath the bungalows, but their construction has trashed the reef. Here and there on the silted seafloor, we come upon wire contraptions that look like cages. They prove to be artificial reefs fabricated to grow coral. Most coral species broadcast-spawn. Their larvae float freely and attach to rocks or to the bony corpses of their own kind.

Overwater bungalow construction, the spoor of negligent civilization, devastates the selfsame coral that island travelers venture abroad to enjoy. The fringe of coral reefs surrounding islands is also the only natural object to stave off rising seas. It is one of the vulgar ironies at the core of tourist travel, the activity of loving a geography or an environment to death. If nonhunters find it hard to fathom how hunters can claim to love their prey, tourists likewise often misconstrue how the fulfillment of their desires can result in the step-by-step extinction of the landscapes and seascapes that give them most joy. Coral grows slowly, NOAA says, adding only fractions of centimeters yearly. As many as ten thousand years are needed to form a reef.

High atop a hill on the resort grounds, we walk to view a chapel and luxury spa. The path is paved and steep, reserved for golf carts toting customers to spa. Our bikes are not allowed. On our sweaty walk, one cart overtakes us on its way uphill and slows to pass. Pretty woman Julia Roberts smiles within it. She is heading for an indulgence. The spa is bustling, the church empty of customers, its only tenants four boxes of new air conditioners. The old church coolers had rusted out in the salty air. Few people must come to these islands with intentions to worship.

We turn a corner and gasp to see the extinct volcanic peaks rise across the lagoon. The sight is more like a movie than like life. The views here, as the saying goes, are to die for.

Polynesia's humidity conjures its lush abundance, fecundity, and evolutionary innovation in the growth of plants and flowers. Bananas bunch out from a tree whose leaves spread broad as doors. At the center of each bunch, a purple inflorescence bulges, a flower spike that dangles at the same angle as a phallus, inviting us to view the contours of that common fruit anew.

The scents on these islands are intense, the vanilla like no other. Tahitian gardenia or tiaré flowers are woven into fragrant blossomed garlands, like leis, or pressed to make an oil and dabbed on as a musk perfume. The high cost of processing Tahitian gardenia, like the cost of Polynesia itself, excludes its use in all but niche perfumes. It is made when tight tiaré blossoms are infused in coconut oil for days. A flower behind the right ear signifies romantic availability.

At home we fact-check Amber's claim about the Kardashians. Sure enough, a magazine article mentions the TV show *Keeping up with the Kardashians*—a fit slogan for certain patrons of such resorts. "While the entire family stayed in Tahiti's signature overwater bungalows," the 2011 article enthused, "Kris and Bruce Jenner and Kim Kardashian and Kris Humphries enjoyed Hilton Bora Bora Nui Resort & Spa's two $5,000-a-night Presidential villas, the only two-story overwater villas in French Polynesia." Such rapt reportage rattles my misgivings anew.

As one who shuns TV, I find the title revelatory—*Keeping up with the Kardashians.* Some tourists must feel a flush of pride to affiliate with megacelebrities and walk the same paths they walked. My stupefied white angel leans and asks in my ear: how is it we find ourselves following the Kardashians? My darker angel rises on tiptoe and hisses in the other ear that it's gratifying on occasion to toss off caution and spend with lavish abandon.

AN ALTERNATIVE TO RESORTS

Alluring spots like Bora Bora prove hard to get to. Being a guest costs plenty, both in cash and CO_2. For certain kinds of tourists and investors, a solution is available by the name of seasteading. On the face of it, seasteading resembles homesteading, but for well-heeled people who mistrust governments.

When the West was wild, the 1862 Homestead Act gave land away. Much of that land, history tells us, was wrested from Indigenous people. In a similar spirit, but without the blunt genocide, the Seasteading Institute urges comers to "reimagine civilization." The website assures investors that islands may be manufactured and tethered inside waters no one owns. The tethers will allow the seasteads to buck rough weather, including cyclones, and avoid the rigors of sea rise. In 2017, ministers in Tahiti endorsed a memorandum of understanding, or MOU. That MOU allowed a tax-free floating city to be sited in the Atimaono Lagoon far to the south on the island of Tahiti, on the condition that the project could muster funding and get timely underway.

One brain behind the notion is former Google engineer Patri Friedman. He is classed as an anarcho-capitalist and a libertarian. His Seasteading Institute requires buy-in. Investors may "exit state reach." They help fund intentional communities designed for abiding in open seas. They may address "rising sea levels, overpopulation, poor governance, and more. . . ." Those ellipses at the sentence end invite investors' rich imaginations to fill in the blanks.

Friedman has the support of PayPal founder and billionaire Peter Thiel. He is another libertarian. Thiel supports Donald Trump and by 2022 had become one of the Republican Party's largest donors. Their seasteads can "feed the hungry, clean the atmosphere, cure the sick, and enrich the poor," the site says. If it all sounds a little too much like the technocratic rebirth of Christ, an open mind is key to taking a good look at the technological proposal. Why Tahiti? The waters are calm, the labor cheap. The international tourist presence and energy is abundant. Visitors might create precious PR for the enterprise. Interested travelers who cannot commit to seasteading full-time might favor periodic vacations on a floating Club Med.

Wouldn't it be nice to allow the waves to lull you to sleep every night? To see the Pacific stretching out all around, not just out from terra firma where you are confined? Sue Joerger harbored such dreams when she took up residence on a sailboat twenty years ago on Shilshole Bay in Seattle. Now she has grown weary of "the conversion of a nice old neighborhood into junky condos and the Port of Seattle constantly raising our moorage rates 2–4% per year."

Seastead promoters aim to excite ideological investors to envision a future accountable to fewer of such pricey forces than their landbound brethren are. Promoters of these mobile fantasy islands, it is tempting to say, have a covert eye trained on the travel trade. If too few investors choose to live full-time in floating custody on the water, others might invest in time-shares there. The Seasteading Institute website, resembling a kind of crowdfunding for the wealthy, displays a bright-red "Donate" tab top right. Why anyone would choose to donate might rightly mystify.

The MOU with Tahiti soon ran into choppy waters. Locals worried that the planned community will contribute little or nothing to the economy. That it will leak sewage to the sea and invite a flux of interlopers and their rank baggage. Tahitians whose livelihoods rely on water quality—fishermen, shrimp farmers, whale-watching outfitters, parasail providers—are rightly suspicious of what might be motivating other American promoters like Friedman and Thiel.

In February 2018, the government of Tahiti declared the signed agreement null and void, the MOU expired due to inactivity. Two months later, hundreds of people marched to protest the Seasteading Institute and its schemes, despite assurances by their government that it was gone.

The would-be colony in French Polynesia appears to be DOA, a corpse that will not float. The people won that struggle. As the aphorism goes, though, you can win the battle and still lose the war. Economic times will tell whether seasteads find a welcome in Tahiti in the long term.

On a realistic level, can the visionary entrepreneurs at the Seasteading Institute honestly insist that technological prowess will advance enough to withstand nature's incursions? That it can weather them sustainably and over long periods of time? Have entrepreneurs forgotten how Hurricanes Katrina and Rita demolished 115 oil platforms and damaged fifty-two others?

One of my favorite sayings, reduced to bumper-sticker schtick, is "Nature bats last." That means nature will have the bottom of the last inning and thus come out on top. I am no actuary, but I can envision few insurance executives who would write policies for seasteading's cause.

IDLE TIME ON MO'OREA

The last island we visit is Mo'orea. We bunk at the Sofitel Moorea la Ora Beach Resort. Like all the other four resorts or hotels where we stay, breakfast is included. Tourists swarm the buffet, angling to stuff in enough to last them through the day and minimize outlays later. The *petit-déjeuner* proves not to be so *petit*. Eyes prove larger than the stomachs to fit food in. Plates are heaped, chow discarded. The waitstaff neither expect gratuities nor have any way to request them. Cash is not on hand here. Plastic is the medium of exchange.

One hopes the waitstaff can squirrel away some food, rather than stand back and watch it thrown away. So many questions vex tourist travel's impact on Indigenous locals. Do our dollars elevate them above subsistence lifeways? Or do our dollars instead squelch traditions? Internally combusting their way to a resort job might make more economic sense than tending coconuts like some of their ancestors for generations have done. If fried pork rinds prove more available and affordable in convenience stores than fresh fish, then obesity requires less explanation.

For all the tainted attitudes I bring to industrial-scale tourism, as Edward Abbey put it in characterizing the booming Four Corners region in the US, this Sofitel Resort preserves its private marine environment well. Its overwater bungalows were built fifty-five years ago. Underwater wildlife is abundant, coral reefs as thriving as any we have seen upon four seas. If sea cucumbers are an indicator species, the water quality is wholesome. It certainly looks clear.

The sea cucumber has a squishy, elongated body and leathery skin. It is a creature made for reproducing. It creeps along the bottom of the sea. From one end a single branched gonad protrudes. It is a biological illustration of the twin Polynesian themes of fecundity and plenitude.

Cucumbers are both gathered wild for human consumption and cultivated on farms. The Chinese market for these creatures exceeds $60 million annually. As we snorkel, we see hundreds of sea cucumbers oozing below schools of fish both large and small that sparkle by.

Some species of pollution can't be seen, though. The French generated ill will by nuclear testing nearby. People were displaced, radiation broadcast. Thyroid cancer and leukemia rates are high. Leery of liability, the government stymies research. More bad news about radiation could hamstring tourism. Mo'oreans yearn for certainty about the maladies that afflict them.

Genome scientist Keolu Fox at the University of California at San Diego, a Kānaka Maoli, a Native Hawai'ian, is trying to help. He arranges meetings. He interviews churchgoers. He stops people in the streets. "What if we can differentiate between cancer that is caused by exposure to nuclear radiation and cancer that is inherited normally? That's powerful," he said. "What if I could show that the effects of nuclear radiation are transgenerational?"

For many occupants of islands, as I was on Vashon Island in Washington State, beliefs are hardwired that isolation defends and protects. Winds and tides, many people believe, can transport waste of any kind away. Oceans thus become dumping grounds for all manner of trash.

At the Sofitel dive shop, we sign on for an expensive whale-watching tour. Aboard the boat, amid high wind and breakers, we hang from swaying stanchions and lounge high on a canopy. We pitch sideways with the waves. Reed drinks provided beer. Karen gets seasick. No PFDs are either mentioned or seen. Polynesian regulations seem much laxer than in the States.

Our basso captain of African extraction, Max, soon spots dolphins. He approaches slowly and invites us to swim and see them at firsthand. His French-born lieutenant, Sophie, clad in wetsuit head to toe, urges us to take the plunge as well. She jumps in first. Instead of scissoring, she pumps her legs like a mermaid or a dolphin through the towering waves. Her kick is known as a mermaid kick, and she looks every bit the part. Her big fins enable her to move. Sophie completed a degree in film studies in France. Polynesian internships like hers, fun jobs after college, are common for young French people as a bridge or gap into the world of solid work.

Once Reed follows Sophie, I mask up. "Go now, my friend!" Max bellows to me above the wind, and I go. We three swimmers close in on the basking dolphins. The underwater sight when they ghost down to evade us proves otherworldly. Films on television and the Web cannot replicate the first-hand rush. Through rollers five feet high, I turn back to the boat. I see the deck, I sink in troughs, I see the deck, I stroke along, till finally I reach the lunging ladder. Flinging my mask aboard, I haul my spent self in. Shivering a bit, I towel dry and catch my breath.

Then Captain Max sees flukes flash.

He motors near the spot where the imprint of the whale flukes makes the roiled water's texture differ from the surface all around. Max cuts the engine. He lets the boat drift. Silence prevails from us eight French, Italians, and Americans. We wait, watch, and hope. Forty yards away, a humpback cow and calf leap fully out and splash back down. A communal whoop rises from the boat. Four of us are seasick and droopy, but everyone perks up at the sight of the whales.

These are calving grounds, the calf a month old, the water a half mile deep. Other skippers motor nearby to treat their clients to the sight, but the humpback family shows itself no more. Regulations stateside would never allow Max to approach so close to the whales, nor to swim his clients in the two-thousand-foot depths and rolling waves. We have received what we came for, the sight of a massive whale family breaching. We are ecstatic. We have achieved our hoped-for *santosha,* a Sanskrit word for utter acceptance and contentment.

WHO ARE WE?

At our core, we are most interested in the ecology of the places where we travel. But the relative confinement of our lodgings in the Tahitian islands has hamstrung us. So has the politesse that governs life in ostentatious resorts. We made those travel choices. We must live and learn from them. To choose posh hotels and resorts instead of homestays is a mistake. By island-hopping we have neglected the advice to travel slowly, spend locally, and venture off the beaten path.

During our resort stays, few paths outside the Pacific Ocean prove to be available to stray from. We spend good time in the ocean's shallows and depths. But to travel slowly, as NatGeo advises, would outstrip our limited financial means to see so many places at one go.

We are behaving like tourists, because the vacation we laid out for ourselves is in fact a tour by any other name. The only difference is that we have hired no tour guides or travel agents.

Interrogating travel in Polynesia, we have seen firsthand the ways that others choose to venture in remote locales—as tourists, not as travelers. In ethical terms I've come to distinguish between touring and traveling in much the same way I distinguish between hunters and shooters. Travelers settle into foreign experiences and absorb them. Tourists wring the sponge and rush on.

Prolonged exposure therapy to travel, practiced on the hop for a quarter century, has had a positive effect on me. Now I can manage to relax as a traveler. Now I can climb on planes, trains, boats, cabs, and vans with nary a shivering for it. I can keep racing thoughts at bay about the tons of invisible particulates we generate. Travel aversion need not be a lifetime affliction.

While unfolding for journeys, while capitulating to paths, I have come to conclude I have no quarrel with travel itself. My quarrel is with unreflective tourism, with those who shoot at anything that moves. As a born-again nonhunter, I have come to avoid that type of society. Time to step back and take a long view of our weeks on *The Happy Isles of Oceania,* as Paul Theroux titled his book about traveling the South Pacific. Theroux pitched a tent, paddled a kayak, bartered for goods, and offered his readers a macroscopic marine-scale view.

My family traveled differently in French Polynesia. When we were not following the Kardashians, we were following the French. The finest tourist lodgings were ours to revel in. They made for a lifetime trip we will not repeat. We flew from island to island, ate luau, and grew grateful for French rosé—made when skins of red grapes touch the wine for a short time.

Like rosé wine, we got pink from the sun. Rosy, never lobster-red. We have had skin malignancies removed. We've learned our solar lessons. To appear pale used to be the height of fashion, but tans grew in esteem after Coco Chanel, the French fashion designer who gave her name to a fragrance, showed the world her tan after she took a Mediterranean vacay. Suntans intimate a life of Riley, the proletarian need to labor all but forgotten. Never mind the annoying matter of inviting melanomas. Our friend the oncologist Corliss Newman slathers her family in sunscreen below and clads them in sunproof long-sleeve shirts above. She will take no chances.

From our respective obligations as busy professionals, Karen and I could afford only a brief time in Polynesia. By mistake we practiced a culturally insulated form of travel. We were at a loss on how to come to know the Polynesian people. We learned it would be much better to get acquainted with locals, much sweeter to stay in resident lodgings instead of isolating like our fellow resort-goers preferred to do. These locals, though, do not tender short-let rentals as a rule.

We knew only resorts. One of my goals was to see the region through tourist eyes and pry wide tourist minds. In doing so I learned that those who enjoy the most privilege and wealth prefer to cocoon in private—quite the opposite of those who travel to socialize with others in the close quarters of cruise ships, for instance. The German sociologist Georg Simmel found one key feature of modern city life to be the ways we continue to exist as strangers to one another. The same is true of international tourist travel, in my slender and selective experience.

If or when my family takes another pass at the happy isles of Oceania, we will do it from the deck of a sailboat. We will pack our own food, keep our own counsel, see the sea up close and personal, and avoid the maximum-consumption ethic of resorts. We still might not come to know the locals as well as we like, and so our isolation may still have that shortcoming. And in May 2022, we enjoyed such a trip when good friends chartered and skippered a catamaran and wove us through the Exuma Islands between Nassau and Georgetown in the Bahamas.

Consumers like every other, we aim to become more mindful, more conscious of what we buy, of whom we meet, of where and how we go. Because every dollar spent is a minuscule political act, we hope to effect change vis-à-vis our spending habits, or at least do little or no damage where we go, in our growing awareness as members of an intentional global community.

18

Making Landfall

There we were: bodies and souls packed into a mess hall in Belize on the last night of our lives. Huddled in a structure convulsing on sticks above the Caribbean Sea. Raindrops drove sideways and wind slammed our remote outpost in bursts. Across from me my family sat, their plates of fish untouched. Our thumbs lay latched on the table's edge, our ears tuned to the storm's advance, heads bent, brows beading from humidity and strain.

It was the winter solstice, December 21, 2012. It was also the Mayan Apocalypse, the world's end as the ancients foretold it, a cataclysm Indigenous people had foreseen. Those ancient seers disagreed on the force and form the cataclysm would take. Solar flares, an asteroid hitting Earth, a reversal of global rotation might all befall. If you credited some of those who foretold the apocalypse, the coastlines of the planet's largest water bodies were likely to see tsunamis sweep in. Big waves would crash, would make landfall. And when they did, woe betide the puny humans who had chosen to take shelter there.

The worst hurt would be sure to occur where the Maya people flourished. The flat land of coastal Belize, its lack of vertical relief, exposes it. So does its absence of rivers. The region's susceptibility to cataclysm is legendary. My mind's eye ratified those dire claims. For all we knew, the projected planetary apocalypse might even take the shape of a smoldering norovirus. Our only certainty was that we were feeling nauseous at the dining table.

To worsen our numerological timing, we had arrived on the twelfth day of the twelfth month of 2012. After touring the mainland, we clambered aboard a deep-draft diesel craft in Belize City. Our destination: a string of coral islets to the east, on the outer limits of Belize, part of a Caribbean storm belt where sixteen hurricanes had killed twenty thousand people over twenty-eight years.

In an image straight out of horror schtick, I envisioned the bones of human casualties stacked up and gathering sand on that ring of former coral, that skeletal heap of marine invertebrates, that remote Turneffe Atoll where we were sweating and silent before our meal.

As this book has made clear, I have never relished travel. I agree to international outings to please my spouse. Mine is a tender gesture, a token of devotion, no matter how white-knuckled I might be. Everyone *loves* to travel. Whole industries are dedicated to travel's propagation. Moreover marriage, like politics, is the art of constant compromise.

*　*　*

Underwater volcanoes called seamounts begin the lives of atolls. Pimply volcanic fissures or hotspots leak and lift from the seafloor. Corals thrive around them, both at sea level and below. Primal coral colonies die, and new ones grow on the remains of their ancestors, even after the originals have been bleached by climate variability or trashed by hurricanes. Trapping sand, fostering vegetation, reef-built atolls foster shaky habitat for marine creatures and people. Much like lava does when it sizzles out to sea, dead coral can generate new land.

But atolls can be vulnerable places in anything but tender weather, and Belize has three of the only four atolls in the Western Hemisphere. Turneffe, the largest of them, is a fragmented ten by thirty miles in size. For a December week in that watery "New World"—as Shakespeare's contemporaries named the Americas—we booked resort time to scuba, snorkel, and explore.

Shakespeare's 1611 play *The Tempest* bobbed to the surface of my consciousness as we boated for an hour to that easternmost seaboard of Belize. Only Shakespeare could have crafted notable poetry out of drowning. Only he could have fashioned earworms out of verse. The most relevant lines come from a song by Ariel—that servant-spirit who flits about the heads of shipwreck victims in the play. Ariel sings or whispers truth or nonsense in their ears:

> Full fathom five thy father lies;
> Of his bones are coral made;
> Those were pearls that were his eyes;
> Nothing of him that doth fade,
> But doth suffer a sea-change
> Into something rich and strange.

The wise wizard Prospero, marooned with others on the nameless island, has liberated Ariel from witchy bondage in a tree. The play encourages us to see how magic infused our earliest English literature in the New World. The drama's title, *The Tempest*, denotes a violent windstorm. The word *hurricano*, or *hurricane*, for a storm specific to the West Indies, had yet to come into play.

Charles Darwin wrote specifically about atolls. In his *Structure and Distribution of Coral Reefs*, he defined atolls as "circular groups of coral islets." He named Turneffe Atoll "the most remarkable reef in the West Indies." Only the Great Barrier Reef of Australia exceeds it in size. Darwin's word "islet," for a tiny island, suggests a certain shakiness. It suggests a transience. What hurricanes construct by layering silt and vegetation over coral, hurricanes also can destroy.

Turneffe's human population is sparse. Four resorts, a research center, and several fishing camps made up the only permanent structures when we visited. The word "permanent" need be applied advisedly here, enclosed in scare quotes. When windstorms barrel across those low islets, palms topple, bird nests crumble, human occupants cringe. The worst storms cause obliteration.

Legends on maps ought to caution visitors to abide at their own risk. Italic script beside a hurricane icon on maps might read, *Here be high winds and little of terra firma to obstruct them.*

Decades before Darwin, Alexander Hamilton underwent a Caribbean cataclysm. The future coauthor of *The Federalist Papers* worked as a clerk in 1772 for a mercantile firm on the island of St. Croix. Only seventeen years of age, he was homesick when a tsunamic hurricane struck. In such a severe meteorological event, thunder and lightning and great waves combine.

Hamilton's tsunami heaved ships far inland, some of them hundreds of yards. Their masts shattered, gunwales crumpled, hulls turned upside down. Hamilton wrote about the fearsome ordeal in a letter to his father. His father read the letter from an outpost farther south in the Caribbean. The namesake musical, *Hamilton*, immortalizes that period of the young man's life.

Massive waves flowed inland, Hamilton wrote, leveling plantations and homes. Upland soil liquefied and flowed seaward in the opposite direction, much like a volcanic lahar.

His report of the tsunamic hurricane compounded my misgivings. He echoed ancients who had prophesied, with numerical certitude, the date of the Mayan Apocalypse. "In a word," he wrote, "misery in all its most hideous shapes spread over the whole face of the country."

The relevant song from the musical *Hamilton* is titled "Hurricane." Its refrain line is "I wrote my way out." Lin Manuel-Miranda contends that Hamilton wrote his way off the island, into history, and back stateside with his compelling letter. "When I was seventeen, a hurricane / destroyed my town," Manuel-Miranda's lyrics assert. "I didn't drown / I couldn't seem to die / I wrote my way out." He sees Hamilton as a forerunner of hip-hop artists who pull themselves up from obscurity and poverty to gain great accomplishment and acclaim. Miranda, coincidentally, is also the name of the wizard Prospero's daughter in the Shakespeare play *The Tempest*.

Alexander Hamilton's mentor in St. Croix, the Presbyterian minister Hugh Knox, recommended his protégé's letter for publication in the *Royal Danish American Gazette*. The florid letter offered a "divine rebuke for human vanity and pomposity," wrote Ron Chernow, whose biography of Hamilton inspired Manuel-Miranda to write his musical stage play.

Hamilton's readers got a spiritual scolding. His eloquence and piety so impressed the locals in St. Croix that they started a financial subscription—an early variety of crowdfunding—to pack away the future US treasury secretary to New York to continue his formal education.

Natural phenomena like hurricanes and tsunamis inspire devotional writings. In his letter Hamilton recalled, "The roaring of the sea and wind, fiery meteors flying about it in the air, the prodigious glare of almost perpetual lightning, the crash of the falling houses, and the ear-piercing shrieks of the distressed, were sufficient to strike astonishment into Angels." Thoughts and prayers are commonplace responses today. Petitioners on social media implored their families and friends to "Pray for Houston" in the fatal aftershock of Hurricane Harvey. Category-4 Hurricane Ida, striking sixteen years to the day after Katrina devastated New Orleans, peeled off roofing and left millions of residents in Louisiana and Mississippi without power in 2021.

Recalling the adage that there are no atheists in foxholes, terrors stirred by conflagrations in the clouds train true believers to find fresh errors to confess. "The scenes of horror exhibited around us," Hamilton wrote, "naturally awakened such ideas in every thinking breast, and aggravated the deformity of every failing of our lives."

Evangelical preachers and alt-right firebrands interpret cataclysms in the Gulf of Mexico as unpaid debts come due, as just desserts levied righteously on humankind. Environmentalists sometimes fall into kindred pits of recrimination by bombastically naming every atmospheric catastrophe the product of our industrial extravagance, the fruit of our unwisdom and our greed.

In the decades since Hamilton and Darwin wrote, though, climate change *has* made our coastlines more susceptible. In the years 2016 through 2019, a record was set when at least one Category 5 hurricane hit each year. Cataclysmic storms devastate in greater proportions than before. Hurricane Katrina in 2005, Sandy in 2012, Harvey, Irma, Maria in 2017, Dorian in 2019, and Laura in 2020 offer fresh reminders, in both expenses and in deaths, of our changing climate.

Among the costliest natural disasters in US history, Hurricane Ida in 2021 inflicted $75 billion in damage, Hurricane Katrina, $182 billion. The Gulf of Mexico and the Caribbean are living laboratories that insurance firms are watching closely as weather extremities trend north.

Some deniers and skeptics are insisting that there's no need for alarm. That such storms are "five-hundred-year events," even "one-thousand-year events." Never mind the seeming fluke that so many such storms should have made landfall in such a short time. Dozens of unfortunates perished in Sandy and Dorian, hundreds in Harvey, thousands each in Katrina and Maria.

The needy always get hit the hardest. The poor have always taken it on the chin. The film *Beasts of the Southern Wild* is a gritty allegory of Hurricane Gustav's impact on subsistence-level families south of New Orleans on Isle de Jean Charles. That swampy province, dubbed "The Bathtub" in the film, is being evacuated voluntarily today due to sea-rise.

Six-year-old Hush Puppy and her father in the movie wade dreary swamps to try to stay alive. I saw the film in the company of academic scholars with whom I'm friendly. They rejected that cinematic commentary for its squalor. Had I wanted to quarrel, I would have said the squalor in the movie is the purpose and point. The rough beasts that tusk across Louisiana's flooded landscape personify our dearth of ecological forethought and flaws in our social systems. Travel is implicated in the squalor of the characters in *Beasts of the Southern Wild*. The oil refineries that loom in the backgrounds of the film are helping to fulfil our addictions to mobility.

My family's sojourn on Turneffe Flats in Belize was the last Central American visit we would make in 2012 before we flew back home to the States. Those aptly named flats, on the slender tip of a north-facing isthmus, expose its occupants to violent weather on all sides.

In the dining hall I sat silent with Karen and our boys. The hot fats on our plates of fish were congealing before my eyes. Their oily surfaces winked as they grew cold. I dabbed my brow. When windstorms make landfall, the terrain can fall. It can fail. The soil can slump, it can become a slurry, slip to the sea, we hopeful sojourners right along with it. My gut and agitated fancy confirmed those facts. If, as the old myths say, gods still regulate the region's weather, then the original inhabitants of Belize might achieve some retribution after centuries of conquest.

* * *

Belize became a Crown colony named British Honduras in 1862. A century later, that last English protectorate in the Americas gained some independence. Named Belize in 1973, it became a Commonwealth realm in 1981. Queen Elizabeth II acted as its head of state. Most residents are mestizos, mixed Spanish and Maya. African and European Creoles speak varied dialects of English, while the Garifuna people descend mostly from Carib people and Africans.

Belize is a Bangladesh in miniature, a country whose luckless geography has set it up for disaster. Both nations feature flat and low-lying land, massed populations, widespread poverty, and a dearth of defensive infrastructures. In *For the Time Being,* my mentor Annie Dillard wrote, "It took only a few typhoon waves to drown 138,000 Bangladeshi on April 30, 1991."

Belize is becoming a colony for North America. Yankees are buying up the nation for investments, retirements, and escape. Some North Americans are building tourist attractions, carving out condos, throwing up second homes, or winging in to revel as if there's no *mañana.*

Ecological ethics try to guide us to do what's right, and we harbor hopes that wisdom will prevail, but those hopes fade when we come to expect jets, planes, taxis, vans, golf carts, and boats to be available on demand. When foodstuffs need to be flown in to meet the high expectations of elites like us, then sustainable travel truly has become an oxymoron.

My family is a demonstrable part of the problem. Enticed by natural wonders of the world, we swimmers and ecotourists grew fascinated by the nation of Belize. We yearned to experience its barrier reef. We longed to chance it, even if we had to teeter on that Central American isthmus, even if the weather tried to shrug us off. Storms might huff, puff, and crack their cheeks in greeting. The weather might challenge our bravado and shudder our structures.

Around the dining table at Turneffe Flats resort, the Mayan Apocalypse loomed large in mind. Our fellow travelers, their faces blanching, did not seem to be any hungrier than we were. Chairs were pulling away from the table. Our chance companions were slowly scattering back to their individual cabins, their rustic holiday cocoons on stilts. It was as if our fellow diners were being spun by a centrifuge, whirled by an unknowable force away from the eye of a storm.

On the table's edge our thumbs rested, like so many skate deterrents bolted to a bench. As if, by force of will, we could deter the storm from coming, thwart it from stripping us of our fun.

Too much sun had afflicted some of our companions. Several of them had been scuba diving, others casting lines from open boat decks most of that hot day. Fans of fly-fishing had been hoping to hook tarpon, permit, or bonefish on the tide flats. Sunlight had refracted off the water and inflamed their faces, peeled their skin in strips. Several of them looked fried. Waves had churned them, too. The digestive systems of our fellow tourists might have been made shakier from their deep-water dives. Maybe the resort cuisine was tainted. Maybe a clever shipboard virus had stowed away. Or maybe—superstition hissed and whispered—the Indigenous gods were bending from above to pluck the flimsy tinsel from our wings.

Walking to the mess hall after dark, we had seen bats droop like furry fruit. Had we read those mammals better, we'd have picked up on the weather. They knew the storm was coming. Under palm fronds they bunched and huddled in clusters to brace against the advancing storm.

Karen and I were worried we had imperiled our kids. One son twelve, the other fifteen, they were growing jaundiced right beside us at that table. Chase had gamed his way across Belize on a handheld computer, mindful of little else besides its pulsing screen, trying in his own way to assuage the pains from the car crash that had lacerated his scalp and caused a brain bleed. Reed had taken scuba lessons with me back home in eager preparation for our tropical stay.

A branch cracked and whacked the shell of the building. Sweat slicked the crown of my head. Karen never gets sick. She fancies travel anywhere and all the time—from dusty towns in the American West to Mediterranean watering holes. Despite a background of rough-and-tumble sports in school, she was growing pale right across the table from me. Her image shimmered, as if we had entered a cloudy fantasy by Poe. We shot glances above the heads of our kids. Unseen forces were having their way, were taking charge. The known world had turned topsy-turvy.

In crisis times the faces of the afflicted and the fearful gleam less green, as the old cliché will have it, than pallid and pasty, sagging and drained. Ruddy blood empties from extremities and pools in the trunk. How might medical science explain such transformations? At the end of a cycle foretold by Indigenous prophets for a millennium, the facial features of my family were drooping and caving, like so many jack-o-lanterns left outdoors too long.

* * *

Before Columbus made landfall, blood was thought to nourish the Indigenous gods. Parched in a salty land, buffeted raw by windstorms, Belizean deities demanded propitiation. Sacrifice took many forms, but only highborn prisoners could make the grade. Some had their hearts torn out on altars. Others underwent decapitation. Still others were fated to be swallowed alive by sinkholes that the Spaniards named cenotes. Those cenotes also often served as burial chambers.

The Spanish conquest of the Yucatán and other regions south of Mexico began in 1527. Maya warriors wielded bows and arrows. They hurled stones and flint-tipped spears. Their cotton armor did little to repel the Spaniards' lances, rapiers, and crossbows. The Maya patron of war, Pax, displayed jaguar paws above its ears and a dislocated lower jaw. Unlike the same-named Roman goddess of peace, this Pax was disposed to vomit blood in hectic rites.

Caricatures of Indigenous folk-art peeped out everywhere we went. Horologists and mathematicians had been reduced to knickknacks and gewgaws, tchotchkes and gimcracks. Reduced to icons imprinted on our eyes luring us to buy them as keepsakes, tote them home.

Comic drawings on airport walls in bas-relief, on T-shirts and nylon caps, in museums rank with mold, reminded us English has become the national tongue. Imperialism and its close kindred tourism invariably abase the Indigenous people. We saw them at their tasks. We watched them labor every day as maids, cooks, grounds crews, and silent skimmers of swimming pools.

On the mainland, guides and drivers toted us to snorkeling hotspots and temples. *Gracias por sus propinas*, their longhand signs entreated, encouraging us visitors to give them tips. Boys split coconuts so we could sip the milk and eat the flesh. Putting on my bravest face, I underwent abasement with them by posing for photos. In the shadow of the Mayan Apocalypse, liberal guilt had me in its grip. First-world privilege was tainting every sip and bite of paradise I tried.

Near our rental on the mainland, a lanky teenager lived. Dogs bellowed at us from the beach house occupied by Eduardo's family. He offered to guide us, no mention of *propinas,* to secret habitats to glimpse birds and fish. He pointed out hidden lizards we walked by. Under his guidance, our head-injured offspring Chase unglued eyes from his tiny screen and reveled in the tropical world. Eduardo's most conspicuous gift was to open coconuts with a machete and a grin.

A fringe hypothesis holds that the Mayans and Aztecs have returned from the dead, from their outdated former lives. Reincarnated, they have adapted themselves to modern ways. Some of them hawk pieces of the past, whether real or invented, if only to get by. In Chiapas, Mexico, not far away, the Zapatista craft woodcuts, paint murals, and cultivate a revolutionary solidarity.

US neocolonialism is the third tsunami to siege Belize. It is the third cultural wave to make landfall. Colonial tourism followed onslaughts by Spanish invaders first and occupation by the British military second. With luck our US presence might only alter Indigenous lifeways rather than destroy them. Our US national aims these days have shifted from seizing territories outright to influencing foreign governments to advance our economic and strategic interests.

Just as disturbing, our industrial vapors cause international atmospheric commotion. If you credit the vast consensus of climate scientists, that is, if you believe we humans are contributing to a changing global climate. As a major contributor of atmospheric carbon, the US bears the lion's share of atmospheric recognition. The businessmen who run Turneffe Flats opened the resort as encore enterprises for themselves after making their fortunes in the states.

When Hurricane Mitch blew through Belize in 1998, it reached winds of 180 miles per hour. Keith followed in 2000, Earl in 2016. Bits of atoll dislodged on each visitation. White-sand beaches vanished, crocodile-nesting sites suffocated under sudden silt transported by big storms, coral gardens expired and bleached dead white in time. Manatees in mangrove forests do better.

On one excursion we saw them lolling, those bewhiskered mermaids of "chaos and old night." Their undersea adaptability proves fortuitous. Their blobby shapes offer nothing humans crave—neither oil, tusks, hides, nor frolicsome behaviors. They do face other threats when we collide with them in watercraft, entangle them in fishing gear, and nibble at their habitat.

The owners of Turneffe Flats chose to rebuild, storm after storm. Or, rather, their insurance policies afforded them rebuilds, elevating already sky-high client rates. After Mitch made landfall in 1998, the island was a mess, they admitted—boat dock destroyed, imported beach sand sucked out to sea. Again in 2016, the onshore dock, the dock-house, and the fueling station all went down, as did twin seawalls and twenty large palms. Sixty tons of lumber had to be hauled in that year, twenty-five yards of concrete poured. During COVID-19 times, entire properties like theirs were seen to be on offer for group rents at cut-rate.

Entrepreneurs prefer to call such atolls islands. In doing so, they enact a subtle PR and offset a likelihood of liability. Some of the major maps even contradict one another. Some of the major maps disagree on whether to call Turneffe an atoll or a ring of actual islands.

Competing with the promotion tracts, activist agendas come into play. Activists challenge the impacts of tourist development on Indigenous people and on ecology. Risky businesses generate issues that need to be managed or spin-doctored by US-minted MBAs. Resort owners then shift to a defensive form of PR known as "issues management." As Darwin noted, atolls are unstable islets, a loan word from French to denote a diminutive kind of island, a less-steady kind.

At the time we visited, a nongovernmental organization for the atoll had been founded. One of its first lobbying campaigns was wrapping up. All the atoll's 131,000 hectares had been protected as the Turneffe Atoll Marine Reserve. Victory for the forces of sustainability!

Within three years, though, a fresh business venture had violated every guideline agreed upon for the reserve. That surreptitious venture breached many of the newly implemented laws. Quickly, before anyone could clang alarms or slow the contractors, speculators had deforested five acres of stubby and salt-loving mangrove trees. Their contractors crept in and dredged a harbor, carved out a seaport, and redistributed the dredge spoils—rock, sand, shells, coral—to elevate the acreage. Silt and mud from such covert and illegal excavations plume out to sea.

A nonprofit land trust filed suit against the developers and the relevant agencies. The Belizean ambassador to the US did not return my email or phone call asking about the status of the spat. No legal traction was afforded me, of course; I was reaching out from an alien nation and from afar. Legal proceedings can hang for ages when they entail such low priorities as land use. Then, too, the damage to the ecosystem had already been done. The property soon came back to market, advertised as a prime site for a fishing resort, a potential competitor to Turneffe Flats. No doubt it will sell and sell again, no matter how encumbered legally it might be.

Between 2 and 7 percent of the planet's saltwater marshes and mangrove forests are being destroyed each year, even though they store, or sequester, fifty times as much carbon as tropical forests do by area. Speculators like those on the Turneffe Atoll need to prevail only once, whereas ecologists need to triumph time after time in sustainability battles. Indigenous Belizeans will be survivors in the long term, but capitalist developers can also be tenacious.

* * *

It is a human construction, this *making landfall*. Travelers in past centuries used the phrase to denote the solace offered by terra firma after weeks or months of ocean travel. Sailors have always welcomed solid land after protracted time at sea. Those ancient mariners, sighing relief in eloquent accounts, equated solid soil with respite and salvation. Poet Ann Stanford, speaking at a scholarly conference, epitomized landfalls in the colonial mind as prototypes of earthly hope. Today, *making landfall* takes on sinister connotations: storms, not people, make landfall now.

Hurricanes—those hectic counterclockwise velodromes of wind—are assigned people's names. Female names till 1978, male names as well today. We humanize, or anthropomorphize, big storms. If the old salts used to pray that landfalls would come their way, landlubbers on tropical shorelines in these latter days pray just as fervently for the hurricanes to stay away.

The semantic range of the phrase *making landfall* has widened to indict the natural world. The seven seas, those incubators of wind, decline to be compliant highways for our commerce and pleasure craft. Seafaring can be arduous, as my late son Braden and I know firsthand. Marine ecologies used to merit submission and respect, but that respect often evaporates in the tourist trade. Technical hubris now puts at risk wild species, Indigenous locals, and tourists on atolls.

As I tumble through unfamiliar lands, a relentless out-of-placeness often pesters me. A reflexive ache or disorder overtakes. In a facsimile of innocence, I try to interrogate myself at such times. Looking in the mirror, I ask what I am doing abroad. In Belize I was being dined on a remote atoll, salt-encrusted, sapped from snorkeling a bleached coral garden, my brave face bending at the edges. The rinsed swim gear I had laid outside to dry was getting drenched.

To outlive the atmospheric onslaught in a fever dream that stormy evening, to survive the savage storm in my subconscious, I strapped my family high on palm trees. That way they would not wash away, as a quarter-million people did in the Indian Ocean on December 26, 2004.

Homer's Odysseus, longing to wallow in the Sirens' sonic splendor, demanded to be fastened to his mainmast. As a mariner I would have commanded the singers all to lie quiet, the Aegean surf to suspend its surge. Cocooned in a cabin built on stilts, my family suffered no cataclysm, despite centuries of prognostications. The pundits had sounded false alarms. The new millennium broke, welcome light arrived, and the structures that housed us all held up.

For the time being, the Turneffe Atoll in Belize continues to be accessible for well-heeled tourists. If you go, you will pay a pretty farthing for the privilege. From the resort shore you will gaze out to the northeast, toward Jamaica, the quarter from which those big storms drive.

Acknowledgments

My cast of contributors to this project is vast. The greatest thanks must go to Karen Lindholdt, née Palrang, who talked me down from the clouds of doubt and got me on those big old jet airliners year after year. She abetted my empirical research into tourism, against my skittish instincts and judgments. Our sons Reed and Chase also often went with us abroad, as did our older offspring, Braden, while he was still with us. My sisters, Diane Reiersgard and Jill Sullivan, also supplied their unflagging support and stories, Diane as a seasoned international sojourner who has put the travel habit on hold to explore her Whidbey Island home.

Many people welcomed my family and me or conferred vital firsthand information. Judy du Plooy went beyond the standard duties as the host of a destination resort by taking me under her wing to educate me on Belize. Pierre Lagayette and his wife, Marie-Paul Lagayette, were warm, generous hosts at the Sorbonne Université and at restaurants in Paris. Bart and Lindell Haggin served as tour guides through the Big Island of Hawai'i and bunked us in their condominium. Steven Garmanian and the Urban Raptor Conservancy fed me meaty details about Cooper's hawks. Simmons Buntin, *Terrain.org* editor, ran early versions of "The Trumpets of Solitude" and "Making Landfall," nominating the latter for the John Burroughs Essay Award.

Other friends also served me well. Erika Zaman gave an interview on the Houston Fire, Becky Brown toured me through that fire's site, and Laura Ackerman supplied details about coal and oil transport. Tim Stewart, longtime resident of Thailand, explained several of its idioms and critters. Waterkeepers Lee First, Sue Joerger, and Jerry White inspired me about the wonders of water and activism to keep bays and rivers healthy. Edward Byrnes's numerical savvy developed key statistics. Jennifer Ekstrom helped me learn the twists and turns of Burning Man dance. Spokane Tribe member and colleague Margo Hill fueled the name change from Fort George Wright Drive to Whistalks Way. Rich Landers publicly and politely traded words on the ethics of hunting. David Sohappy Jr. and his daughter Loretta built on the history of Indigenous rights provided to me by attorney Tom Keefe, who represented members of their tribe. Dr. Gary Gleason helped me understand the uncanny draw of doom tourism. My father, Harold, left far too soon for me to thank him personally for cultivating my appreciation for the great outdoors.

Many friends and colleagues sharpened draft chapters of this book. Alan Weltzien and Igor Klyukanov read thousands of words generously and incisively. David Tagnani and Dan Butterworth from Gonzaga University improved my thinking and syntax. Anthropologist Fred Strange conferred his expertise on all things Indigenous; without him, I'd have been far out of my ethnic depths. Former Buddhist lay monk Galen Leonhardy conveyed sweet kindliness and care. James Hathcock and Georgia Tiffany reminded me, as only the best friends can, that old-school rules about written composition still and always will apply. Jon Gosch stepped up to the editing desk, and environmental educator extraordinaire Laird Christensen taught me a ton.

Among those who helped in the drafting stage, my research assistant Lilian Seitz ably gathered data and shared her technical communication skills. Zac Thorp and Sage Workman, both with the Spokane Academic Library, fetched dozens of books for me during high COVID-19 so that I never had to enter libraries. For the gifts of time, I owe boundless gratitude to the Northwest Institute for Advanced Study at Eastern Washington University, which relieved me from classroom duties on key occasions to pursue this project to its end. Jenny Keegan at Louisiana State University Press offered sound advice, patience, and faith in this work. Behind every chapter lie the example, the presence, and the inspiration of my mentor Annie Dillard.

Selected References and Notes

INTRODUCTION

Throughout these references and notes, I favor online over print resources, in large part due to the global accessibility of the World Wide Web. Likewise, I offer only authors, titles, and publishers for those sources (instead of site addresses or URLs) due to the confusions that arise from so-called reference rot, including references that have been strategically withdrawn.

Judy du Plooy tells her family story online at "Belize Botanic Garden." She sold her namesake du Plooy's Jungle Lodge to the Muy'Ono Resorts chain, which rebranded the property as Sweet Songs Jungle Lodge and added a zipline and a beverage bar. After the sale, Judy stayed on and devoted herself to the property's extensive Botanic Garden. The opinion Judy shared with me—that "sustainable travel is an oxymoron"—benefits from fuller explanation.

An "oxymoron" is a figure of speech that produces a contradictory effect, while anything that is "sustainable" is capable of being perpetuated. A foremost instance of sustainability is the Seventh Generation Principle, from the Iroquoian, or Haudenosaunee, confederacy. The goal of that Indigenous principle is to manage natural resources and social institutions to sustain them for present and future generations. Online corporate co-optations of the phrase "seventh generation" have all but eclipsed the original Indigenous usage, which appeared in early 2022 as the twentieth hit in Google. For Judy du Plooy, then, the two words "sustainable travel" function to contradict or cancel one another out. Travel, she means, can never be considered sustainable.

The funeral for the Okjökull Glacier took place on August 18, 2019. The story can be found in *The Guardian* newspaper under "Iceland Holds Funeral for First Glacier Lost to Climate Change." University of Berlin aerodynamics professor Julien Weiss, attending the event with his wife and young daughter, reported: "You don't feel climate change daily. It's something that happens very slowly on a human scale, but very quickly on a geological scale." The plaque for the glacier reads: "In the next 200 years all our glaciers are expected to follow the same path. This monument is to acknowledge that we know what is happening and what needs to be done. Only you know if we did it." The Rhône glacier in Switzerland is draped every summer with white fleece blankets to reflect the sun and slow the ice-melt, as reported by Michael Hardy in *Wired,* May 26, 2020. The detail about fleece blankets draped on ski slopes in Switzerland is documented by Arnd Wiegmann and Brenna Hughes Neghaiwi in "Wrap up Cool: Blankets Help Stave off Glacier Melt on Swiss Ski Pistes" in *Reuters,* Aug. 27, 2021.

Rick Steves's most pertinent book is *Travel as a Political Act* (2009; New York: Avalon Travel/Perseus, 2018). In it, and in a YouTube video by the same title, Steves asserts that "we gain empathy for the other 96 percent of humanity" when we as travelers grow politically aware. A leader of travel tours himself, Steves dodges problems inherent in commercial tourism, though he does acknowledge in the book that "the 'corporate' version of travel is about having fun in the sun, shopping duty-free, and cashing in frequent-flyer miles" (11). He is the founder and owner of Rick Steves' Europe, a tourist travel business that brought some thirty thousand people to Europe each year before the pandemic. Online sources gauge his net worth at $10 million.

Before the pandemic, a "Record 93 Million U.S. Citizens Traveled outside the Country in 2018," wrote Hannah Simpson on Apr. 3, 2019, for Skift, a media company that provides market services for the travel industry. In "COVID-19 Travel Industry Research" for January 2021, the US Travel Association reported that "travel spending totaled a mere $679 billion in 2020, an unprecedented 42% annual decline (nearly $500 billion) from

2019." Air travel revenue continued its decline in 2021, estimating a mere 43 percent of levels compared to the year 2019.

The matter of cruise-ship contamination of air and water can be found at *Forbes* under "Cruise Ship Pollution Is Causing Serious Health and Environmental Problems." Under "EPA: Limit Plane Deicing Chemical Runoff," *NBC News* reported that "Airports across the country spray millions of gallons of deicing chemicals onto airliners. The deicing fluid can turn streams bright red and create dead zones for aquatic life." The neologism *solastalgia* originated with Australian professor Glenn Albrecht and others who detailed it in their article "Solastalgia: The Distress Caused by Environmental Change," *Australasian Psychiatry* 15, no. 2 (Feb. 1, 2007).

Space considerations limit profiles of leading climate activists here. The most pertinent work by George Monbiot is "On the Flight Path to Global Meltdown," in *The Guardian*, Sept. 21, 2006. His book *Heat: How to Stop the Planet Burning* (London: Penguin, 2006) is also relevant. His article "Flying Is Dying" vanished unaccountably from the Web in 2021. The stated goal of 350.org is to "build a powerful climate movement."

Greta Thunberg refuses to fly due to carbon emissions generated by air travel. She sailed from England to New York in September 2019 to the UN Climate Action Summit aboard the solar-powered racing yacht *Malizia II*, then back from Virginia to Lisbon on the sailboat *La Vagabonde*. The pandemic raised the stakes of air travel, as Francesca Street reported for CNN on Nov. 10, 2021, in her article "The travelers who are turning their backs on airplanes."

The Pacific Northwest's extreme heat dome in June 2021 received widespread coverage. On July 23, 2021, the *New York Times* ran the article "Deaths Spike as Heat Wave Broils Canada and the Pacific Northwest," and on Oct. 11, 2021, the *New Yorker* issued "72 Hours under the Heat Dome," defining a heat dome as "a high-pressure system in which hot air is trapped over a single geographic area." Most Pacific Northwest apartments and homes have no air-conditioning, unaccustomed as residents in the region are to heat that exceeds 100°F.

The notion of vertical travel has been theorized by several French and English writers including by Charles Forsdick, "Vertical Travel," in *The Routledge Research Companion to Travel Writing*, ed. Alasdair Pettinger and Tim

Youngs (Oxfordshire, UK: Taylor and Francis, 2019), 99–112, and by Michael Cronin in several books and articles including *Across the Lines: Travel, Language and Translation* (Cork, Ireland: Cork University Press, 2000). Forsdick, in a useful imagistic definition, wrote that vertical travel is "the worm's-eye view as opposed to the bird's-eye view, and consequently [it] tends to intensify the relation of the traveller to their environment, rather than rendering them apart or aloof from it" (104). The "pleasures of the local," which I recommend here as cures for tourism, are synonymous with vertical travel.

The 2020 Central Park incident involving Christian Cooper, the Black bird-watcher, occurred the same weekend as George Floyd's arrest and murder. Bystanders filmed both incidents and posted videos to social media. Cooper's ordeal, for this discussion of travel, shows how disparities in race, class, and gender can complicate outdoor recreation. The Cooper ordeal has generated its own Wikipedia page, "The Central Park Birdwatching Incident." The poem that foreshadowed the Cooper incident, "9 Rules for the Black Birdwatcher," appears in *Orion Magazine* for 2013. That poem's author, Clemson University professor J. Drew Lanham, who is Black, wryly laments the absence of diversity among naturalists. Lanham followed the poem with a video titled "Bird-Watching While Black," which is available on YouTube.

Attention to diversity and equity in public lands is growing. In Leslie Jamison's "Taking on Edward Abbey: An Interview with Amy Irvine," in *Paris Review* for May 23, 2019, Irvine spells out hazards for women outdoors. The quotation from Rebecca Solnit may be found in her book *Wanderlust: A History of Walking* (London: Granta, 2014). Joe Kanzangu traced the phenomenon of exclusionary travel privileges back more than a century to the South Side of Chicago and the death of Eugene Williams, who was attacked while rafting on Lake Michigan, in "The Lack of Diversity in Outdoor Rec Is Systematic and Disconcerting," in *High Country News*, Sept. 2, 2021. "Until the 1964 passage of the Civil Rights Act," Kanzangu wrote, "Black people in many states were legally barred or subjected to segregation at national and state parks, and other public lands." For statistical data, see also the National Health Foundation summation titled "Breaking Down the Lack of Diversity in Outdoor Spaces," July 20, 2020.

For more general data about recreation on public lands, see "2020 Outdoor Participation Report," by the Outdoor Industry Association, on

Dec. 31, 2020, which reports that only half of the US population took part in outdoor recreation in 2019. Those numbers increased during the 2020–21 pandemic, when many Americans regarded indoor spaces and mass travel as hazardous. The Oregon-based group Brown Folks Fishing was launched in 2018. Reporting on US national parks, Tiffany Midge listed the most egregious tourist follies in "Idiot Invasion; Outhouse Fail; Rim-to-Rim Rule Rupture," *High Country News*, June 1, 2022. One of her sources coined *tourons* to underscore moronic behaviors by certain tourists.

My resource for the World Tourism Organization statistics, both for inbound international tourists and for deaths by airline travel, is "Our World in Data: Tourism." The International Civil Aviation Organization, as a specialized funding agency of the United Nations, offered the numbers for carbon dioxide emissions from jet airliners.

Besides the many books on dark tourism, see DarkTourism.com, "a comprehensive guide to 'dark-tourism' destinations worldwide. Covering nearly a thousand individual places in 114 different countries." Timber King Outfitting in the Canadian province of Alberta tantalizes customers by advertising on its website, "Hunting wolves in the winter can be tough and takes patience, it's often referred to as the pinnacle of ones [*sic*] hunting career when a wolf is harvested." Timber King conducts "baited hunts which means you'll be sitting from early morning until dark (7–8 hrs.). Our box blinds are comfortable, insulated, and heated."

Marilynne Robinson's opinion on touring the homes of famous authors is found in Casey Cep, "Marilynne Robinson's Essential American Stories," *New Yorker*, Oct. 5, 2020. Chimamanda Ngozi Adichie's speech "The Danger of a Single Story" is available as a TED Talk. Michael Colglazier's promotion of travel to other planets has been reported widely, including by Michael Sheetz and Sarah Whitten, "Meet the Former Disney Executive Taking over as Virgin Galactic's New CEO," on the CNBC website.

The news item about France discouraging tourists and Instagram influencers from its Calanques National Park appears under the title "As Tourists Return to Europe, Some Top Destinations Want Fewer of Them," *Washington Post*, July 2, 2021. Research by French-language consumer group UFC-Que Choisir finds that planes emit seventy-seven times more CO_2 per passenger than trains do on journeys that last less than four hours.

"Major U.S. Airlines Commit to Carbon Neutrality by 2050" may be found at *Reuters* for March 30, 2021. The *NatGeo* advice for traveling vanished, inexplicably, from online access sometime in 2021.

1. THE SPRAY AND THE SLAMMING SEA

The location for the salmon-fishing narrative in this chapter—the entrance to the Strait of Juan de Fuca—has claimed many vessels over years. The mouth of the strait is especially treacherous in foul weather. In 1906, the SS *Valencia*, lost in rain and fog, smashed into nearby Vancouver Island. Trying to disembark in the ensuing havoc, 136 passengers and crew drowned or were battered on rocks. See David Wilma, "Graveyard of the Pacific," in HistoryLink.

Vicki Talbott responded in a text message that she had experience with the paranormal before our son vanished. After his disappearance, her interest in becoming a medium grew, after "Braden started leaving messages on the answering machine." Her communication with those on the spiritual plane often involves instrumental transcommunication (ITC), that is, messages from the afterlife received and stored on electronic devices. For more details on these phenomena, see *Calling Earth* on Vimeo, a ninety-five-minute video that features accounts of Braden and Vicki and sound/visual recordings left through telephone, computer, digital recorder, and television.

Kiowa novelist N. Scott Momaday describes "reciprocal appropriation" as a way of seeing with the eye of the heart and the mind. In that Indigenous prescription for gaining knowledge, "man invests himself in the landscape and at the same time incorporates the landscape into his own most fundamental experience." Find Momaday's statements in his article "Native American Attitudes to the Environment," in *Seeing with the Native Eye: Essays on Native American Religion*, ed. Walter H. Capps (New York: Harper and Row, 1976), 80.

2. PADDLING LAKE MISSOULA

Taxonomists often respond slowly to political changes. In 1998 the squaw-fish was renamed the northern pikeminnow, or Columbia River dace (*Pty-*

chocheilus oregonensis). Hundreds of US geographic sites—including mountains, rivers, lakes, and islands—likewise began to be stripped of the word *squaw* in February 2022, a process that was led by Secretary of the Interior Deb Haaland, the first Indigenous person ever to serve as a cabinet secretary. *Lymantria dispar,* formerly the European gypsy moth, was likewise renamed the spongy moth in 2022.

University of Chicago geology professor J Harlen Bretz made his breakthrough discovery about the Ice Age floods in 1923. His seminal article, discoverable online, is "The Channeled Scablands of the Columbia Plateau," *Journal of Geology* 31, no. 8 (Nov.-Dec. 1923): 617–49. A few years later, addressing the Geological Society of Washington, DC, Bretz presented his research in person and caused some controversy. Pardee, in the audience, remained silent in fear for his career. At the age of eighty-two, Bretz received the telegram ("We are all now catastrophists") from those few geologists still alive who had withheld their support of him for all those decades.

The Gaia Hypothesis has found many adherents among scientists. Editors Stephen H. Schneider and Penelope J. Boston write, of the scientists who contributed to their massive anthology, "In fact, they suggest that life on Earth provides a cybernetic, homeostatic feedback system, leading to stabilization of global temperature, chemical composition, and so forth" (xiii), in *Scientists on Gaia* (Cambridge, MA: MIT Press, 1991). The Gaia Hypothesis is articulated by its originator, James Lovelock, in *Gaia: A New Look at Life on Earth* (1979; New York: Oxford University Press, 2008).

The word *Anthropocene* derives from the Greek root *anthropo,* for "human," and *cene* for "new." It suggests that humans are a geological force of nature. Robert Macfarlane wrote skeptically of the Anthropocene's apologists in "Generation Anthropocene: How Humans Have Altered the Planet Forever," *The Guardian,* Apr. 1, 2016. Travel writing over centuries has contributed mightily to commodifying the environment, as Michael Cronin has written in *Eco-Travel: Journeying in the Age of the Anthropocene* (Cambridge: Cambridge University Press, 2022), 22.

Theodore Winthrop praised pork in his novelized memoir, issued posthumously in 1862, available in the book I edited and published as *The Canoe and the Saddle: A Critical Edition* (Lincoln: University of Nebraska Press, 2006). The Gregory Pardlo poem "Problema 3," in his collection *Digest*

(New York: Four Way Books, 2014), is the source of the quotation from him. The patchwork quotation from Tolkien derives from the Peter Jackson film *Lord of the Rings*.

The statistic about cash flows from gambling on reservations, which exceed those from Atlantic City and Las Vegas, is found widely online and in the article by Dana Smith titled "Gambling in Antelope Valley: Do Players Need More Options?," *Antelope Valley Times*, Aug. 6, 2019.

The history of Lucretius and his theory of atomism are presented in detail by Stephen Greenblatt in his Pulitzer Prize–winning book *The Swerve: How the World Became Modern* (New York: Norton, 2011). The 1833 painting *The Titan's Goblet* has defied a wide consensus of art historians. The Metropolitan Museum of Art in New York City, which houses the painting, categorizes the painting as a "romantic fantasy."

3. THE SECURITY OF DIRT

Zoë Schlanger, in "Dirt Has a Microbiome, and It May Double as an Antidepressant," published by the news organization *Quartz* on May 30, 2017, reports that treating mice with friendly bacteria normally found in the soil produces similar effects to antidepressant drugs. Schlanger was reporting upon research published in a recent issue of *Neuroscience*.

On the increased stress for airline carriers, crews, pilots, and passengers during the pandemic, see Kyle Arnold, "An Aviation Psychologist Explains Why COVID-19 Is Causing Havoc for Passengers and Crews," *Dallas Morning News*, Aug. 16, 2021.

Harvard University professor, psychologist, and philosopher William James published *The Varieties of Religious Experience: A Study in Human Nature* in 1902. The book collects edited lectures he delivered between 1901 and 1902 at the University of Edinburgh.

4. SHRUB-STEPPE, POTHOLE, PONDEROSA PINE

Dave Foreman's book referenced here, cowritten with Earth First! cofounder Howie Wolke, is *The Big Outside: A Descriptive Inventory of the Big Wilderness Areas of the United States* (New York: Ballantine, 1984).

Col. George Wright's name was stripped in 2020 from a road in Spokane, Washington. That road that was renamed Whistalks Way, taking the name of the warrior woman whom Wright widowed when he hanged her husband and other Yakama Indians in 1858. See "Fort George Wright Drive Changed to Whistalks Way," Spokane Tribe of Indians, Feb. 4, 2021.

The story on toxic Hanford insects is Linda Ashton's: "Radioactive Bugs Found at Nuke Site," Associated Press, Oct. 21, 1998.

5. THE TRUMPETS OF SOLITUDE

When the Port of Seattle completed expansion of the Seattle-Tacoma International Airport with a third runway in 2008, at a cost of $1.1 billion, hundreds of homes were bought out and the residents forced to move. Schools closed, including Sunset Junior High, which I attended.

The poems by Wallace Stevens whose fragments I quote in this chapter are "Notes toward a Supreme Fiction" and "The Snow Man." The book by Jerry Mander, *Four Arguments for the Elimination of Television* (New York: William Morrow, 1978), argued that television can never be reformed due to the problems inherent in its technology and the medium itself.

Polish-born writer Jerzy Kosinski's novel *Being There* (New York: Harcourt Brace, 1970) led to the 1979 film of the same title, whose screenplay Kosinski cowrote with Robert C. Jones. Directed by Hal Ashby, the film starred Peter Sellers and Shirley MacLaine. The film was inducted into the National Film Registry for its cultural significance. Kevin Decker published *Who Is Who? The Philosophy of Dr. Who* (Chicago: Open Court, 2010). David R. Coon published *Look Closer: Suburban Narratives and American Values in Film and Television* (New Brunswick, NJ: Rutgers University Press, 2014). Barry Lopez published *Arctic Dreams: Imagination and Desire in a Northern Landscape* (New York: Knopf Doubleday, 1986). Sut Jhally published *Advertising and the End of the World* (Brockhampton, MA: Media Education Foundation, 1997).

The wildlife documentary television series *The Crocodile Hunter*, hosted by Steve Irwin, began on the Animal Planet Network in 1996. Claims about the circumstances of his death were made in the anonymous article "Cameraman Justin Lyons Reveals Steve Irwin's Last Moments: 'I'm Dying,'" *Sydney Morning Herald*, Mar. 10, 2014.

The 2013 documentary film *Blackfish* exposed the mistakes made by SeaWorld that resulted in the death of trainer Dawn Brancheau in 2010. The film was pulled from Netflix under questionable circumstances that caused some commentators to suggest SeaWorld petitioned Netflix to remove it. In 2016, bowing to public pressure, SeaWorld Entertainment said it would no longer breed orcas or have them perform crowd-pleasing tricks. Compare the recent news reported by Chris Morris, "Ringling Bros. Circus Is Back after a 5-Year Hiatus—but without Animals," online in *Fortune*, May 18, 2022.

The original *Wild Kingdom*, aka *Mutual of Omaha's Wild Kingdom*, was a documentary television program from 1963 until 1988. *Grizzly Man* is the 2005 documentary film by German director Werner Herzog, coproduced by the Discovery Channel film arm Discover Docs. The quotation about Steve Irwin by Jimi Izrael vanished online in 2021.

6. ECSTASY, EUPHORIA, TRANSPORT

The quotation from the Russian ballerina has also vanished from the Internet.

The Dionysian Mysteries of ancient Greece and Rome entailed dance and the occasional use of intoxicants to loosen inhibitions and social restraints. Dionysus was the Greek god of grape-harvest, winemaking, wine, fertility, orchards, vegetation, insanity, and ritual madness. Among the Romans he was known as Bacchus. His was a mystery religion, an outlet for slaves and other marginalized people. Its principles were lost with the decline of polytheism.

Ecstatic dance as a recreation, like the Dionysian Mysteries, encourages partakers to abandon themselves to rhythms. Abandonment can lead to a condition of energetic meditation and an ecstatic state. Physical exertion and endorphins compound the group energy or gestalt.

Tom Robbins published his first novel, *Another Roadside Attraction*, with Doubleday in 1971. His pseudomemoir, *Tibetan Peach Pie: A True Account of an Imaginative Life* (New York: HarperCollins, 2014), recalled that one of his intentions in that first novel was to re-create the 1960s, "to mirror in style as well as content their mood, their palette, their extremes, their vibrations, their profundity, their silliness and whimsy." A profile of Tom Robbins noted: "With the possible exception of [Jimi] Hendrix, Robbins is the top emissary of arts and letters whose rise to prominence can be traced to the Washington of the 1960s. But unlike Hendrix, who died at 27, Robbins is still dispensing all sorts of wisdom at 86." Find the article as Bob Young, "Mark Twain with an Illegal Smile," Washington Secretary of State, 2018.

7. BRONCOS IN THE SALON

Sir Roger Scruton died in 2020 at the age of seventy-five. After we met in 2004, he published many more books, including two in 2015 and another two in 2016. The *Rappahannock News* reported on his death, in "A Remembrance: Sir Roger Scruton (1944–2020)," that "One of the things that attracted Roger to Virginia, and Rappahannock in particular, was his passion for foxhunting. This area is renowned as the cradle of the American foxhound. Roger wanted to experience it for himself, especially as the sport had been gelded in his native England." Scruton was knighted in England at the 2016 Birthday Honours event for his "services to philosophy, teaching and public education." Thomas Babington Macaulay, the 1st Baron Macaulay, made his wry observation about bearbaiting in his *History of England*, vol. 1, chap. 3.

On rodeos as reenactments of bygone frontier lives, see John Livingston, *Rogue Primate: An Exploration of Human Domestication* (Boulder, CO: Roberts Rinehart, 1994). Livingston writes of rodeo there: "Events purport to be illustrative of the traditional work of cowboys, but they would be more accurately described as the romantic cowboy mythology that persists in our society thanks to movies and television. Rodeo is very hard on animals" (155). Livingston continues, "The cowboy needs the wild in order to demonstrate his ability to subdue it" (157). The enduring cowboy myths, and their reliance on animals, may be seen in the Academy Award–winning 2022 movie, directed by Jane Campion, *The Power of the Dog*. That film is based on the same-titled 1967 Thomas Savage novel, a book that opens with the castration of a bull calf.

The source for Renato Rosaldo's phrase "imperialist nostalgia" is *Culture and Truth: The Remaking of Social Analysis* (1989; Boston: Beacon, 1993), 69.

Anthony McCann tells the story of the 2016 right-wing occupation of the Malheur National Wildlife Refuge in his book *Shadowlands: Fear and Freedom at the Oregon Standoff* (New York: Bloomsbury, 2019).

8. MY CLIMATE CHANGE

Stephen J. Pyne is a leading scholar on wildfires. His *Fire in America: A Cultural History* (Seattle: University of Washington Press, 1997) set a standard for comprehensive fire research. His later book *The Pyrocene: How We Created an Age of Fire and What Happens Next* (Berkeley: University of California Press, 2021) makes bolder claims about humankind's carbon pollution and unnatural suppression of fires as factors in the rise of devastating conflagrations.

Mauri S. Pelto, professor of environmental science at Nichols College in Massachusetts, founded the North Cascade Glacier Climate Project in 1983. The project's website gives this definition: "Mass balance is the difference between the amount of snow and ice accumulation on the glacier and the amount of snow and ice ablation (melting and sublimation) lost from the glacier. Climate change causes variations in temperature and snowfall, changing mass balance." Sublimation, in this context, denotes the conversion from a solid (ice) to a gas (vapor) in the absence of an intermediate liquid stage. Studies of causal connections between travel-generated carbon and the various climate-change indicators, such as the shrinking of planetary glaciers, promise to grow in importance as provocative topics for future researchers.

American glaciologist Wendell Tangborn (1927–2020) pioneered contemporary interpretations of winter and spring water-storage capacity involving temperate glaciers. Tangborn's research has far-ranging implications for drought cycles in the intermontane West. Hydroelectric utilities have used his streamflow forecasting model for three decades to predict runoff in the Columbia River watershed.

Former California representative Richard Pombo, who served from 1993 to 2007, until he was voted out of office, chaired a task force dedicated to overhauling the Endangered Species Act. Pombo is now a lobbyist for mining and water interests. His book *This Land Is Our Land: How to End the War* on *Private Property* (New York: St. Martin's, 1996), coauthored with former *Sacramento Union* editor in chief Joseph Farah, detailed his environmental politics.

Microplastics pollute by entering natural ecosystems from cosmetics, clothes, containers, and industrial processes. Microplastics are small enough to migrate from water to air and back again within precipitation and evaporation portions of the water cycle. NOAA researchers find microplastics in oceans, lakes, snowfall, and rainfall. Microplastics can also "biomagnify," by moving up food chains and concentrating in ever-greater quantities as they do. Nonprofits striving to diminish marine plastics include Algalita Marine Research, Five Gyres Institute, Plastic Oceans International, Plastics Pollution Coalition, Plastic Soup Foundation, and Surfrider.

The 2015 billboard that read "Public Land: Log It, Graze It or Watch It Burn" was hired by the Stevens County Cattlemen's Association, part of an orchestrated effort by beef producers in western states to enhance public relations and expand grazing allotments on public lands.

Tim Flannery, a fellow at the Melbourne Sustainable Society Institute, is a public scientist. His book *The Future Eaters: An Ecological History of the Australasian Lands and People* (New York: George Braziller, 1994) tracks how humankind has altered ecologies. Flannery's book *The Weather Makers: How Man Is Changing the Climate and What It Means for Life on Earth* (New York: Grove Atlantic, 2005) outlines the history of climate change, forecasts its impacts over the next century, and recommends what to do to avert cataclysms. In 2019–20, Australian bushfires killed thirty-four people, consumed more than 3,500 homes and other structures, and killed or displaced hundreds of species of flora and fauna.

The initialism "B.A.U." by Elizabeth Kolbert appears in her article "The Climate of Man III," in the *New Yorker*, May 9, 2009. The perpetuation of B.A.U., or business as usual, is a primary goal of business continuity planning, where it originated and has currency. On the matter of the violations that cost Volkswagen so much in cash and public relations, see Clifford Atiyeh, "Everything You Need to Know about the VW Diesel-Emissions Scandal," *Car and Driver*, Dec. 2, 2019. The case of the Rev. George Taylor is reported, among other sources, by Kip Hill, "Spokane Climate Activist

Can Argue He Was Forced into Trespassing Train Protest, Supreme Court Rules," *Spokesman-Review*, Aug. 7, 2021. Attorney Karen Lindholdt, who was ready to represent Taylor pro bono in a jury trial in 2021, found the suit dismissed at the insistence of Northern Pacific Railway—a dismissal that has set a welcome precedent for climate activists.

9. SURVIVOR TREE

The sculpture *Jean de La Fontaine* by Pierre Julien has been housed in the Louvre Museum in Paris since 1960. The sculpture shows the poet holding a folio of the manuscript "The Fox and the Grapes," a poem he based on the Greek slave Aesop's famous tale. The sculpture, carved from marble, was commissioned in 1782 and unveiled in 1785. A photographic reproduction of it is available through Wikimedia Commons. William Blake's poem "The Tyger" was published in 1794 as part of his *Songs of Experience* collection.

10. SHOOTERS AND THE TOOLS THEY USE

Greek philosopher Aristotle wrote his *Nichomachean Ethics* around 340 BCE. The American writer Sinclair Lewis published his satirical novel *Main Street* in 1920. Aldo Leopold began as a professor of game management in the Department of Agricultural Economics at the University of Wisconsin in 1933. The English distinction between hunting and shooting—quite different from mine—is reported by Michael Brander, *Hunting and Shooting* (New York: Putnam's Sons, 1971), where the distinction is class-based. Hunting was mostly done by proles; shooting, by members of the upper classes. Cabela's, a specialty retailer of outdoor recreation merchandise, was acquired in 2017 by Bass Pro Shops in a $4 billion deal.

Robotic decoys for law enforcement have become so effective at apprehending poachers that Custom Robotic Wildlife in Wisconsin now has specialized in making them. In 2020, the Pew Charitable Trusts reported that the long decline in hunting license sales has had negative environmental consequences by diminishing funding for conservation programs: "Hunters in the United States numbered nearly 17 million in 1980. By 2016, the number had fallen to 11.5 million, according to data from the U.S. Fish and

Wildlife Service. That survey found that 90% of hunters are male, 97% are white and most are 45 and older—a sign that future funding losses could be steep as more hunters age out of the sport and the country becomes more racially diverse." The Pew article is "The Pandemic Created New Hunters. States Need to Keep Them."

At the same time that new hunters are being courted, research shows that raptors are dying in record numbers. Bald eagles, hawks, vultures, and other birds of prey ingest lead from shotgun pellets that lodge in the flesh of wounded birds and animals. They feed on the dead or wounded prey that get away from hunters; they ingest the neurotoxins in that lead. "It's similar to the neurological damage suffered by children who consume lead-based paint and other lead sources," wrote Rita Giordano, in "Bald Eagles Are Being Poisoned by Lead Ammo in Hunted Animals. Could Copper Bullets Be the Fix?," *Philadelphia Inquirer,* Feb. 3, 2022.

11. HAWK WATCHING

Forensic ornithologist Carla Dove works in the Smithsonian National Museum of Natural History in Washington, DC. See the article titled "Her Name Says It All," in the *Montanan,* the University of Montana's alumni magazine. It names Dove, an alumna, as "the country's leading expert in microscopic feather identification, studying bird collisions with airplanes for the sake of making travel safer." Each year she receives some eight thousand parcels of snarge—"a bunch of ick and stuff," as she describes it. Her specialized neologism *snarge* describes the gathered guts and bone and feather fragments. The fact that laboratories are needed to troubleshoot collisions between birds and planes says much about the magnitude of air transport in the twenty-first-century international economy and its impacts on nature.

The Urban Raptor Conservancy of Seattle, instead of making permanent captives of birds of prey like falconers do, works to study raptor habits and habitats, to propagate the birds in a wild state, and to help them survive in the midst of contemporary urban environments.

The book referenced here by Rick Bass, *The Ninemile Wolves: An Essay* (1992; Boston: Houghton Mifflin, 2003), follows the fortunes of a pair of wolves that appeared near the author's home in northwestern Montana and led to a reintroduction project. Their reintroduction, and later in-migration to other states, has become a lightning rod for controversy throughout the Northwest. Some states want to eliminate them outright, reprising the pattern that occurred a century ago throughout the Lower 48. See my op-ed "Managed by Rifle" in *Inlander*, Dec. 5, 2012, about an agency-endorsed extermination of a wolf pack in Washington State.

Helen Macdonald's *H is for Hawk* (New York: Grove, 2014) is the best-selling nonfiction account of how the author, an experienced falconer grieving the sudden death of her father, trained a goshawk that helped her recovery. The book was so popular it led to the documentary film, *H Is for Hawk: A New Chapter*, as part of the BBC's Natural World series in 2017.

Genesis 1:28 is the source of "rule over the fish of the sea, the birds of the air, and over every living creature that moved upon the ground."

12. TIDINGS FROM THE VIRUS

Nora McGreevy's article "Scientists Propose a New Name for Nature in the Time of COVID-19: The 'Anthropause,'" *Smithsonian*, July 1, 2020, is my source for that nonce word or neologism. Washington State University graduate student Alissa Anderson's research on Canada lynx enhanced by the pandemic has been widely reported; one example among many is Teresa Byrd, "Study Catches Glacier's Elusive Lynx—on Camera," *Hungry Horse News*, Feb 26, 2020. On a similar theme, John Brunton reported, "'Nature Is Taking Back Venice': Wildlife Returns to Tourist-Free City," *The Guardian*, Mar. 20, 2020. See also Rob Picheta, "People in India Can See the Himalayas for the First Time in 'Decades,' as the Lockdown Eases Air Pollution," CNN, April 9, 2020. Coinciding with those news reports, Delia Gallagher wrote, "Pope Says Coronavirus Pandemic Could Be Nature's Response to Climate Crisis," CNN, Apr. 9, 2020.

On the specifics of air travel and the climate crisis, see Tatiana Schlossberg, "Flying Is Bad for the Planet. You Can Help Make It Better," *New York Times*, July 27, 2017. Erin Florio is quoted in a *CBS This Morning* television news report titled "How 'Overtourism' Can Strain Popular Tourist Destinations." Regarding the alleged centuries that will be needed to recover from humankind's industrial excess, search Donald Worster, "Another Silent Spring," Environment & Society Portal, *Virtual Exhibitions* no. 1 (April 22, 2020), in the Rachel Carson Center for Environment and Society.

Responsible Travel, a self-described "activist travel company" founded by Justin Francis in Brighton, England, made the short documentary film *Crowded Out: The Story of Overtourism*, which profiles Professor Fabiola Mancinelli. That film, available on YouTube, includes Francis's analyses of overtourism quoted here. The *Business Insider* story "Influencer Marketing: Social Media Influencer Market Stats and Research for 2021," was posted on July 27, 2021. On passenger enplanements, see Bureau of Transportation Statistics for the various years under review. The story about the German woman angry at tourists who come to visit the site of Nazi atrocities at Dachau is told by Rick Steves in his *Travel as a Political Act*, 3rd ed. (2018), 76.

The comparison made by Dr. Anthony Fauci, likening cruise ships to incubators, is found in the article by David Leonhardt, "When Coronavirus Hit, Why Did Cruise Ships Keep Sailing?," *New York Times*, April 27, 2020. Gay Courter's statements about being coddled on a cruise ship during the pandemic can be found in the article by Yaron Steinbuch, "Novelist Quarantined on Diamond Princess Says 'Real Hero' Is Cruise Ship's Pastry Chef," *New York Post*, Feb. 11, 2020. *Midway* is a photo series made by Seattle-based artist Chris Jordan about plastics pollution mortality in seabirds. Excerpts from the series are searchable on YouTube.

The statement comparing college dorms to cruise ships, by Terry Hartle, then senior vice president of the American Council on Education, is available online in the article "With Virus, U.S. Higher Education May Face an Existential Moment," *PBS News Hour*, May 1, 2020. Elizabeth Becker's exposé of the travel industry is titled *Overbooked: The Exploding Business of Travel and Tourism* (New York: Simon and Schuster, 2013). Find "Methane Pollution," on the David Suzuki Foundation website, for statistics on the global sources of that invisible gas.

For Nathaniel Hawthorne's 1846 short story "Earth's Holocaust," search his book *Mosses from an Old Manse* on Project Gutenberg. Samuel Taylor Coleridge's "Rime of the Ancient Mariner" is available on the Poetry Foundation website.

On the financial rescue of cruise lines during the pandemic, search Eli

Moskowitz, "Critics Argue That U.S. Government Should Not Bail out Cruise Liners," in Organized Crime and Corruption Reporting Project. Moskowitz is also the source for the 1 percent tax rate paid by the average cruise line. On financial consequences of COVID-19 within the cruise line industry, see "CMV Becomes the Third Cruise Line to Go out of Business in a Month," in the *Maritime Executive* for July 20, 2020.

13. TRACKING CAPTAIN COOK

Turtle Island, for certain Indigenous peoples, refers to the continent of North America. Oral histories from the upper Midwest account for planetary creation as originating when a turtle supported the planet on its back. The turtle accordingly has been regarded as an icon or embodiment of life itself. Gary Snyder won a Pulitzer Prize for his collection of poetry and essays titled *Turtle Island* (New York: New Directions, 1974), a literary accomplishment that would be more difficult today, due to growing proscriptions against cultural appropriation.

The references to sobbing captive turtles, and the use of ashes from the animals for restoring hair, come from an English natural historian's account, which I edited and published as *John Josselyn, Colonial Traveler: A Critical Edition of "Two Voyages to New England"* (Lebanon, NH: University Press of New England, 1988), 29–30, 78–79.

Rachel Feltman reported on the antiquated sport of turtle riding in "Ever Wondered What It Would Be Like to Ride a Sea Turtle through the Great Barrier Reef?," in *Washington Post*, July 1, 2015. Celmara Pocock wrote about it in greater depth in "Turtle Riding on the Great Barrier Reef," in *Society and Animals* 14, no. 2 (2006): 129–46. Both items are available online. Sea turtles received protection in the United States and its waters under the 1973 Endangered Species Act, which lists the green turtle and others as endangered. Illegal also now is the importing, selling, or transporting of turtles or products made from turtles. The image of Charles Darwin riding atop a tortoise—one of the less-admirable practices of the esteemed naturalist—is recorded in the Elizabeth Hennessy book *On the Backs of Tortoises: Darwin, the Galapagos, and the Fate of an Evolutionary Eden* (New Haven, CT: Yale University Press, 2019).

The quote from Thoreau, about preferring a pumpkin over a velvet cushion as a seat, appears near the beginning of "Economy," the first chapter of *Walden* (1854). Thoreau was jailed for a day and night in 1846 for refusing to pay a poll tax, or head tax, on the grounds that the money might be used to support either slavery or the Mexican War—both of which he publicly opposed. Mark Twain's semi-autobiographical travel novel *Roughing It* appeared in 1872.

Much of my information about the final voyage of James Cook's twin ships HMS *Resolution* and *Discovery* comes from "Captain Cook Killed in Hawaii," *History.com*, February 10, 2021, and from C. G. Cash, *The Life and Voyages of Captain James Cook* (London: Blackie, 1905). The Alfred North Whitehead quotation may be found in his book *Science and the Modern World* (New York: Mentor, 1948), 17. A person who herds cattle in Hawai'i is a paniolo, which was a local pronunciation of *espaniolos*, meaning Spaniards. Mexican vaqueros were brought in during the nineteenth century to teach the locals how to manage imported beef cattle.

14. A MAYAN APOCALYPSE

Encyclopedia Britannica reports, in "Chac: Mayan Deity," that "Chac, Mayan god of rain, [was] especially important in the Yucatán region of Mexico where he was depicted in Classic times with protruding fangs, large round eyes, and a proboscis-like nose." During our sojourn in Belize, my family and I boated to Xcalak, Mexico, for lunch. On the ghost city of Tikal, see Alex Fox, "Why Did the Maya Abandon the Ancient City of Tikal?," in *Smithsonian* for July 2, 2020. Lakshmi Supriya reports: "The leading theory is that the Maya suffered a series of severe droughts around 800–1100. New evidence suggests there may have been another reason: severe tropical storms," in "Severe Cyclones May Have Played a Role in the Maya Collapse," *Smithsonian*, Sept. 3, 2020. Theories proliferate about why the Maya civilization ended. The hypothesis about diminished longevity due to female sacrifices is mine.

Carl de Borhegyi curates and illustrates a website, Breaking the Mushroom Code, as a repository for research that he has undertaken with his son Stephan. Among their most original discoveries is the connection, illustrated in the iconography of the Maya, between psychoactive mushrooms and toads. Michael Pollan complements some of the Borhegyis' research in his book *How to Change Your Mind: What the New Science of Psychedelics Teaches Us about Consciousness, Dying, Addiction, Depression, and Transcendence* (New York: Penguin, 2018).

Jamaica Kincaid's book *A Small Place* (New York: Farrar, Straus and Giroux, 1988) focuses on her birthplace, the island of Antigua. That book indicts the tourist industry and the island's legacy of British colonialism. Kincaid said she was banned for five years from that country after the book was published. She even worried she might be murdered if she returned.

In 2009 the Puget Sound, the Strait of Juan de Fuca, the Strait of Georgia, and an intricate network of connecting channels and waterways in British Columbia and Washington State were collectively renamed the Salish Sea by the US Board on Geographic Names.

15. LOVED BADLY ON YOUR BANK

Wanapum means River People. That Indigenous band is enrolled in the federally recognized and confederated Yakama Nation. The Wanapum Heritage Center is Mattawa, Washington. See Stephen Emerson, "Wanapum People after Smohalla," HistoryLink, Sept. 15, 2010. Natalie Angier's article "The Wonders of Blood" appears in the *New York Times* for October 20, 2008.

King County in Washington State illustrated and narrated the Kent Valley flood event online as "Green River Flood of 1959." On Boris Tokin and his claims about the benefits of tannins, see Rebecca Lawton, "The Healing Powers of Nature," in *Aeon*, Sept. 8, 2018. On the straightening and diking of the Duwamish River, see "Duwamish Waterway Map Superimposed on a Map of the Formerly Winding Duwamish River," HistoryLink, Feb. 20, 2001.

The states of Oregon and Washington have introduced legislation that would approve psilocybin for medical use, decriminalize it, or eventually legalize it. Decriminalization efforts began in the United States in the second decade of the millennium. Denver decriminalized the substance in May 2019, followed by the California cities of Oakland and Santa Cruz. The title of the poem by Sylvia Plath which I quote in this chapter is "Mushrooms."

Billy Frank Jr. is recognized as a Washington State hero. A national wildlife refuge near Tacoma, a building owned by the Nisqually Tribe, and a street in Bellingham have all taken his name. See Robert O. Marritz, "Frank, Billy Jr. (1913–2014)" in HistoryLink, and Gabriel Chrisman, "The Fish-in Protests at Franks Landing," in the Seattle Civil Rights Labor History website. A related article is Timothy Egan's "On the River Bank with Billy Frank Jr., Indians and Salmon: Making Nature Whole," *New York Times*, Nov. 26, 1992.

To survey decades of backlash to Indigenous sovereignty in the Pacific Northwest, search Chuck Tanner, "Bigotry, Calls for Violence, Follow Protest of Tribal Treaty Fishing," Institute for Research and Education on Human Rights, May 13, 2016. The "usual and accustomed places" legal guarantee for tribal fishing rights may be found at "Treaty: Promises between Governments," posted by the Columbia River Inter-Tribal Fish Commission.

The Richard Hugo poems are available by searching Google Books for *Making Certain It Goes On: The Collected Poems of Richard Hugo*. Ripley S. Hugo, Lois Welch, and James Welch edited for publication *The Real West Marginal Way: A Poet's Biography* (New York: Norton, 1992). The Duwamish Tribe website illustrates its longhouse and cultural center.

Ernest Hemingway's "Big Two-Hearted River," part of his short story collection *In Our Time*, was published in 1925. His novel *A Farewell to Arms* was published in 1929. The Wild and Scenic Rivers Act was enacted by Congress on October 2, 1968. The act reads, in part, that it is "the policy of the United States that certain selected rivers of the Nation which, with their immediate environments, possess outstandingly remarkable scenic, recreational, geologic, fish and wildlife, historic, cultural, or other similar values, shall be preserved in free-flowing condition, and that they and their immediate environments shall be protected for the benefit and enjoyment of present and future generations."

The only biography of David Sohappy currently is mine: "Sohappy, David (1925–1991)," available in HistoryLink for Feb. 22, 2019. The documentary film of Sohappy's life, *River People: Behind the Case of David Sohappy*, discoverable on YouTube under the title "David Sohappy," was written and directed by Michal Conford and Michele Zaccheo (New York: Filmakers [*sic*] Library, 1991). In "Salmon Scam," the Northwest Power and Conservation Council chronicles the 1982 sting that made the Sohappys, father and son, captives.

The Wanapum spiritual leader Smohalla is profiled by Cassandra Tate in "Smohalla (1815?–1895)," HistoryLink, July 11, 2010. See also Carlotta Collette, "A Visit with the River People of Hanford Reach," *High Country News*, Dec. 8, 1997, and Jennifer Ott, "U.S. Congress Passes American Indian Religious Freedom Act on July 27, 1978," HistoryLink, Dec. 22, 2016. David Sr.'s granddaughter, Loretta Jane Sohappy, a Gates Scholarship recipient, earned a master of public health degree from Eastern Washington University in 2020. Gates Scholarships are awarded to outstanding minority high-school seniors from low-income households.

Mortality rates inherent in catch-and-release fishing depend on species and size of the fish caught and released, as well as sporting pressure on the water in which they are caught. See Debbie Drews, "Like a Fish out of Water," *Outside Bozeman* (spring 2016): 70–74. "Debilitating hook injuries can reduce a fish's ability to feed by 50%," Drews wrote. She continued, "Multiple captures of individual fish, common in many trophy-trout fisheries, further compound the issues of sub-lethal injury." Montana, and Bozeman in particular, are meccas for fly fishermen. Drews concludes, "On the upper Madison alone, 20,000 fish die each year from hooking mortality." The quotation from David Quammen may be found in "Synecdoche and the Trout," in *Wild Thoughts from Wild Places* (New York: Touchstone, 1998), 25. Implications for sportfishing as a hurtful aspect of tourism need further exploration.

The Albeni Falls Dam Visitor Center, referenced in this chapter, is promoted on a website that enjoins the reader to "Visit North Idaho," an area it names "The Northwest's Playground." Some tourists, including motorcyclists, consider dams to be attractive tourist destinations. The Tankside Dam Tour is one such group whose dam tours make for "A Dam Fine Experience." MotoQuest is another motorcyclist group that tours dams, and EagleRider is yet another.

The movie *Smoke Signals* was released in 1998. Writer Sherman Alexie is a member of the Spokane and Coeur d'Alene Indian Tribes and has won a National Book Award. The film's director, Chris Eyre, speaks, in an interview with Michael Jones, of his difficulty filming the waterfall scene. Find the interview in *Filmmaker* magazine under the title "Alien Nation." Alexie's poem "That Place Where Ghosts of Salmon Jump" was commissioned in 1995 as public art for Spokane's downtown library. Carved on a polished granite floor in a spiral, the poem starts at the spiral's outside and winds inside to arrive at the poem's end. The poem was reprinted in Alexie's book *The Summer of Black Widows* (Brooklyn, NY: Hanging Loose, 1996).

On March 16, 2005, Cassandra Tate wrote a timeline entry for HistoryLink titled "Native Americans Begin 'Ceremony of Tears' for Kettle Falls on June 14, 1940." The Indigenous purpose of the ceremony, Tate wrote, was "to mourn the loss of their ancestral fishing grounds, soon to be flooded by Grand Coulee Dam on the Columbia River in Central Washington." The anecdote about Walt Toly, who promoted Expo '74 in Spokane and enlisted the auto executives, appears in "Testimony of John Osborn," April 22, 2008, on the website WaterPlanet.

The Thomas Cole canvas *Falls of the Kaaterskill* was completed in 1826. Held in a private collection, it is searchable in reproduction online at WikiArt. The waterfall proved to be such a tourist attraction that a dam was built, and fees were paid, to see the water in action, as reported in the anonymous and undated article "Kaaterskill Falls and the Bayard of Dogs," *Atlas Obscura*. Z. Vanessa Helder, Washington State's leading practitioner of the visual art movement dubbed Precisionism, is profiled in an article by David F. Martin in HistoryLink, posted Sept. 9, 2008. Selected paintings from the Bureau of Reclamation Art Collection, including the artists whom I name, are searchable via the webpage "American Artist and Water Reclamation," a collection of paintings whose backstory I tell in "The Fine Art of Bureaucracy," *High Country News*, Jan. 14, 2009, and in greater detail in "From Sublimity to Ecopornography: Assessing the Bureau of Reclamation Art Collection." *Journal of Ecocriticism* 1, no. 1 (Jan. 2009): 1–25.

On the website titled Clark Fork Delta Restoration, see the clickable "About" tab for the euphemistic language on "altered hydrologic conditions." Franker language can be found in the smaller print there: "This erosion is the result of wave action and water level fluctuations of Lake Pend Oreille due to the operation of the Albeni Falls dam." The group sponsoring the restoration project is Idaho Fish and Game, an agency that is caught between the Bonneville Power Administration, which sells the power generated by the dam; the sporting industries that include boaters, hunters, and people who fish; homeowners along the lakeshore who use the water for their recreation; and the needs of the ecosystem in the degraded delta.

A 2002 study of disparate impacts to Indigenous people from Hanford pollution was reported in an Everett, Washington, newspaper, accessible online as "Hanford Exposed Tribes, Study Says." On the impacts to orcas in the Salish Sea, see Meilan Solly, "Pacific Northwest Orca Population Hits 30-Year-Low," *Smithsonian*, July 10, 2018.

Information on the ecological hazards of dams through gasification is widespread. Lois Parshley reported on the greenhouse gases and dams in "The Allure and Perils of Hydropower," *Undark Magazine*, Nov. 13, 2017. A newer report by Tara Lohan, "Dam Accounting: Taking Stock of Methane Emissions from Reservoirs," is found in the *Revelator*, April 25, 2022.

An explanation of dam breaching as a solution to salmon recovery, in a video for Oregon Public Broadcasting, is available on YouTube as "Salmon vs Dams." Lynda V. Mapes, in an article illustrated by photos and video, reported the successful aftermath of the Elwha River dam breaching in "Elwha: Roaring Back to Life," *Seattle Times*, Feb. 13, 2016. Plenary speaker Laura Wildman, as part of the 2015 International Conference on Engineering and Ecohydrology for Fish Passage, discussed creative vandalism and legislative efforts to remove dams, in her presentation titled "The Evolution of Pro-Active Dam Removal in the U.S. over the Last Quarter Century." Success stories about dam removal are widespread in print and on the Web.

The Columbia River Inter-Tribal Fish Commission shares its online "Restoration Projects" for salmon in the Columbia River Basin. An outcomes summary of the case involving culverts as barriers to salmon migration can be found under "AG Ferguson statement on culverts decision." On the topic of barges used to try to recover flagging salmon populations, see the Northwest Power and Conservation Council item "Fish Transportation."

16. NOMADS OF THE SEA

The "Maldives of Thailand" comparison, published on a Trip Advisor page titled "Ko Lipe," goes back to 2013. Such a comparison would be surprising to find today due to the overtourism that has afflicted the island. The Urak

Lawoi people, found only in Thailand, are animist in their beliefs, holding that every sea, bay, and beach has a spirit that needs respect.

Political unrest, kept out of sight in Thailand's tourist-dependent economy, contradicts the nation's verbal logo, according to David Stout, in "Thailand Was Never the Land of Smiles, Whatever the Guidebooks May Have Told You," *Time*, Feb. 12, 2014. Searching the internet in late 2021, I found the first eight hits for *jai yen* (which is Thai for "cool heart") have been appropriated by a variety of commercial interests.

Influence marketers, especially travel influencers, have faced challenges since the pandemic curtailed worldwide travel, as discussed in "These Travel Influencers Pivoted during the Pandemic," by Stephanie McNeal in *Buzzfeed News* for June 29, 2021. Continuing through the spring of 2022, the borders of Thailand remained mostly closed to tourists. The phrase "the locals," as applied to servers in Koh Lipe restaurants, is used by self-styled "celebrity and influencer" Shayan Safai in his blog *Dose of Life*.

A profile of the longtail boat is found on the Snorkeling Thailand website under "What Is a Thai Longtail Boat" (*sic*). The capacity of the Lawoi to see underwater is analyzed by scholars Anna Gislen et al., in "Superior Underwater Vision in a Human Population of Sea Gypsies," *Current Biology* 13, no. 10 (May 13, 2003): 833–36. *CBS This Morning*, on the world's top tourism spenders in 2017, reported China outstripped the USA by almost twofold, at US$258 billion versus US$135 billon, in "How 'Overtourism' Can Strain Popular Tourist Destinations," a video on YouTube.

The water guardians we met in Thailand are part of the nation's Natural Resources and Environmental Crime Suppression Division. BBC News twice reported on the effects of the overtourism caused by the Leonardo DiCaprio movie *The Beach*, in "The Beach Nobody Can Touch" (March 4, 2017) and in "Thailand: Tropical Bay from 'The Beach' to Close until 2021" (May 9, 2019). Across two decades in Thailand, a series of animal-abuse offenses occurred in its many tiger-petting zoos, where millions of tourists paid for photos with tigers. Allegations of chaining, whipping, doping, killing, and illegally removing microchips tainted the zoos. See, for example, "Thai Tiger Temple's Long History of Controversy," *BBC News*, June 1, 2016.

Wat Hantalay is the only Buddhist temple on Koh Lipe. Its monks acknowledge the Urak Lawoi as the island's original inhabitants and as practitioners of religious rites based on honor of the natural world and ancestor worship. Citizens of Bali hold the macaque monkeys sacred. In early 2021, when it became clear tourists would not soon return, those monkeys, habituated to tourist handouts, became aggressive, according to Firdia Lisnawati and Niniek Karmini in their article "With No Tourist Handouts, Hungry Bali Monkeys Raid Homes," AP News, Sept. 4, 2021. Visits to the Sangeh Monkey Forest had averaged six thousand per month before the pandemic, but they dropped off to around five hundred, until the country banned foreign travelers altogether in July 2021.

A story about sovereignty activists for the Urak Lawoi people appears online as "Sea Gypsies Still Seeking Justice," in *Bangkok Times*, Jan. 20, 2020. Anchalee Kongrut wrote about a special curriculum on Koh Lipe, which helps Lawoi students understand their culture, in her "Tribal Education" article published in *Bangkok Post*, May 18, 2015. Mark Sweeney wrote "BBC to Buy out Lonely Planet," in *The Guardian*, Feb. 18, 2011. The tab titled "Tourism Notes," under *UNWTO—The World Tourism Organization*, gives 1934 as the date that the International Union of Official Tourist Propaganda was created.

John Everingham's photoblog disappeared from the internet late in 2021, a disappearance explicable since he began spearheading, with his son Ananda, a tourist enterprise called the Beachfront Club. The feature film on John Everingham, *Love Is Forever*, premiered in 1982 and starred Michael Landon as John Everingham; his son Ananda was born that same year. For the "jinx-dispelling ritual," see the Anchalee Kongrut article cited above.

The quotation by William Faulkner comes from his short story "A Rose for Emily," in his *Collected Stories* (New York: Random House, 1950). The quotation by Anne Sexton comes from her poem "Rowing," in *The Awful Rowing Toward God* (Boston: Houghton Mifflin, 1975).

17. ISLAND TIME

South Pacific, quoted in the chapter epigraph, is the popular Rodgers and Hammerstein Broadway musical from 1949, and its film adaptations in 1958 and 2001, based loosely on James Michener's Pulitzer Prize–winning novel, *Tales of the South Pacific* (1947).

Malena Ernman; her husband, Svante Thunberg; and their daughter Greta Thunberg cowrote *Our House Is on Fire: Scenes of a Family and a Planet in Crisis* (London: Penguin, 2018). The quotation comes from an excerpt of the book published as "Malena Ernman on daughter Greta Thunberg: 'She was slowly disappearing into some kind of darkness,'" in *The Guardian*, Feb. 23, 2020.

The excerpt from the unpublished letter by James Norman Hall is used by courtesy of Mara Bohman, who shared it from her family records. The quotation on the disappearing shoals of Tahiti is found in an article by Jon Bowermaster, "The Fragile Paradise That Tahiti Used to Be," *New York Times*, Feb. 18, 2007. On the climate refugees in Louisiana, see Carol Davenport and Campbell Robertson, "Resettling the First American 'Climate Refugees,'" *New York Times* May 2, 2016, as well as Bob Marshall, "Losing Ground: Southeast Louisiana Is Disappearing, Quickly," *Scientific American*, Aug. 28, 2014. Hurricane Ida in 2021worsened their condition.

The statement by United Nations Secretary-General António Guterres is searchable as "The UN Secretary-General Speaks on the State of the Planet," *United Nations*, Dec. 2, 2020. Among the abundant research on the impacts of rats as avian predators in the South Pacific, see Quiterie Duron et al., "Invasive Rats Strengthen Predation Pressure on Bird Eggs in a South Pacific Island Rainforest," *Current Zoology* 63, no. 6 (Feb. 22, 2017): 583–90.

The quotation about Tahiti's stereotype as "a hotbed of unbridled sexual pleasure" may be found online in Sylvie Largeaud-Ortega, "Nordhoff and Hall's *Mutiny on the Bounty*: A Piece of Colonial Historical Fiction," in an essay collection edited by Largeaud-Ortega and titled *The Bounty from the Beach: Cross-Cultural and Cross-Disciplinary Essays* (Canberrra: Australian National University Press, 2018), 133. On the matter of the passage that Herman Melville's publisher censored from his first novel, see Robert Sullivan, "Excerpt from *Typee*," Penguin Random House website.

Tahiti Tourisme North America's PR Newswire is my source for "The Legendary Island of Bora Bora in Tahiti Featured on *E!*'s Hit Show *Keeping up with the Kardashians*," Aug. 17, 2011. On the growth rate of corals, see "Important Fish Habitat Formed by Slow-Growing Corals May Recover More Slowly in a Changing Climate," NOAA Fisheries Jan. 12, 2017.

"Locals Oppose Tahiti Floating Island Project," an anonymous article published in *Radio New Zealand* on Feb. 20, 2018, states, "The French Polynesian government appears to have lost its enthusiasm for the world's first floating islands." Along with the website for the Seasteading Institute and its Floating City Project, see Elisavetta M. Brandon, "Are Floating Cities a Real Possibility?," in *Smithsonian* Aug. 12, 2021.

The Happy Isles of Oceania, published by Paul Theroux in 1992, is an account of a trip Theroux took by kayak through the Pacific Islands shortly after the breakup of his first marriage. On the inadvertent "invention" of suntanning by Coco Chanel, see Sophie Wilkinson, "A Short History of Tanning," *The Guardian*, Feb. 19, 2012.

18. MAKING LANDFALL

The statistics on fatalities from tropical storms in the Caribbean and Central America are found on the website of Organization of American States, "Chapter 12: Hurricane Hazards," which calculates twenty thousand deaths from hurricanes between the dates of 1960 and 1988 alone. The ranking of the costliest storms in the nation's history is available in the graph titled "Most Expensive Natural Disasters in the United States as of December 2021," at Statista. By a large margin, the top six costliest disasters all occurred within the first two decades of the present century.

Alexander Hamilton's letter to his father may be read at Founders Online, in "From Alexander Hamilton to the *Royal Danish American Gazette*, 6 September 1772." The song "Hurricane" from the Broadway show *Hamilton* is searchable on YouTube as "Hurricane—(Original Cast 2016—Live)." Ron Chernow's biography of Hamilton is accessible as "Alexander Hamilton—Ron Chernow (2005)" on the website Publicism. *Beasts of the Southern Wild* is a 2012 film directed by Ben Zeitlin.

9 780807 179499